Prepared

Unlocking Human Performance with Lessons from Elite Sport

Paul Gamble PhD

Prepared: Unlocking Human Performance with Lessons from Elite Sport

© 2020 Paul Gamble

ISBN (paperback):   978-1-7752186-6-1

IBSN (e-book):   978-1-7752186-7-8

This book is dedicated to my dad; most of what I know about leadership, and the parts of managing people that I get right, I learned from you, Father...

Thanks also to the coaches and practitioners whose wisdom features in this book, including the no doubt many instances that are unattributed!

Finally, coaching is an art that is acquired and continually refined from working with athletes, so I am hugely thankful to the athletes I have been privileged to serve and who continue to enlighten me...

Contents

Prologue

To understand *human performance* we need to recognise it is an endeavour that is not restricted to the narrow confines of sport. The pursuit of excellence in performance is not exclusively the domain of athletes and those who operate in elite sport, but is rather the hallmark of high performers in all sectors. The central premise of this book is that the elements, principles, and processes that we associate with high performing individuals and teams in sport are transferable to leadership, management, and more broadly to our professional and personal lives beyond sport.

This book thus takes an all-encompassing view of human performance. The chapters that follow seek to apply wisdom from coaching and preparing athletes in ways that translate to the reader's professional and personal practice in whatever realm they operate in. Whilst the content of the chapters that follow are of course highly relevant to those who are directly engaged in the realm of sport, the themes presented are equally applicable to professionals in other domains.

For the benefit of those readers who are not involved in sport, it seems a good idea at the outset to make the case for a book that uses the lens of coaching and preparing athletes to explore what it contends are universal themes and lessons. In my head it does not seem a huge reach to apply wisdom from coaching and the principles derived from preparing athletes to human performance in other sectors. Nevertheless, I recognise the need to articulate the 'why' behind this contention, before we move on to consider what exactly the salient lessons are, and how we might apply them.

Something that resonates with many people is the notion that sport serves as a metaphor for many of the challenges we face in work and life. By extension, the practice of coaching and the process of preparing athletes have direct parallels to the domains of leadership, people management, and human performance in other spheres. It is interesting to note the prevalence of 'business' books on leadership circulating among leaders and coaches in sport, and in a circular fashion books examining high performance sports teams and coaching have started to appear among the selection of business and leadership titles! Perhaps the notion that wisdom derived from coaching and athlete preparation might translate more generally to work and life is not so outlandish after all.

CROSSING DOMAINS...

I have been fortunate to encounter some exceptional coaches across a host of different sports. What strikes me is that these individuals possess some traits in common. One shared trait is that they are not bound by the conventions of the sport or coaching manual 'wisdom'. Rather these individuals bring a unique perspective and seek applicable knowledge from different realms and disciplines. Another feature in common is that they had highly successful careers in other domains, aside from their involvement in sport. For instance, the head coach I worked with at the start of my career (he was actually player-coach at the time) is a medical doctor by profession, and continues to maintain a medical practice in his native South Africa. Other exceptional coaches that come to mind include a professional actor, a software developer, and a teacher. This echoes the themes of applying knowledge acquired from other realms, and the propensity for wisdom and principles to transcend domains, which are central to the present book.

Similarly, the trials of preparing and competing over time prompt athletes develop certain 'meta-abilities' to regulate themselves in order to be successful in this highly challenging environment. These experiences hereby equip the athlete with tacit knowledge and higher level tools that readily transfer to other competitive and high pressure domains such as business. Importantly these tools are not only applicable at a surface level, but have been empirically shown to translate to other facets of life outside sport [1]. As such, these higher order skills are pertinent to any aspiring 'high performer' who strives for excellence in performance, regardless of what sector they operate in.

The qualities and abilities developed in a sporting career are accordingly recognised and highly valued by those in the realm of business and commerce. Many high performers in these realms have themselves competed or at least taken a keen interest in competitive sport. For instance, in 2015 the online financial and business publication *Business Insider* ran a feature that noted many prominent CEOs shared the distinction of having a decorated sporting history at high school, college, or even professional level. These observations once again demonstrate the link between sport and business. It also reinforces our theme that human performance extends beyond athletics.

WHAT LESSONS CAN WE TAKE FROM COACHING..?

The world of sport and coaching undoubtedly holds a fascination for leaders in business and commerce. There are numerous parallels we can draw between sport and business from a variety of perspectives. We can relate coaching and practices from the realm of elite sport to leadership and people management in various sectors.

It is no coincidence that resources on leadership and management in business look to sport for examples of best practice. In 2012 the Harvard business school undertook an in-depth interview and study of Sir Alex Ferguson, the highly acclaimed manager of Manchester United Football Club, which has since become one of the most widely read case studies they have produced. The New Zealand All Blacks rugby team has similarly been used as a study of organisational culture and performance excellence.

Exceptional coaches have much to teach us about many things in life. I was struck by this during a conversation with a highly experienced and well-travelled tennis coach, who is presently responsible for the development of young players in Canada. In the course of the conversation, he remarked that he increasingly found his time off the court was spent counselling not the youngsters but their parents on matters of life and business. He expressed his incredulity that the practical advice he was dispensing was not obvious to the audience he was counselling; the guidance he was providing he felt was common sense and the solutions struck him as simple and straightforward.

Such interactions exemplify what I have observed over the two decades I have spent in elite sport. Based on these experiences, I feel there is simply a need to connect the dots in order to relate this wisdom to other contexts. At the culmination of each chapter I invite the reader to engage in some reflection in order to do just that, in order to apply the principles presented to the constraints of the specific environment the reader might be operating in.

The notion that observing head coaches in sport can provide lessons in organisational leadership for business and society in general is not a new idea [2]. As the authors of a 2011 study remarked, 'there is a growing body of literature promoting the transfer of elite performance principles from the sporting domain to the business domain' [3]. Over the past two decades it has also become increasingly common for leaders in business to seek out mental skills coaches and sports psychologists, and enlist their consulting services to assist with teamwork initiatives and change management [4]. Indeed *performance psychology* is increasingly well established and accepted practice in business and other domains beyond sport, including the medical profession.

THE ROLE FOR COACHES BEYOND SPORT...

Continuing this theme, over the recent period it is becoming common practice to engage a coach as part of developing leadership and management skills. In the business domain the title employed is 'executive coach' or 'business coach'. The more generalist 'life coach' role has also become well established, serving individuals across all professions. Indeed, many enlightened organisations have started to employ individuals on staff in the role of 'coach' to work with selected employees to develop leadership, communication, and other relevant skills.

In January 2009 the Harvard Business Review published a Research Report entitled "What Can Coaches Do For You?" [5] to explore this trend. In the article the authors offered some tips for choosing a coach, to help ensure readers are getting value for their money. This raises an interesting question. How do we select and evaluate whomever we choose to enlist as our 'coach' unless we have some understanding of coaching? Fortuitously, aside from coaching athletes, I have invested time coaching coaches and mentoring practitioners across disciplines, and the chapters that follow will lend some insights on this front.

Leadership is ultimately coaching, and coaching is effectively leadership. On a more fundamental level, there is an element of coaching in much of what we do in work and life. Effectively we are all coaches in different contexts. Similarly, the processes and practices we use to prepare athletes to perform in competition and endure the stresses involved have more general application beyond sport. It follow that the principles and methods employed have application to human performance in all domains.

HUMAN POTENTIAL...

Biological performance and human limits are *plastic*; in other words, they are not fixed but are rather malleable. The difference between our genetic potential and what we actually exhibit is represented in the distinction between *genotype* and *phenotype*. Epigenetics describes the process whereby the environment, external stimuli, and the activity that individuals engage in switches on genes, and shapes growth and the adaptation that follows exposure to stressors and other stimuli. Epigenetics thereby regulates which traits, properties, and abilities are expressed. Essentially, the extent to which we realise our genetic potential (genotype) is determined by what we do and what conditions we are exposed to (phenotype).

In the context of sport, the process of training and the training sciences seek to provide the stimulus and steer adaptation to extend the athlete's physical and physiological capacities to their genetic limits, as we try to ensure they express their full performance capabilities. But the reality is we have no real concept what the limits of human performance might be. As the saying goes, records are made to be broken, and every feat of human endeavour simply reveals what might be possible. In the wake of a watershed moment when one athlete breaks a barrier of human performance (such as the four-minute mile) a surge of others follow.

Another key takeaway is that different aspects of human performance (such as resilience) emerge as a consequence of the inputs, conditions, and experiences we are exposed to. This fundamental principle applies to performers in all realms of human performance, not just athletes. It follows that we should seek to take a progressive and systematic approach to providing the stimulus to develop these qualities in a directed way, just as we do with athletes.

PHYSICS AND PHILOSOPHY IN HUMAN PERFORMANCE...

A wise and highly seasoned coach remarked to me that coaching and athlete preparation are effectively a blend of physics and philosophy. The coach in question is Dan Pfaff, who in 2018 was inducted into the United States track and field coaches' hall of fame. The 2016 Rio Olympic Games was the tenth Olympic championships Dan has attended as coach to a long and distinguished list of athletes across multiple events. It is a huge source of pride and accomplishment that Dan has become both a friend and mentor over recent years, and Dan's wisdom features at various points in the chapters that follow.

The physics part of Dan's wisdom seems straightforward. As coaches we are after all dealing with the mechanics of movement. Mechanical effectiveness determines how high we jump, how far we fly, and how fast we move. The element of mechanics in sports injury is similarly evident. There is a reason that these injuries occur simply through exposure of performing athletic tasks such as running over time; and mechanics is a big part of this. However, on a more fundamental level, physics is central to the notion that there are laws of motion and principles that apply universally. Regardless of the traditions of the sport, or the special talents of the individual, all of us are subject to the same fundamental physics. No sport and no athlete is above physics or exempt from the laws of motion.

The philosophy aspect might be less self-evident, until we consider that when preparing athletes we are not dealing with machines, but complex adaptive biological organisms with a mind attached. This adds a huge degree of complexity and brings a huge degree of uncertainty. Coping with complexity and uncertainty brings us into the realm of philosophy. Similarly, coaching of any kind involves interacting with humans and communicating messages in various ways, both verbal and non-verbal. In turn this necessitates managing perception and how these messages are received. The dynamics of these interactions mean we must consider our own emotional state as well as that of the athlete. Once again this brings us into the realm of philosophy, as it relates to the mind.

Turning our gaze away from sport, the coalescing of physics and philosophy can similarly be found in other domains. Whatever sector you work in, you will typically find there are fundamental inviolable laws and essential 'physics' that govern market forces and workflow processes, analogous to the laws of motion. As with coaching in sport, once identified the essential laws of motion for your specific domain serve as the lens through which you view the realm in which you operate. This lens provides both clarity and depth of understanding.

The philosophy part, as it relates to humans and our interactions with them, likewise applies across domains. Returning to the Harvard Business Review research report on coaching in business [5], it was interesting that the authors noted that coaching in this context combines elements of consulting and therapy. I have often remarked that in many instances my work with athletes feels as much like counselling as coaching.

SO WHAT IS IT YOU DO..?

Naturally, this is a question I am often posed upon meeting new people, but it is less straightforward to answer than might be expected. During my career to date, I have essentially made it my business to not easily fit into a particular 'pigeon hole'. There is a rationale for this: performance and sports injury do not respect boundaries between disciplines or discrete domains, such as physiology, biomechanics, or motor learning. Given that performance and sports injury are the spaces I operate in, it seemed to follow that I should also not be constrained by a particular discipline or area of specialism.

So, rather than staying within the confines of physiology, biomechanics, the more nebulous catch-all 'sport science', 'strength and conditioning', or sports coaching, I have chosen not to stay in my lane. Over the course of my journey to date, I have chosen to explore in depth whatever area was required by the athlete and the scenario I encountered. My scope of practice is therefore the aggregation of these experiences and learning across multiple fields.

Sadly, I am not sure coming up with an ever-growing array of new titles is necessarily the answer, and in general I struggle with self-appointed titles. For instance, with some incredulity I learned recently that a company chairman and former colleague had anointed himself with the title 'Chief Visionary'. Inevitably what I end up saying when asked is simply that I am a coach; this is the term that I feel best captures what I do. When pressed to elucidate, I generally say that my role is to prepare athletes to compete, and I also work with injured athletes to return them to performing in competition. It is often at this point where the conversation devolves in a question and answer round:

- so you're a physio?

- no.

- oh, you're a personal trainer?

- no. I work with athletes.

- so strength and conditioning?

- well, yes that is part of what I do – but beyond making athletes stronger in the gym, a big part of what I do is work on other elements of athleticism such as movement mechanics

- so you coach sport?

- well, yes and no – I coach track and field athletics (and I used to coach rugby union), but I work with athletes in all sports, including artistic athletes; for instance, I work with a ballerina at the Bolshoi, yet I am certainly not a ballet instructor

blank stare

You see my predicament... However, I contend that you, the reader, could also describe yourself in the same terms: the odds are that you too are a coach of humans. If you reflect on many of your day to interactions, it is likely you will observe some element of coaching. This might be in the form of directing others, instructing, influencing, or simply engaging with the human in front of you and building rapport.

THE JOURNEY BEHIND THIS BOOK...

My early background was in team sports; growing up I played essentially any and all team sports that involved a ball, regardless of the shape, eventually settling on rugby union and rugby league football. I was a high achiever at school, but sport was the field that I could foresee capturing my attention for the decades to follow, so I baffled my teachers by choosing to pursue sport and exercise science at university, and after my undergraduate studies embarked on a PhD. Around this time I began my career as a practitioner working in professional sport with a rugby union team in the English Premiership. Initially I was employed as an applied sport scientist, and very soon I moved into the realm of strength and conditioning, working with players in the gym and on the field to prepare them for the rigours of playing a contact sport against other large humans. In the decades since I have embraced the opportunity to work with athletes across all sports and individual pursuits. This journey initially took me from England to Scotland, then across the world to the southern hemisphere, and latterly to North America.

My experience coaching sport began with coaching rugby union at university and club level, and somewhere along the way I fell into coaching track and field athletics, eventually coaching athletes to world level (culminating with attending the 2017 World Athletics Championships as part of the New Zealand team). I had not competed in track and field, so I took the unconventional 'outsider' path to acquiring the necessary technical knowledge and practical coaching skills, which involved a lot of independent study, as well as applied learning derived from working alongside some exceptional coaches. This path served me well as I was not bound by the coaching manual established ways of doing things, or the conventional wisdom in the sport!

Being the sport coach is a different endeavour to being a member of the athlete support staff, not least due to the fact that you (hopefully) hold ultimate authority over the other practitioners involved, and also ultimate responsibility for the outcome. These experiences thus prepared me well for the leadership and senior management roles I moved into as my career progressed from head coach and national lead positions to working in the capacity of coaching director and finally director of performance. During the time, the transition felt quite natural; after all, a major element of leadership and people management is coaching. This is a theme that we will return to often!

As an aside, my experience coaching track and field athletics also opened my eyes to how much room remains for athletes even at the top level to develop their athletic capabilities. In some ways working with track and field athletes ruins you for returning to work with athletes in other sports. Once you have coached sprinters, jumpers, and throwers, with some notable exceptions team sports and racquet sports players are just no longer impressive purely as 'athletes'. Equally, what this illustrates is the huge amount of scope there exists to enhance athletic performance in these sports – to essentially turn them into bona fide athletes in their own right. My experience is that this applies even to professional athletes at the highest level. For instance, I recently worked with a ten-year veteran of the National Basketball League who remarked he had not previously been exposed to the fundamental movement mechanics that we were working on.

My contention with this book is that there is equally a huge amount of untapped potential that we can realise with respect to human performance in general, simply by assimilating lessons from coaching and the world of elite sport. I have been fortunate to interact with some of the best coaches and practitioners in their respective sports and observe how they practice. A big part of coaching is simply paying attention. I have been able to make best use of these observation and experiences, as well as the insights that have been shared with me, in creating the content of this book.

Aside from being agnostic in how I practice, I am eclectic in where I source information. As you, the reader, will discover in the chapters that follow, I seek inspiration and draw insights from a host of different realms. I have come to subscribe to the 'outsider-insider' approach. Essentially this involves pairing the fresh eyes and unconventional thinking that an outside perspective can bring with the in-depth knowledge of context and subject matter expertise that comes with full immersion. It is my contention that such a blend offers a path to original but calibrated insights.

Finally, given that human performance and the topics we explore in the chapters that follow represent an endeavour for humans by humans, it also seems apposite to capture some of that story from a more personal perspective. To that end, examples from my own journey appear throughout each chapter. I will also invite you, the reader, to reflect and consider how the themes presented relate to your own experience. Ultimately this will be a necessary step in order for you to apply the principles and derive insights within the context of the realm in which you operate.

INTO THE BREACH WE GO…

The period during which I was inspired to write much of the content for the chapters coincided with the parallel project to bring *Prepared Athlete Training & Health* into existence to bring elite expertise and support to aspiring athletes locally in Vancouver, BC. A host of family, friends, and colleagues generously lent their support, input, and skills to help make the independent coaching venture a reality. This book therefore hopefully embodies the spirit of adventure and collaboration that spawned these parallel projects.

To guide the reader, the book is divided into four parts. In contrast with conventional approaches that go from 'micro' to 'macro', we begin with the environment in which you operate, and close with managing yourself as an individual. There is a rationale for this. Effecting change begins with the environment over which we have stewardship. Ultimately achieving success and steering the course over time however requires understanding and managing ourselves, in order to that we have an undistorted view of the external world, make good decisions, and interact successfully with others.

The opening section thus deals with the imperative of creating and maintaining a performance environment. The second part explores themes on leading and coaching others. The third delves into principles and practice in relation to coaching intervention, and draws on lessons from athlete preparation. The final part focusses on managing ourselves.

Part One: Creating the Environment

Both the working environment and motivational climate have a considerable bearing on behaviour on a group and individual level. As the saying goes, we are to some degree the product of our environment.

In our role as leader within our domain, we have stewardship over the environment in question. Similarly, if we are in a management role, often a major part of what we manage is the environment in which our team operates.

Whatever the setting, the climate that is created under our watch is ultimately our responsibility. If we are seeking to effect change the environment is accordingly where we must begin…

The 'C' Word

The word 'culture' is often thrown around in the context of teams and organisations. It seems everybody is talking about culture. Despite being a nebulous term and intangible in nature, culture is cited over and over again by leaders in sports and business alike. Everybody seems to be in agreement that culture is critical to success in different realms, even if we are not necessarily clear on what it is. Culture is simultaneously cited as both the root cause and universal solution to all ills. With the chapter that follows we will try to get a handle on the 'C' word. More importantly we will attempt to get to the bottom of what creates culture, and explore how we might go about effecting a change in team or organisational culture.

A WORKING DEFINITION...

"Culture remains one of the most vaguely deployed terms in social science"

– Cruikshank & Collins [6]

Culture has been described as a phenomenon of *social cognition* [6]. To break this down, culture is based on subjective factors, including perceptions, attitudes, and associated behaviours. By extension, organisational culture is the summation of these elements within the group as a whole, albeit prominent individuals and those in positions of influence tend to have an outsized contribution. Culture is also dynamic, and somewhat fluid, given that both those who make up the group and their attitudes and behaviours can change over time. That said, once established the culture within an organisation is notoriously recalcitrant to change.

MISSION STATEMENTS...

Almost every company has a mission statement. It has seemingly become important for teams and organisations to publicly declare their 'core values'. A couple of years ago, a national sports institute that I had some dealings with went one step further and proudly shared their 'culture plan'.

It is a wonder that teams and organisations are so quick to make these declarations, seemingly unconscious of what is at stake. It is like an incantation, as if reciting the words will miraculously make it so. Yet this act of declaration can have major consequences. Invoking the words and committing them to paper raises the stakes exponentially.

In the case of the aforementioned national sport institute, the lesson became 'beware the coach who can read' (for I was that coach).

As leaders we need to choose our words carefully when we are speaking of culture and related aspects. This is the case particularly when they are the right words.

CORE VALUES, CORE PURPOSE...

Culture is said to be values-based and purpose-driven. Many extend this logic to assume that we simply need to declare our values and define our purpose, et voila! Culture sorted! Sadly, this is not so.

As with the ubiquitous mission statement, we now hear the terms 'core values' and 'purpose' incessantly. Yet it is only recently that I have come across a definition (courtesy of Jim Collins in his book 'Good to Great' [7]).

To paraphrase, core values are those we will not compromise under any circumstances. By this definition, very few teams or organisations exhibit core values in practice.

Similarly, what constitutes our 'core purpose' is that which we will not waver from under any circumstances. Once again, such unwavering purpose is very rarely demonstrated in action.

WORDS AND ACTIONS...

By definition, value and purpose are demonstrated in our actions rather than our words. We might describe or declare what we aspire to; however the current state of affairs is already evident and observable. When we talk about creating a performance culture, we need to reckon with the existing culture that is already established. Every organisation, department, or team possesses a collective culture. After all, team or organisational culture is nothing more than the amalgamation of the perceptions, attitudes, and behaviours of the staff. Hence, from the time the group is assembled, the culture of the collective quickly becomes established, and is reflected in a top-down fashion in day to day behaviours, actions, and interactions.

I vividly recall attending a question and answer session with Chip Wilson, the founder of *Lululemon Athletica*, who had been invited to share his wisdom with the senior leadership and management staff of a commercial sport and health organisation that I was part of. The question was posed to Chip on how we might go about instilling the organisational culture that we aspired to. For context, the organisation had been in full operation for five years at this point. Chip's expression immediately betrayed his incredulity at the question, and he said that if he was the founder, he would be very concerned. It was his belief that the opportunity to establish organisational culture was during the early days. Chip went onto to say that given that our organisation was already five years in at this point, the culture was already firmly embedded, and as such it would be very difficult at such an advanced stage to make any significant change. The senior leadership were suitably discomfited by Chip's response.

In this context, as we already noted, making a grand declaration is inherently a high risk strategy. We need to acknowledge and reconcile how our words contrast with the present reality. Without doing so, what we are effectively doing is inviting those around us to take part in a collective illusion.

By extension, once we have stated our intent, there must be action to back it up, otherwise such bold statements can soon prove fatal for our credibility. In failing to match words with action, many great 'culture change' endeavours are frequently doomed from the outset.

"Don't explain your philosophy. Embody it"

– Epictetus

Actions always trump words. Absolutely all members of the team or staff must have clarity around what standards and behaviours are expected from them. But once again, these standards and behaviours must also be modelled in a top-down fashion, and consistently reflected by the actions of those in leadership positions at all levels of the organisation.

Declaring values (and outlining desired behaviours) may therefore seem easy in the short term, but has major medium- and long-term consequences. In the majority of cases, what has been declared, be it 'core values', 'core purpose', or 'shared vision', is not reflected in day-to-day actions. In order to be reflected in the culture of the team or organisation these elements must be evident in daily practice. Almost invariably there is a failure of implementation.

DETERMINING CURRENT REALITY...

As noted, from its inception, any group naturally develops a collective culture. Once again, there needs to be a reckoning with the culture that is already established in order to set about instilling whatever core values and core purpose we aspire to. As such, to effect any change in culture requires a readiness to face the present reality, and in turn we need to be willing to discover what is happening at ground level.

The challenge for those at the top of any organisation is that there is inevitably some degree of separation from what is happening on the ground. There are other challenges to contend with for those seeking to learn the unvarnished truth. One such challenge is that team members and staff will tend to tell those in leadership positions what they assume their superiors want to hear. A related challenge is the tendency for staff members to 'manage up', and paint a more favourable picture than what is evident in reality.

Those in leadership positions must be mindful of these challenges, and ready to be resourceful in their intelligence-gathering efforts. For instance, employing an 'inside-outside' strategy is one way to help calibrate and corroborate the insights provided by staff internally. Bringing in somebody who is independent and not beholden to the organisation to spend time to observing and gathering data from the staff can provide this outside perspective. The 'insider data' is also strengthened by having both internal and external reviews; on occasion, staff will be more comfortable being open about their concerns and more forthcoming with critical feedback with somebody who is not involved with the organisation.

Where this approach can fall down, as I observed on two different occasions with the same organisation, is when the independent person is subsequently hired by the organisation following the review. This places those staff who shared their views on the understanding that the information was privileged and there would be no repercussions in an invidious position. To avoid this, from the outset it should be made clear to all parties that the independent external person will remain independent of the organisation both during and following the review process.

Clearly any internal or external review can only happen periodically, and most often reviews are only instigated in sport and in business following an adverse outcome or poor results, at which time it is arguably too late. Similarly there is a need to stay connected with the reality on the ground in between those times. Red flag mechanisms offer a way to help remain in touch with the reality on the ground on an ongoing basis. The protocol is that any member of the team, regardless of seniority, is able to flag issues or alert the leadership to anything pertinent at any time. For this system to be successful it is critical to be clear that there are no sanctions for doing so, and then demonstrate that this is the case, in order to build trust among the staff to come forward with their concerns.

Clearly, in order for this to work, team members or staff must have confidence that they will be heard (and that there is some readiness to take action based on the intelligence provided). Once again they must have faith that there will not be any sanctions or negative consequences to coming forward. One way to encourage confidence might be to provide an option to provide information anonymously.

BEWARE IMPOSTERS...

It is true that values steer behaviours. However it is naive to assume that what a person or organisation declares to be their values will automatically be reflected in their actions. Rather the behaviours we observe (particularly during interactions with those who can do them no harm) shed light on the true values of the person (or organisation). Actions are always more illuminating than words.

It is a similar scenario when it comes to purpose. Being part of something greater than oneself is a route to commitment and meaning. However, this assumes a level of humility. A prerequisite is the ability and willingness to put ego aside.

A person's true commitment to the cause can be observed, particularly at times when they think nobody is watching. If a member of the team (or leadership group) is ego-driven and motivated by their own status invariably this will be reflected in their actions. In this way, a person's true 'core purpose' is generally clear to the skilled observer, regardless of what has been declared.

Paradoxically, those who say the words most often tend to be the people who fail to act accordingly – or indeed may behave in a manner that is contrary to the ideals espoused. Parroting the words becomes a tactic; they are used as armour to protect the individual from the consequences of their contrary actions that inevitably follow.

Conversely those who exemplify the desired team ethos rarely feel the need to say the words.

So take note of those individuals vigorously nodding during team meetings when matters of culture are being discussed. There is a chance that these people are your problem.

TEAM SELECTION (EJECT PROBLEM PASSENGERS)...

Let us briefly return to Jim Collins' study of organisations who made the transition from *good* to *great* [7]. What was observed is that it all begins with finding the right people; thereafter momentum builds from purposeful action. Interestingly, the authors observed that under these conditions 'alignment' with team values and purpose largely takes care of itself, without the need for any special strategy or investment of resources.

The authors put the personnel piece of the jigsaw in more simple terms: make sure you have the right people on the bus; next make sure they're in the right seats. However, the inescapable corollary of this proposition, which was also observed in practice, is that the leadership also must identify those who do not demonstrate the right character and behaviours, and then take appropriate action. In other words, the leadership must act to get the 'wrong' people off the bus.

Instilling 'core values' and 'core purpose' into the culture of the team ultimately requires the discipline and the will to eject those who are contrary to these ideals (and/or do not meet standards required). This applies particularly to those in the upper echelons.

"They say it's mostly vanity that writes the plays we act…"

– Mark Knopfler

Those people who are the problem, or an obstacle to the solution (or both), are often star performers otherwise. These individuals may be highly competent or even excellent in their work, but are nevertheless evidently driven by ego and advancing their own personal agenda. The reticence of the leadership to get rid of a star player is understandable; however, this is also the biggest impediment to effecting any real change. The mantra of team sports (outside of the US anyway) is that no player is bigger than the team. Put another way, no player is so good that the positive of their contribution to the team outweighs the insidious negative impact their conduct has on the collective over time.

DEATH BY A THOUSAND CUTS…

Always it is beguilingly easy to take the soft option. On the surface it often seems far less stressful to take the compromise option. We need to recognise this for what it is. At best we are failing to uphold standards; at worse we are actively appeasing or indulging those who are the issue. Funnily enough this strategy never helps our situation.

Whilst opting not to act might seem to involve less pain in the short term, ultimately the cost in terms of ongoing damage to the wider team is far greater. This scenario has been described as 'short term easy, long term hard'.

We can illustrate this syndrome with the analogy of the choice between amputating the limb (to eradicate the disease), versus death by a thousand cuts. The former scenario admittedly involves considerable short term pain; however we live to fight another day and thereafter have the opportunity to rebuild having resolved the issue once and for all. In practice the latter scenario (death by a thousand cuts) is most often preferred, after all the prospect involves far lesser short term pain. However, in doing so we ignore the fact that the ultimate outcome is we end up dead.

So often we prefer to defer acting until another day, in some distant hope that the issue will spontaneously resolve itself. This delusion is comforting. Moreover, for those in the hot seat, deferring or deciding not to act is clearly less discomfiting. Once again, we need to appreciate the consequences that are borne by others while we delay. Failing to discipline and ultimately eject problem individuals is harmful and can ultimately be fatal to the credibility of the leadership in the eyes of the rest of the staff.

APPLYING STANDARDS INSIDE-OUT AND TOP-DOWN...

As we have spoken about, the values and purpose that are declared must be authentic. These ideals must also be rigorously adhered to. Subscribing to a vision and endorsing a shared purpose are somewhat meaningless without establishing and maintaining clearly defined standards of practice and conduct.

As we have noted, culture is effectively defined by the day-to-day conduct and behaviours of all members of the team; however, it is shaped especially by those in leadership positions. We must demonstrate values and purpose that we espouse through our own actions. By extension, all members of the group must be granted the shared responsibility to hold those from the top down accountable to these standards.

Indeed it is crucial that those in positions of authority are held to a higher standard; it follows that those in senior leadership positions are held to the highest standard of all. Those towards the top of the organisation chart have a major bearing on the collective culture. They have proportionally greater scope to influence (or impede) culture change; and their actions impact a greater number of people within the team or organisation.

"Just because it is common sense does not mean it is common practice"

— Gilbert Enoka

Whilst most follow this logic, very rarely are these principles applied in practice. Tenure and standing in the organisation almost invariably confers privileged and protected status.

Once again, failing to be consistent when it comes to the crunch can be fatal to our credibility and undermines the legitimacy of the leadership. Those who believe in the purpose most fervently will be the first to become disenchanted when they see those ideals being violated without any consequences.

I have personal experience of this scenario. After being recruited by an organisation in a newly created director role in my initial information gathering it quickly became apparent from speaking with a representative sample of the existing staff that things were at something of a tipping point. Having enthusiastically bought into the vision they were sold during the hiring process they were becoming increasingly disillusioned by the realisation that this bore no resemblance to daily practice. Indeed they were dismayed to observe decisions and actions taken by those at the top of organisation that were entirely contrary to the declared vision, values, and purpose that they had subscribed to and strongly identified with. I dutifully reported these findings to the senior leadership. I also highlighted that the most staunch believers (i.e. the very people we needed to keep on side) were feeling the disconnect most keenly. Sadly, despite best efforts this trend largely continued, and within a year most of the key team members who were truly assets to the organisation had moved on (and with them went the best hope of salvaging the situation).

As noted, our task is not so much a matter of 'creating alignment' or motivating the troops. Rather we must avoid demotivating the staff, or provoking disillusionment among the 'right' people who we will need to move the team or organisation forwards. Ultimately this requires that we take the necessary action to deal with problem team members, regardless of (and indeed because of) their status.

Standards must be consistently applied, not just when it suits us. It is naive in the extreme to think people aren't watching.

CONVICTION AND COURAGE...

Most often the problem is not that those leading the team do not possess the right values, but rather that we are simply not willing or able to summon the strength of will and conviction to do the hard part and translate our beliefs into action. Essentially those in leadership positions must have the stomach to do what is necessary.

There are some hallmark traits of leaders who are able to change organisational culture and take their team from mediocre to great. Chief among these is an indomitable professional will to do what is necessary, tempered with uncommon personal humility.

Many otherwise good leaders essentially kill any chance of real progress with kindness. In essence they don't have the heart to make discomfiting decisions, particularly when it comes taking action to jettison those who are toxic elements in the team environment.

IN CLOSING: YOU ARE WHAT YOU REPEATEDLY DO...

"Greatness is largely a matter of conscious choice..."

— Jim Collins, Author of 'Built to Last' and 'Good to Great'

To develop the idea framed in the above quote further, I would contend that greatness is in fact a matter of a series of conscious choices (followed by action) on a day-to-day basis.

Despite 'culture' having become ubiquitous in the language of teams and organisations, in reality the vast majority fail in the implementation.

Culture is not particularly complicated. But it does involve hard work every day. As such, instilling a high performing culture (or altering existing culture) requires a great deal of will and conviction. In practice, it involves difficult decisions and discomfiting actions. It is understandable that the majority fail to execute, or rather choose the easy option, ultimately preferring not to execute when it gets hard.

Culture is a matter of actions rather than words. Establishing culture is a cumulative and iterative process. Borrowing from 'Good to Great' one final time, we can use the analogy of a heavy flywheel, whereby momentum very gradually builds as a result of impetus applied repetitively in a consistent manner over time. A great deal of sustained effort is required to overcome the initial inertia and get things moving, but once we have some momentum and things are travelling in the right direction it takes relatively less effort to keep the wheel turning.

Finally, those who truly wish to change culture have no need for declarations. Whilst there is a need to relentlessly share our vision, we communicate our values and demonstrate our purpose in our daily actions. The grand statements and surrounding fanfare that typically heralds 'culture' initiatives are not only superfluous but may be counterproductive from a credibility viewpoint.

REFLECTING AND CONNECTING THE DOTS...

How is culture catered for in your organisation?

What culture initiatives have been undertaken in teams or organisations you have been part of? To what degree do you believe they were effective?

Have you observed culture initiatives or approaches that have proven effective? If so, to what do you attribute their success?

To what extent do you feel organisational culture is a top-down, versus bottom-up phenomenon?

Based on your answer, do you feel altering existing culture is predominantly a top-down or bottom up process?

If you accept the proposition that culture encompasses the perceptions, attitudes, and behaviours on staff, how would you go about getting an accurate read on these aspects from the staff at any given time?

What strategies do you (or could you) employ to minimise distortion, and ensure that you get a representative view and unvarnished account on the state of play from staff members?

What measures or mechanisms would you employ to monitor the situation over time? Do you have an early warning system?

The Dynamics of the Performance Environment

The working environment within our domain is our first responsibility as leaders. In competitive sport, the motivational climate within the environments that come under our stewardship has a profound influence over the athletes we serve. Beyond the competition arena, the performance environment within a sporting context comprises the practice setting, the training facility, the changing room, and even the treatment room. Clearly the performance environment in other professional domains differs according to the specific context, however, these principles nevertheless have broad application beyond the realms of sport. In this chapter we aim to parse out the key themes, and then invite the reader to consider how these principles might be applied and adapted to the constraints of the 'performance environment' in the particular domain.

PILLARS OF A PERFORMANCE ENVIRONMENT...

The environment in which performers operate has a major bearing on conduct, interactions between team members, and ultimately performance outcomes. If we are striving for excellence in performance we must do all we can to create and maintain an environment that is conducive to this. Sustained success is supported by a performance environment that is built upon commitment to the pursuit and engagement with the process, rather than simply the rewards and satisfaction of achieving the end goal. This is a universal truth that applies to sport, to business, and to human performance in essentially all domains. Clearly the leader is not the only person who contributes to shaping the working environment; a host of individuals at different levels of the organisation will have significant influence over this. However, accountability for the environment ultimately resides with the leadership.

In the case of sport, the supporting cast may comprise a few or the many. In modern professional team sports, for example, the support staff can be of a similar number to the athletes in the playing squad. Beyond team sports, individual sports also ultimately represent a team endeavour, and as such there is often an extensive team of support personnel involved. In each of these instances, all parties involved have a bearing on the environment that is created during practice and in the competition arena. From a leadership perspective, it is thus crucial that these dynamics and interactions support rather than detract from the environment we are seeking to create and maintain.

A performance environment is also a learning environment. The relative emphasis on short term performance output versus learning and development will of course differ to some degree, based on the context – for instance, academy versus senior professional squads in elite sport. This may also vary at different points in time, and will tend to shift according to the proximity of the pinnacle event or competition – an example would be a quadrennial building towards an Olympic Games.

Whatever the domain, the performance environment hinges on all parties involved being aligned on a shared goal and having a common mission. Congruency of aims is arguably more assured in sport, albeit there is still a need for it to be clear and explicit that the coaches and support staff are working towards the same goals. The performer must have faith that the actions of everybody involved is motivated by the desire to make them better.

PERFORMANCE MANAGEMENT...

Establishing a performance environment is clearly a complex undertaking. It is also an iterative process that requires careful and ongoing management. To that end, authors have identified four discrete strands of *performance management*: strategic, operational, leadership of the performance team, and finally individual performance management [8]. Managing the performance environment in turn encompasses organisational structure and related processes, in addition to leadership, management, and one-to-one coaching.

Returning to sport, the duties of a performance director or a head coach are therefore quite extensive, particularly in the case of professional sport teams and national sports organisations. Whilst we tend to think of the role of a sport coach simply in terms of coaching athletes, there is often considerably more to this than meets the eye. Even for a coach of an individual athlete, there are multiple players in the process, as well as different external concerns and stakeholders that might infringe on the training, practice, and competition environments, and so must be managed accordingly.

"What I realised was the need to relentlessly share my vision"

– Adam Krikorian, Head Coach of the multiple Olympic and World Championships gold medal-winning USA Women's Waterpolo team

As noted in the observations shared by Adam Krikorian, strategic leadership in sport, or any performance-focussed domain, begins with consistently communicating the overarching vision for the collective. Beyond that, in order for there to be real clarity, the leadership group must also specify the strategic objectives, process goals, and milestone performance outcomes (with an indication of timelines). The expectations for all parties involved must also be clearly articulated, including the standards for day-to-day operations and general conduct; all should be clearly defined. Coming back to 'relentless' part of the quote, whilst it is important to declare the vision at the outset, this is not sufficient. In much the same way as we spoke about in the previous chapter, purpose, aims, objectives, and standards must be reinforced on an ongoing basis, and continually demonstrated in the actions of the leadership and key individuals within the organisation. This is necessary in order for respective members of the team to identify with the vision and invest themselves in realising the declared end goal.

"Every team I have coached is different but my expectations never change"

– Russ Ross, 7-time NCAA championship winning volleyball coach with Penn State

Operational performance management in essence concerns operationalising these respective aspects, which means creating structures, delineating responsibilities, allocating resources, establishing processes and devising metrics. In essence, the task is to create the capacity, provide logistical support, and develop the operational capability to facilitate a systematic approach to working towards the stated end goal, with appropriate feedback mechanisms to help remain on course. Whilst these terms might be more readily associated with business, we can equally observe each of these respective components in a well-managed Olympic training cycle [9], or in the year-to year planning and operations of consistently successful professional sports franchises.

Leading the performance team begins with the senior leadership team itself, and extends through all levels of the organisation. This includes managing interactions between and within subunits that are part of the organisation, and also social dynamics within working groups. In the case of sport or the performing arts, there must be a degree of harmony or synergy among the group of performers (for example, team-mates in team sports, or training partners in the case of an individual sport). Finally, a head coach or performance director must provide leadership, people management, and coaching to develop the capabilities of each individual. In sport, the head coach or performance director must lead and manage all stakeholders in a 360-degree fashion, never losing sight of the fact that the athletes remain the primary concern, and that every decision, action, and interaction should serve the ultimate mission or performance objective.

In sport and in business the multiple facets of leading and managing a performance environment has necessitated a shift away from autocratic management styles and dictatorial leaders towards alternative leadership approaches. In the business realm the shift towards a knowledge-based economy has been identified as driving this change in approach. This somewhat parallels sport, whereby the skills and tacit knowledge of the athletes is essential to the success of the organisation.

TRANSFORMATIONAL LEADERSHIP...

Transformational leadership has its origins in organisational psychology, but has also been applied to leadership in military settings and to sport over recent years.

The transformational leadership model described in the literature maps well to the four components of performance management outlined in the previous section. The transformational leadership inventory includes a strategic performance management component, namely *inspirational motivation* which pertains to articulating the vision and inspiring others to follow [10]. Similarly, leadership of the performance team is covered under *fostering acceptance of group goals*, *high performance expectations*, and *appropriate role modelling*, respectively. Individual performance management is also a notable feature, under the guise of *individual consideration* and *intellectual stimulation*.

The defining tenets of transformational leadership are an emphasis on inspiring others and a focus on stimulating thought and developing each individual within the group to realise their potential. The central premise is that this approach will ultimately lead to enhanced capability and higher levels of performance on an individual and collective level. Proponents of transformational leadership identify that addressing and satisfying the needs of individuals are important factors that serve to increase wellbeing among individuals with the group [11]. There is also a suggestion that the transformational leadership style fosters intrinsic interest and appreciation of the process among group members [12].

Perhaps the best way to illustrate the concept of transformational leadership is by drawing the distinctions from its opposite, i.e. *transactional leadership*. No doubt many jobs still operate on a transactional basis – i.e. employees are simply there for the pay cheque (and in turn the management regard employees as human capital and as an expendable asset), and work is solely motivated by the external reward (or punishment) that is contingent on the outcome. However, this is clearly not conducive to a performance environment, where meaning is derived from the mission, all parties strongly identify with the collective purpose, and the pursuit has value and is inherently motivating.

A transactional mindset sadly does still exist among certain coaches and practitioners operating in sport at various levels. There are 'prestige driven' coaches and practitioners, for whom the primary motivation is enhancing their own profile and basking in the reflected glory of the athletes' achievements. For these individuals the athletes or the team are essentially treated as a vehicle for their own agenda, and merely serve as a means for their own self-promotion. As the reader may sense, I view these individuals as akin to parasites, and my contention is that they have no place in a true performance environment.

It follows that there are some crucially important character-based selection criteria when assembling the leadership and support team. In the case of sport, these include a mentality of service to the athlete, and the humility to subjugate ego, self-interest, and any individual agendas to the pursuit of a shared goal. Equally, transformation leadership is somewhat reliant upon the levels of intrinsic motivation among individuals within the group. In other words, this leadership strategy to some extent presupposes that group members are intrinsically motivated to some degree and therefore amenable and responsive to this approach. Taking a less generous viewpoint, transformational leadership could conceivably be exploited by group members with a transactional mindset. Accordingly, there is a need for staff members and performers to be similarly recruited and selected based on attitude and work ethic, just as much as skills and expertise.

SERVANT LEADERSHIP...

What defines a servant leader is the philosophy of placing others' needs and aspirations above their own. The servant leadership model has elements in common with transformational leadership, for instance with respect to its emphasis on individual development and personal growth of member of the organisation [13]. The other basis for servant leadership is empowering people. To that end, the traits associated with servant leaders include humility, authenticity, and acceptance [13].

Part of the appeal of the servant leadership idea from the perspective of developing a performance environment is that it is associated with fostering intrinsic motivation and developing capability (individual and collective); both of which are key drivers of a performance environment.

Given the nature of the role of the coach, the servant leadership model would seem to lend itself to application in sport. Servant leadership would seem to apply not only to those at the top of the organisation, but to all staff members who lead departments and serve others in the capacity of coach or practitioner. For instance, in the context of sport, this would include all members of the support staff. By definition these individuals operate in service to the athletes, and so the traits and premise of servant leadership is highly applicable. Once again this contrasts sharply to self-serving coaches and practitioners who seek to benefit personally from their association with the athletes, and claim credit for their success. The notion of servant leadership would in fact seem to extend to all those within an organisation who direct others, including peers and colleagues. The contribution of these individuals certainly needs to be recognised, and often they demonstrate all of the attributes of servant leaders.

Whilst the servant leadership model is highly appealing, it is also somewhat vague and thus hard to operationalise [13]. As a result, there has not been a great deal of empirical study of servant leadership in an applied setting. The dimensions of servant leadership are inherently subjective and it is difficult to objectively evaluate outcomes, and so in some ways the concept is more aspirational than actual. That said, there have been some attempts to study this model in the context of sport, typically in a high school or university setting. Preliminary data based on athlete survey data suggest that the high school and collegiate athletes studied responded better to coaches categorised as servant leaders based on athlete questionnaires [14, 15]. There is also some support for individual traits, such as the apparent benefits of coach humility [16].

HORIZONTAL LEADERSHIP...

Continuing the theme of empowering staff members and performers, horizontal leadership pertains to operating in a more decentralised manner to the more traditional top-down hierarchical organisation structure. From an operational performance management perspective, this approach is more appropriate when striving to create a performance environment in most knowledge and expertise-based domains [17].

"As we look ahead into the next century, leaders will be those who empower others"

– Bill Gates

Directing and instructing are clearly part of the role of the leader or coach. However, direction and instruction only goes so far; ultimately it is the performer who will be operating on the ground, not the coach or leader. Sport exemplifies a field that does not lend itself to a centralised leadership model, when it comes to making decisions and directing actions in real-time; and the same is arguably also true in business and other domains of human performance. From an operational viewpoint a crucial objective in our quest to engender a performance environment is to assign authority and distribute capability where it is required.

"No operation extends with any certainty beyond the first encounter with the enemy"

– Helmuth Von Moltke

Our ability to anticipate what is going to happen, and therefore account for future events in our advance planning, is extremely limited. Once again, this points to the need to provide those on the ground with the capability and authority to respond accordingly as the situation unfolds, as opposed to relying on top-down command from leadership who are removed from the situation. Indeed sport is perhaps the best illustration of this. The opportunities for the coaching staff to intervene and provide direct input under competition conditions are at best sporadic and quite limited in terms of effectiveness. Even in the most structured sports (American football comes to mind) that do allow some opportunity for coaching staff to call plays during breaks in play, the players themselves must still read the situation in front of them and respond accordingly in real-time without external input.

It should be noted that horizontal leadership is something that emerges over time as the project evolves. Essentially the aim to create the conditions for those on the front lines to read the situation and assume the authority to make decisions and take whatever action is necessary. It follows that a key objective for coaches and leaders is to develop performers' capabilities in these areas, with ongoing guidance to enhance and refine their ability to operate and problem-solve independently as they progress.

PEER LEADERSHIP...

Peer leadership can to some extent be viewed as an extension of horizontal leadership. If there is merit in those on the ground assuming responsibility to make decisions and take action, it follows these individuals can also assist with providing leadership to their peers. Peer leadership has been studied in relation to transformational leadership [18], and also shares elements with servant leadership, as noted in the previous section.

"Successful teams are bound together by individual and mutual accountability"

– Yukelson & Rose [19]

Peer accountability is the Holy Grail for organisations who aspire to be high performing. A common observation in relation to the great sports teams is that they did not require the coaching staff to enforce discipline. In great teams the performers themselves impose and maintain standards in the daily environment. Another notable feature that is characteristic of champion teams is that they have leaders throughout the squad. Beyond the realms of sport, these elements of peer leadership are something that all high performing organisations should aspire to. Informal leaders within the peer group not only contribute to raising performance levels among those around them, but also provide the glue to strengthen social bonds as well as helping to regulate dynamics within the group [20].

Something that is worth considering, which oddly is rarely discussed in the literature, is how devolved peer leadership can be attained. As has been famously declared, leaders create leaders, so to some extent this is contingent in part on the leadership and the performance environment that is created under their stewardship. However, this will be a process. An interesting investigation noted that new teams gradually transitioned from a vertical top-down leadership structure to more distributed leadership during the course of the 24-week study period [21].

"Captains are elected… Leaders emerge!"

– Russ Rose, in Yukelson & Rose [19]

Leaders within the group similarly emerge over time. As with horizontal leadership, peer leadership is thus something that evolves and emerges, rather than a situation that we can create or appoint from the outset. Individuals will assume greater responsibility as they demonstrate not only the willingness but also the capability. As individuals within the group demonstrate leadership traits over time the other members of the group will likewise become more inclined to entertain taking direction from them and following their lead [21]. Equally the leadership can assist the process and help cultivate relevant capabilities via mentorship as these individuals make themselves known.

What is also important to note is that peer leadership does not replace leadership from above. For instance, in a sporting context, athlete leadership is not to the exclusion of the leadership provided by the coach. Rather, this is a shared and complementary endeavour. In other words, the benefits of coach- and athlete-leadership are additive [22]. What we are therefore aiming for is a shared leadership model, as opposed to delegating responsibility entirely.

NOT ALL SWEETNESS AND LIGHT…

With terms such as transformational, servant leadership, and humble leadership, the reader of the literature might form an opinion that leading a performance environment is about being warm and fuzzy. Whilst this makes for an appealing narrative, the interpretation in much of the literature is based on surveys and interviews, and are likely somewhat influenced by social norms. Certainly, an exclusive emphasis on socially desirable traits does not entirely resonate with those who have worked in elite sport, or indeed high performing environments in other domains.

From the positivist slant provided in much of the literature it is easy to get the impression that it is desirable for leadership to be yielding, open to compromise, and amenable to conforming to performers' wishes. However, this does not entirely square with my own experiences of operating in elite sport and observing high performing leaders, coaches, and practitioners over an extended period. Of the authors in the sports psychology field who have contributed to the organisational performance literature, I give more credence to Professor Dave Collins, given that he has actually served in a national performance director role (with UK Athletics). Collins and others have provided a counterpoint to the dominant narrative that performance leadership is based primarily on socially desirable traits.

These authors have taken a lead from the business management literature highlighting notable examples of wildly successful entrepreneurs and leaders of organisations who famously exhibit less 'socially desirable' character traits and behaviours. Such analysis demonstrates that prominent industry leaders certainly exploited the *dark arts* in their leadership style, and some engaged in morally questionable management activities to their benefit (Steve Jobs and Mark Zuckerberg come to mind). Investigators have sought to explore the extent to which leaders in performance sport exhibit 'dark' traits in their leadership and interactions, based on insights gathered from athletes [23] and interviews with elite team leaders themselves (head coaches and performance directors) [24]. I should state that I do not fully support the premise of the *dark traits* approach, for instance the mapping of selected traits to extrapolated subclinical traits. Nevertheless interviews with leaders and athletes alike cite recollections of instances where the actions of those in leadership positions indicated miscellaneous dark traits, as characterised. For instance, leaders and head coaches recalled instances of being 'strategically manipulative' to influence the thinking of staff and athletes [24]. They also cited social dominance behaviours in the course of discharging their leadership duties, and a degree of ruthlessness in maintaining values and enforcing standards.

Returning to the contention that leadership relies upon socially desirable traits, my own assessment would be that compromise and conformity have very little do to with instilling a performance culture. I do however agree that there is a need to be a good human; in order to have sustained success requires enduring relationships built on genuine human connection, and so nor do I fully subscribe to the dark arts viewpoint. It should be considered that leaders and coaches might have success in spite of certain traits and behaviours, rather than because of them. Personal integrity, humility, earning the respect of others, and showing respect to them in return, are all absolutely critical (and 'socially desirable') leadership traits and behaviours. However, indomitable will and relentless commitment to the highest standards are equally crucial differentiators, albeit I would take issue with the notion that these constitute 'dark' traits.

A performance environment is built upon non-negotiables. In essence, it is about creating something that others aspire to be part of. As such, all parties who wish to be involved are expected to subscribe to the highest standards of operating, and it should be explicit that they will be rigorously held to these standards. Our goal is therefore to create these expectations, and in order to remain credible we must enforce them.

The suggestion that coaches and leaders are manipulative also strikes me as something of a lazy and misleading characterisation. As we will explore in a later chapter, manipulating the constraints of the environment is fundamental to the coaching process. Similarly, good leaders and coaches effectively influence others' thinking, for instance altering an individual's perceptions to overcome their preconceived notion of what they are capable of, and what is possible. Once again, I would argue that this is somewhat different to 'manipulative behaviour' as generally defined; we need to consider the context.

A performance environment further requires coherence and cohesion between different parts of the organisation, and within the group of performers. Part of achieving this is exercising zero tolerance for internecine disputes that may otherwise develop between departments, disciplines, and cliques that may form within the group. It is important to differentiate such disputes over spheres of influence (turf wars) and competing agendas from the cognitive conflicts and disagreements on matters of substance that are conversely important to the health of the organisation. That said, whatever the (legitimate) issue that is being contested, there needs to be an explicit expectation that all parties will behave like grownups and engage in a respectful way to avoid disagreements escalating and becoming acrimonious. There also needs to be an understanding that these debates should be conducted in the proper forum.

From a leadership perspective, regulating inter- and intragroup dynamics therefore requires careful handling. For instance, the leadership should seek to ensure that favour is not shown to one subgroup over another. Equally there needs to be a readiness to step in and act swiftly and decisively to break up factions and quell petty squabbles that might otherwise develop into rifts within the organisation. Using the dark traits parlance, enforcing and regulating these aspects might arguably constitute 'social dominance' behaviours. Indeed these actions might ultimately include removing repeat-offending individuals from the organisation. Once again, this willingness to do what is necessary in the interests of the group, perhaps akin to what has been termed 'performance-focussed ruthlessness' in the literature [23], is a far cry from simply being agreeable and friendly.

THE CRITICAL IMPORTANCE OF CANDOUR...

Irrespective of leadership style, candid feedback and unambiguous communication is a prerequisite when seeking to create an environment that fosters growth and development of individuals. It should be recognised as a mark of respect when others are frank and honest in sharing their feedback, and make the effort to express views that concern us directly in person. This is a departure in thinking for many. The more conventional narrative is that people are more expressly concerned with not causing offence or harming the person's feelings.

"Rather than love, than money, than fame, give me truth"

– Henry David Thoreau

In a performance context choosing not to share feedback is akin to killing with kindness. It does a great disservice to other team members when we fail to express our concerns or pertinent views, particularly in the case that we have shared these opinions with a third party. Feedback should be direct, consistent, and unambiguous.

"Coach Rose is not afraid to tell it like it is; he is always honest, direct, and to the point with his feedback and constructive criticism, sometimes brutally honest"

– Yukelson & Rose [19], describing Russ Rose, volleyball coach with Penn State, who holds the best win:loss record in NCAA history

There is also an argument that when we choose to spare somebody's feelings, this is actually a selfish, and even cowardly act. This scenario whereby the source professes to care about the person in question but chooses to stay silent to protect their feelings has been described as 'ruinous empathy' in Kim Scott's book *Radical Candor* [25]. In many instances what motivates this behaviour is not in fact how it might hurt the other person, but rather our own aversion to the prospect of dealing with the aftermath in the event that what we have to say does upset them.

The other potential scenario when people choose not to voice critical feedback is that they unabashedly do not in fact care enough about the person to speak up, and might even derive some advantage from allowing the other party to remain blissfully unaware. This has been described as 'manipulative insincerity' [25]. Once again, failing to do what is necessary and provide what is critical feedback can be viewed as a show of disrespect, and demonstrating a lack of regard for the other person, rather than a sign of kindness.

If we wish to operate in a performance environment then all parties should enter into a collective agreement to be candid with each other. As part of this, each individual must consent to entertaining the merits of the feedback or constructive criticism offered, rather than becoming defensive or dwelling on hurt feelings after the event. As with choosing to operate in elite sport, opting to be part of a performance environment requires us to be brave and not be precious in the face of feedback and criticism. If we want to be better, there needs to be acknowledgement that direct feedback and constructive criticism are necessary.

When we seek to be empowered similarly this requires an undertaking to be accountable; any member of the team cannot expect to be granted one without assuming the other. The terms of the agreement need to be made explicit and understood from the outset. Thereafter the expectation of accepting and embracing accountability in exchange for empowerment needs to be rigorously upheld by all parties.

Accordingly, there should be an expectation and explicit permission on the part of all members of the organisation to express the unvarnished truth in a 360-degree manner. This necessarily includes the undertaking to provide direct and honest feedback to colleagues, those they are responsible for, and those in authority within the organisation on a regular basis. For leaders within the organisation this should not be viewed as an aspiration for some vague purpose of culture, but rather as an imperative. Only by cultivating the practice of 360-degree candid feedback can those at the top of the organisation have any real appreciation of the situation on the ground.

TO SUM UP...

There are elements of architecture and engineering in creating and maintaining a performance environment. The architecture part concerns assembling the right personnel from the outset to provide the foundations, and articulating the vision and mission provides the scaffolding for the structure as a whole, with explicit expectations and standards that all parties subscribe to. As architects, we also need to create the sub-structures and processes to operationalise what has been outlined and work towards agreed objectives.

We can regulate the dynamics of the environment thereafter by engineering conditions on an ongoing basis and managing situations as they develop. The engineering challenge is to balance the paradoxical need to empower others but also provide periodic intervention for quality control and to ensure things continue to operate in the desired manner. Such intervention includes strategically deployed assertive (and even ruthless) action as demanded by the circumstances of situations that arise.

The approach to leadership and performance management to some extent will depend on the audience we are working with, and also the context in which we are operating. Even within the context of sport, what has efficacy with a squad of high school or college players will clearly differ to what is required in professional and Olympic sport. These respective environments, including the profile and expectations of the athletes and the dynamics and external considerations involved (such as media and funding partners), are radically different in each case, so it follows we should tailor our approach accordingly. The performance management challenge in professional and Olympic sport for instance requires multidirectional management [26], extending both outwards (media, external stakeholders) and upwards (owners, board of directors, funding bodies, etc.).

REFLECTING AND CONNECTING THE DOTS...

What are your thoughts? How would you rate the health of the environment you presently operate in?

How would you describe the present leadership structure? Which of the models described in this chapter do you feel best applies?

Would you say the present issues with your working environment are chiefly a problem of architecture, or engineering?

If you were tasked with making changes, would your first step be to alter the structure (architecture approach) or how things function within the existing structure (engineering approach)?

To what extent are individuals at all levels of the organisation empowered to take initiative and solve problems? Are there opportunities to encourage and facilitate more of this?

How do you (or could you) seek to ensure that accountability remains a key operating principle within the working environment? How is this presently modelled by the leadership?

To what extent is candour an explicit expectation within and between working groups within the organisation? How is this managed and reinforced?

How effective are the lines of communication and transmission of intelligence from the various branches of the operation to the leadership?

To what extent is the leadership well informed about the real conditions on the ground? What distortion is there? How might this be managed?

Fostering Diversity

Divergence of opinion has traditionally been viewed in less than positive terms: when x and y don't see eye to eye on a particular subject, this is generally seen as problematic (particularly if x or y is in charge). By extension, we hear of the virtues of assembling a group of 'like-minded' individuals. Organisations typically promote compromise and conformity as virtues to foster harmony and unity within the group (as well as obedience). Contrary to this, the wisdom of crowds illustrates the benefits of aggregating judgements from a broad and disparate group of individuals. To further strengthen the case for diversity of thought and experience, 'cognitive diversity' is in fact found to be the major factor that differentiates successful teams and organisations. In this chapter, we explore the paradoxical ways that diversity and divergence in thinking are conceptualised and dealt with, to see what lessons can be learned on a group and individual level in whatever context we work in.

Intuitively it makes sense that having a diverse mix of knowledge and experience within the group will be of benefit. Such diversity should assist how we are collectively able to problem-solve. Using the example of sport, diversity in thinking is helpful to navigate the complexity inherent in working with athletes, and operate in the uncertainty of sport. In business speak, 'cross-functional collaboration' is identified as key for agile problem solving and innovation, rather than operating in 'functional silos'. Yet the conventions of organisations and our own foibles, with respect to how we entertain 'otherness' in terms of ideas and individuals, have a tendency to drive selection and behaviours in the opposite direction from the diversity we seek.

Here we have a paradox: the benefits of diversity in thought and divergence in opinion are apparent on a rational level; yet humans and organisations do not entertain these things in a particularly rational manner. These issues are as evident and prevalent in sport as they are in business. Given the intractable nature of the problem, we have been slow to reckon with the questions and challenges posed at an organisation and individual level in the respective realms of human performance.

WISDOM OF CROWDS...

The wisdom of the crowd phenomenon was noted in Nate Silver's excellent book on the art and science of prediction [27]. What this refers to is that a prediction or judgement based on the aggregation of diverse estimates from members of a large group is frequently superior to the judgement of an individual expert.

It follows that as leaders we should be seeking to leverage the collective intelligence of the group to improve our judgement and problem solving capabilities. On an intuitive level, it makes sense that being able to aggregate diverse knowledge, experience, and perspectives on a problem should help us form superior judgements and devise better solutions, and indeed this is typically the case.

By extension, it is important to note that the 'hive mind' works to best effect when it contains dissenting voices. For the aggregating effect to work there must be diverging opinions. From this viewpoint, the challenge is to ensure the hive mind continues to function in a way that preserves and safeguards dissenting voices.

Specifically, one tendency we need to guard against is 'herding'. Clearly, if the thinking and opinions of individual members of the group become unduly influenced by the prevailing view of the largest or most vocal sub group then they no longer function as independent thinkers, or at least are dissuaded from expressing their independent viewpoint. Once again, as the leader, it follows we need to be aware of our own influence over the group in this regard.

Unfortunately, as a social species, humans tend to be susceptible to peer influence. In effect these tendencies serve to compromise the collective intelligence of the 'hive mind'. Herding mentality, and other group dynamics that lead to our independent thinking becoming 'socialised', tends to negate the range and diversity of opinion that underpin the wisdom of crowds.

THE CASE FOR (COGNITIVE) CONFLICT...

Diversity has been described as a double-edged sword. The main counter argument against a diverse group is the propensity for conflict between members of the group and lack of cohesion as a collective. According to this logic, a homogenous group is deemed desirable on the basis that there will be less potential for conflict between members or subgroups within the team or working group.

As noted in the opening of the chapter, conflict is generally viewed in less than positive terms. On that basis, it seems we need to make the case that conflict is necessary and positive, and therefore something that should be embraced and even encouraged.

In doing so we do however need to make the distinction between cognitive conflict, which is based on the content of the respective arguments and focussed on the task at hand, versus inter-personal conflict that is, well, personal, and thus more emotive and likely to lead to personal animosity. Clearly this can be a matter of interpretation. One of the protagonists might feel the disagreement is based purely on the different viewpoints expressed (i.e. cognitive conflict). The other individual involved may however 'take it personally', so that for them it is an 'affective conflict', which is laden with emotion (hence 'affect') and centres on the individuals involved [28].

The latter 'affective' type of conflict between individuals has the propensity to harm relationships and is thus deemed dysfunctional and potentially destructive. Perhaps this helps explain why the notion of conflict within teams and working groups has such negative connotations for many of us. It is nevertheless crucial that we are able to engage in cognitive conflict in order to leverage the diverging viewpoints of team members. Only in this way can we fully benefit from the collective wisdom of the group during the strategic decision making process [28].

Conflicting ideas (i.e. cognitive conflict) similarly drive innovation within teams and organisations. This is particularly apparent at senior levels of management. Cognitive conflict between members of the senior management team is linked to the likelihood of the organisation to engage in innovation and explore different strategies [29]. Good leaders encourage members of their team to provide alternate viewpoints and argue with them.

SURFACE VERSUS DEEP DIVERSITY...

As reported in the Harvard Business Review [30], studies of executive groups discovered that diversity in terms of more obvious criteria such as age, ethnicity, and gender did not show any correlation to which groups were successful. Rather, it was diversity in terms of the perspectives and thinking of individuals within the group that separated those groups that were most effective. This illustrates the distinction between 'surface' diversity, which is easily observable, and 'deep' diversity that is less immediately apparent, as it relates to less tangible character traits, and the experience, knowledge, and perspective that the individual has accrued over time [31]. What distinguishes these individuals is that they think differently and adopt a different approach to solving problems.

We can adopt a working definition of cognitive diversity that includes acquired knowledge, perspectives, information processing, problem solving, and ability to handle novelty and complexity. Effectively we are looking for the following: knowledge within and across domains; variety of experiences that inform and influence their perspective; how they entertain and process new information; how they think about problems; and how they approach and solve new problems.

BENEFITS OF COGNITIVE DIVERSITY...

One way in which cognitively diverse groups enhance collective wisdom is by group members sharing their knowledge, experience, and perspectives. The degree of knowledge sharing between members of the group is in turn related to the cognitive diversity within the group, so that a more diverse group share knowledge to a greater extent [32]. The composition of the group accordingly has a bearing on their collective ability to make good judgements and solve problems. Cognitive diversity also supports the collective ability to learn over time and respond to changing conditions [33]

Groups that are cognitively diverse are less prone to bias in judgement [34]. The pioneering work of Daniel Kahneman and Amos Tversky demonstrated that as individuals we are prone to common cognitive biases that affect our judgements and our decisions [35]. It follows that making judgements and decisions in a way that incorporates diverging points of view from members of a group will help to combat these individual cognitive biases [36]. Decisions based on the collective wisdom of the group thus serves to reduce decision errors; equally, this is reliant upon the cognitive diversity of the group.

Thus there are a number of mechanisms through which cognitively diverse groups are ultimately able to arrive at better decisions with superior outcomes [37]. Interestingly, the collective decision making of a group that exhibits cognitive diversity also yields more creative solutions.

The collective creativity of the group is further related to the degree of cognitive diversity among group members, assuming we are operating in a collaborative environment [31]. Fostering creativity and innovation is the Holy Grail for those seeking 'organisational agility' to navigate an ever changing environment. Innovation is recognised as a major driver for organisational performance, as well as the means to adapt to changes in the competitive environment or market place [32]. This is as true in competitive sport as it is in the contemporary business setting. In sport the shifting landscape might constitute accommodating rule changes or strategies and tactics adopted by opponents. The competitive environment encapsulated as 'the market' in business and commerce is similarly in a constant state of flux.

There is arguably no more dynamic environment than team sports. Football (or soccer for the North American reader) is perhaps the best exemplar of this, with ten outfield players on each side, very little restriction on movement around a relatively large playing area, and extended periods of 'live' action when the ball is in play. Players require creativity and flexibility to come up with novel and workable solutions in the moment, and this occurs multiple times every game. Moreover, this is not just on an individual attacker-versus-defender basis, but often encompasses a collaborative effort involving team mates in the vicinity, who must recognise the situation and respond appropriately to cooperate in the play as it evolves. Once again, preliminary evidence suggests that teams which are more diverse, with supportive coaching environments that promote individuality and autonomy, demonstrate greater initiative and higher levels of creativity [16]. This is expressed both on an individual basis and in how players perform collectively.

Clearly leveraging cognitive diversity is key to our collective ability to innovate, adapt, and respond to a constantly shifting competitive landscape. In particular, it seems crucial to possess cognitive diversity within leadership groups, especially at senior levels of the organisation.

But given that the 'deep' diversity we seek is not immediately visible, how do we then go about screening and selecting for cognitive diversity?

SELECTING FOR COGNITIVE DIVERSITY...

Hiring should be driven by a desire to enrich and add to the diversity within the collective. This contrasts sharply with the conventional approach of evaluating prospective new hires based on how they might fit with existing culture or group identity. To give an example from my own experience in a senior management role, when recruiting for new staff I was clear that I was seeking to strengthen the team by bringing in individuals with different experience and education from other countries, systems, and environments in relation to our existing staff. My rationale was that we did not need more of the same. I felt strongly that adding what I viewed as much needed diversity in terms of experience and perspectives would ultimately strengthen the team by exposing our existing staff to different ideas and ways of operating. In this way, I believed we could expand individual staff members' horizons beyond what they had become accustomed to when operating within their existing bubble.

Practically, my efforts to recruit for cognitive diversity meant paying particular attention to the education and experiences that candidates brought with them from their academic and professional journey to date. As an aside, an obstacle to recruiting on these criteria are the restrictive policies and procedures in force in many countries when it comes to securing work permits and legal right to work for overseas applicants. Whilst it is an understandable policy on a number of levels, those countries and organisations that give 'native' applicants first priority nevertheless effectively serve to obstruct efforts to recruit for diversity of experience.

That said, these challenges are not insurmountable. And even if we only consider 'native' applicants, those individuals who have invested the time and effort to travel to live and work in different environments and cultures would be favoured when recruiting based on cognitive diversity selection criteria. Deriving the benefits of overseas experience does however appear to depend on the individual having committed to spending a significant period of time working in a foreign country and immersing themselves in the culture, rather than simply visiting or spending a shorter period of time [38].

In terms of traits, what I probe for during the interview process is how the individual responds to challenge, and how they entertain new ideas that might conflict with what they have been taught previously. Similarly, how the applicant speaks to the systems and models they cite as employing in their practice offers important insights. Finally, examining the extent to which they allow for uncertainty in their answers is also indicative.

Ultimately, in order to add to the collective intelligence of the 'hive mind', the individual needs to be not only open to new and conflicting ideas, but also able to retain their independence of thought and resist being unduly influenced by their peer group. Similarly, the individual must possess the courage to express their independent viewpoint, whatever the consensus view of the group, or views expressed by authority figures. For instance, if the individual has an undue need for affirmation or approval this is likely to prove problematic, given it will present a major barrier to expressing the dissenting views that are so vital.

Another excellent criteria employed by a friend and colleague of mine when recruiting staff and selecting graduate assistants is that he looks for individuals who know more than he does within a particular domain or subject area. Essentially he recruits people who can teach him something.

ORGANISATIONAL BARRIERS TO COGNITIVE DIVERSITY...

Operational structure and conventions within organisations typically serve to drive towards uniformity of opinion and a shared approach to both working and problem solving. By definition, this tends to negate or at least discourage diversity within the hive mind. As such, when diverging opinions are expressed this tends to be interpreted as dissent, leading both the opinion and the person who offered it to be received in a correspondingly negative manner.

In a sporting context, the institute of sport model is an example of an organisation that is structurally prone to these problems. Institutions by their nature have an in-built tendency towards conformity in thinking and working practices. This is a consistent theme whatever the particular local version, as I have learned on my travels in different parts of the world.

The problem with promoting a common and shared view of how things should operate is that naturally this serves to constrain how we approach problems. By definition, conformity and uniformity discourages alternative views and approaches. Ultimately, on an individual and collective level, this makes us less able to entertain novelty and cope with uncertainty and complexity. Ironically, novelty, uncertainty, and complexity are the very elements that we need to deal with when working with athletes and in sport; and this equally applies to the dynamic nature and unpredictability that is inherent to business and other realms.

Nepotism and 'jobs for the boys' likewise remains a factor that drives recruitment for coaching and back room staff in professional sport. As a recruitment strategy this is clearly not conducive to cognitive diversity. By definition, granting jobs to others based on shared history and personal relationships is unlikely to bring a great deal of diversity of knowledge, experience, and perspective to the coaching and support staff. If we examine the demise of the Leicester Tigers rugby dynasty over the past decade (previously the dominant force in English rugby and champions of Europe on multiple occasions), the predilection of the club's management to recruit retiring players to the coaching staff has arguably been a contributing factor.

Elite sport is an unforgiving and not particularly congenial environment that does not afford a great deal of tolerance for bruised egos or hurt feelings. By definition, those who operate in the crucible of competitive sport must be ready to entertain conflict and be receptive to being challenged on a routine basis. If you are unduly affected by harsh words, elite sport is not a good career choice. Similarly, leaders in sport do not have the luxury of being comfortable, taking action simply to appease others, or being appeased by those who advise them.

As in business, being successful, or even surviving, requires a readiness of those in leadership positions to face the brutal facts of their present situation. Clearly this is greatly assisted by having a support staff and decision making team who are direct and provide their unvarnished assessments and opinions. Having our chums around us, or being surrounded by a collection of sycophants is not conducive to facing the objective reality of what is required to be successful, and indeed may not be survivable for somebody in a head coach or performance director position.

Excessively dominant or dictatorial leadership represents another barrier to realising the benefits of the cognitive diversity that exists within the group. Domineering leaders likewise tend to constrain creativity and discourage dissenting opinions or open discourse on potential alternative solutions and strategies. There is some evidence that the leadership style and the associated environment can also impact knowledge sharing between team members and the learning that occurs within teams. By definition, intrusive management practices such as micro-managing similarly hinders autonomy, and tends to inhibit others from taking any initiative or making effective decisions in the moment.

Beyond structural constraints, domineering leadership, and management interference, there are also a number of conventions and practices that favour herding and inhibit independent thinking. Examples range from group brainstorming, to working groups and consensus by committee. Whilst decision making and judgement can benefit from soliciting the independent opinions of individuals within the group, paradoxically we need to be careful to mitigate the influence of group dynamics and social pressures when we bring individuals together as a group. In essence we need to actively combat group think in order to leverage the hive mind in ways that helps rather than hinders.

BARRIERS ON A PERSONAL LEVEL...

On an individual level it can be discomfiting to be faced with somebody who sees things differently, and those who express ideas that conflict with our own. It can be unsettling to be exposed to thinking that deviates from what we understood to be true, or confronted by ideas that contradict our present thinking on the topic.

"One big mistake people repeatedly make is focusing on proving themselves right, instead of focusing on achieving the best outcome"

– Shane Parrish

Similarly, when making group decisions and seeking to solve problems there is a natural tendency to become attached to our viewpoint or proposed solution in the face of competing ideas and opinions. As noted in the quote above, our motivation tends to be a determining factor in how we engage in the debate. The question becomes are we most interested in being right, or seeking enlightenment and ultimately arriving at the best outcome?

Without a separation between our ideas and our sense of self we are also likely to take disagreement or criticism of our viewpoint as a personal affront. As with most things, ego is the biggest barrier to realising the benefits of cognitive diversity on an individual and a group level. This is certainly the case when we are part of a peer group, but all the more so when we are in a leadership position.

Unsurprisingly as humans we typically gravitate towards those who see things as we do and have shared experiences in common. It is natural for humans to seek affirmation, so we find it comforting to be around like-minded individuals. These tendencies do however make us prone to cognitive biases which lead us to be less receptive to alternate viewpoints and others who see things differently than we do. As humans, we typically favour sources and information that correspond to the opinions and viewpoints that we subscribe to, and we tend to discredit and disregard the rest.

To compound these tendencies, in the era of smart technology, websites and applications are also constantly monitoring and learning our preferences, views, and biases in order to curate what we see when we use a search engine and browse social media. Essentially these websites and applications take our views, preferences, and biases and reflect them back at us, providing only confirming information sources and filtering out the rest. These algorithms are literally telling us what we want to hear. In this way, our own echo chamber is created for us, even when searching and browsing 'independently'.

SOLUTIONS AT AN ORGANISATION LEVEL...

The drive for 'agile' innovation is prompting those in business to reassess conventional vertically-aligned, top-down hierarchical organisational structures. More enlightened organisations are moving towards decentralised and horizontal organisation structures. The merits of this approach for sport and high performance athlete support teams are also becoming recognised by pioneers such as Teena Murray, who recently joined the Sacramento Kings NBA franchise.

"If you're going to build a strong culture, it's paramount to make diversity one of your core values. This is what separates strong culture from a cult: the commitment to promoting dissent"

– Adam Grant, in 'Originals: How Non Conformists Move the World'[38]

Returning to a major barrier, arguably the most telling factor that differentiates organisations and teams is how they entertain dissenting voices. The truth is that dissent is a necessity. Certainly it is essential to the health of cognitive diversity within the organisation.

The best illustration of the potency of dissent for stimulating deeper consideration is that a dissenting view that proves to be wrong still serves to promote superior collective decision making, so that the group ultimately arrives at a better solution [38]. Essentially it almost doesn't matter what the dissenting opinion is, or its veracity, as long as there is one.

Given that the function of the hive mind is dependent upon team members expressing dissent, in a circular fashion this does of course require there to be diversity of thought within the team. Moreover, the dissenting opinion needs to be authentic [38]. The counterpoint or minority view needs to be advocated with conviction, rather than for the sake of it. This explains why attempts to hack this process by nominating a devil's advocate to argue for an arbitrary counterpoint fails to replicate the benefits of meaningful dissent. Playing devil's advocate ultimately doesn't work; the dissenting voice needs to be genuinely advocating the alternate position [38].

Equally what is also important is how members of the decision making team entertain and respond to cognitive conflict. A level of trust between members of the group is necessary [37], not least to ensure that conflict in ideas and opinions does not escalate to conflict on a personal or emotional level. Clearly there do need to be rules of engagement, in order to avoid arguments and debates becoming personal as far as possible.

That said, there is also an onus on each individual member of the group to engage with disagreements in the spirit of healthy debate, rather than taking it as a personal slight when others express dissenting views. In other words we need to subscribe to the idea of cooperative disagreement. This does require putting personal concerns aside, and agreeing to prioritise the needs of the collective. Sadly it is increasingly rare to find those who are willing to subjugate their own concerns for the benefit of the group. This underscores the need to recruit well and select team members based not only on what insights they bring, but also how they entertain diverging views.

Arriving at a functional outcome similarly necessitates a readiness on the part of each member of the group to commit to whatever decision is ultimately arrived at [37]. Fostering a less 'ego-involved' environment will certainly help with this endeavour.

Whilst structural changes are an important step to remove some of the constraints to collective intelligence and to help derive the benefits of cognitive diversity, ultimately those in positions of authority remain in control and so need to be part of the change.

"It doesn't make sense to hire smart people and then tell them what to do. We hire smart people so they can tell us what to do."

— Steve Jobs

So can we expect authoritarian leaders within sports organisations to cede their power and step back to realise the benefits of autonomous working groups and decentralised decision making? Well, it seems unlikely those turkeys will spontaneously vote for Christmas. Ultimately Darwinian processes, perhaps survival of the most adaptable or agile, are likely to drive this evolution in sport, as in business.

That said, there are examples within elite sport of notoriously authoritarian head coaches evolving to a more collaborative approach in order to continue to be successful at the highest level, in part having been prompted to do so by esteemed colleagues who challenged them. According to anecdotes shared by colleagues, such examples include Steve Hansen, who in recent years has become one of the most successful national team coaches in the history of the dominant New Zealand All Blacks rugby team.

"I don't believe anything really revolutionary has been invented by committee"

– Steve Wozniak

Finally, there are numerous opportunities to amend operating practices in our quest to preserve and protect independent thought. Collaboration is not exclusively a group exercise. Doing everything by committee is not effective or efficient. In order to foster real creativity and innovation, individuals need space to work independently. On the one hand, collaboration is a group problem-solving exercise to develop solutions together. Equally, ideas need time to geminate, and individuals need the opportunity develop their ideas free from scrutiny and judgement before presenting them to the group. On that basis, we should rather think of collaboration as both a team sport and an individual pursuit. What is clear is that individuals need the space to develop their independent thoughts in order for the group to benefit.

FOSTERING DIVERSITY WITHIN OURSELVES...

Perhaps a more tractable problem is to consider what can we do to foster cognitive diversity within ourselves? Attaining a range of experiences will naturally bring different insights. There are numerous examples from various fields and disciplines that demonstrate how investing time living and working overseas yields considerable benefits in terms of originality and creativity [38]. Being exposed to a range of perspectives likewise provides different insights that allow us to better understand the puzzle we are seeking to solve.

However, to realise these benefits we must remain alert in order to avoid finding ourselves in an echo chamber. Being surrounded by people who see things the same as we do might be reassuring on some level, but it adds nothing to our understanding of the problem, and certainly does not help generate alternative solutions.

In order to take advantage of having exposure to diverse viewpoints and ways of thinking we must recognise and resist the urge to immediately discredit and dismiss views that are contrary to our own. Acquiring a wider and more diverse array of mental models that we are able to bring to a given problem will clearly be to our advantage. It is also a useful exercise to consider the counterpoints and work through the counter arguments to whatever view we might hold. In this way we can probe and interrogate our own thinking for flaws in the underlying logic, and consider all perspectives on both the problem and prospective solutions. This practice will not only allow us to have more conviction in our ultimate solution, but will also make us better equipped to navigate uncertainty and unpredictability.

"Avoid having your ego so close to your position that when your position falls, your ego goes with it"

– Colin Powell

As noted previously, our ego will be the biggest barrier to realising the benefits of cognitive diversity. Separating our ego from our position, both when advocating our viewpoint and in the ultimate outcome is therefore crucial. Better yet, parking our ego at the door will make us better able to engage in debate without being hampered by having our ego involved during the discussion.

It has been identified that over-specialisation is a growing problem within different industries, and you could argue that this equally applies to the professions within sport. There are an ever growing array of titles and specialist roles within athlete support teams, each with their designated area of specialism and responsibilities within their scope of practice.

I would argue that having an area of specialism is not the problem with over-specialisation. Possessing deep knowledge of one or more single area defines us as a specialist. Conversely, having both an awareness and level of knowledge across domains and disciplines makes us a generalist. I have written before about the need as coaches and practitioners to be both a specialist and a generalist.

"Try to learn something about everything and everything about something."

— Thomas H. Huxley

Deep knowledge in our specialist area remains crucial – teams greatly benefit from having 'subject matter experts' in their respective domains. However, possessing the cross-domain knowledge of a generalist enables us to avoid our specialism from skewing our thinking and constraining our perspective on the problem. We can operate most effectively and leverage our collective wisdom to best effect when subject matter expertise is accompanied by a broad understanding and level of awareness across domains and disciplines.

LESSONS BEYOND OUR CHOSEN DOMAIN...

Looking outside our particular domain is often more instructive than limiting our scope of learning and investigation to within the bubble of our particular profession or 'industry'.

From a personal perspective, I have no urge to keep up with trends or whatever the current fad is within the 'industry'. Concentrating too much on current trends within the field or what others are doing within our domain inevitably leads to unwarranted peer influence on our practice, and ultimately constrains our thinking.

Through interactions with colleagues it is quite possible to remain peripherally aware, but not concern oneself too much with what others in our field are doing. I increasingly pay more attention to lessons and examples from outside of the profession or domain, and I frequently find inspiration from other fields. Reading and hearing those who operate in an 'unrelated' domain, such as business, investing, or some other field of 'knowledge work', often provides lessons that are highly pertinent to my own areas of practice. Indeed the present book is an exemplar of this approach.

TO SUM UP...

In the interests of the collective wisdom of the hive mind we need to be ready to embrace cognitive diversity. Fundamentally, this means recognising the value of otherness. Practically, this necessitates entertaining diverging views and ideas, not in spite of but because of the fact they may be contrary to what we have been exposed to previously. It also means actively seeking out those with differing backgrounds, experience and education for the insights they can bring.

For those who work in a realm as uncertain as sport and with beings as complex as athletes we should seek different perspectives and different ways to think about the challenges we encounter. This equally applies to all domains of human performance. There are many ways to conceptualise a problem. Different perspectives allow us to get a more rounded view and improved understanding of the puzzle. The potential solutions are also many and varied; as we are likely to realise when we allow ourselves to be exposed to differing sources and alternative thinking.

On an individual and a group level embracing cognitive diversity will necessitate a change in how we deal with divergence in views and how we think about disagreement. In essence we need to recognise the inherent value of diverging views and disagreement in ultimately making us better able to innovate and improving our collective ability to handle novel problems. On that basis we should invite and encourage alternative viewpoints in order to realise the value of dissenting voices. Personally it is rare that I agree 100% with anybody on any given topic. And that's okay. In fact it is healthy. It is also not a personal slight to those involved. It is entirely possible to respect both the individual and their point view despite the fact I don't necessarily agree with it.

In general it is not safe to assume there is wisdom in the conventions or the present consensus viewpoint in our chosen field. I would argue we should not pay undue attention to how others within our field are operating. We should rather give liberty to our eyes and ears. Cognitive diversity means being eclectic in our input. Giving ourselves the freedom to roam and explore other domains helps to develop the generalist knowledge to complement and provide perspective to better apply our subject matter expertise. We should look to more established professions when searching for wisdom, and be attentive to the lessons and principles from other domains that may have application to our own field.

Finally, cognitive diversity and free thinking requires courage. It necessitates the strength to resist pressures to conform in order to remain independent thinkers.

Ultimately if independent thoughts are to be heard they must first be voiced. We must therefore have the courage to express our independent viewpoint, irrespective of the prevailing view of the group, and regardless of how it might be entertained by our peers and those in authority.

REFLECTING AND CONNNECTING THE DOTS...

How do the themes and principles relate to your working environment?

Is the value of cognitive diversity and challenge recognised and celebrated in your organisation?

To what extent does the leadership group where you operate presently act to support exploration and innovation in thinking and working practices?

What opportunities do you see to better leverage cognitive diversity in your specific context?

How is dissent or challenge entertained in your environment presently?

Within your sphere of influence, how might you lead the way? Is there merit in inviting peers and staff to challenge your thinking and propose alternative views?

How might you encourage those around you to receive diverging opinions and dissenting views more positively?

What is the best forum to introduce the concept of cooperative disagreement?

Is there merit in introducing a social contract between members of the group, whereby they agree to challenge and be challenged by each other, with rules of engagement for cognitive conflict?

What reflections do you have on a personal level? To what degree is it important for you to be right, versus arriving at the best outcome irrespective of who was responsible for the idea that won out? How confident would you be that your colleagues and staff would corroborate your answer on this question?

Combating Binary Thinking and Polarised Debate

In the previous chapter we outlined the merits of diversity of opinion, dissent, and cognitive conflict. However, to derive these benefits there is a need for discourse and forums to debate different ideas, present diverging viewpoints, and engage in healthy disagreement. Sadly, each of these elements seems to be in decline, not only within wider society, but also in academic and professional circles. For professionals who spend any time on social media it is easy to get the sense we are in the death throes of intellectual debate. In this chapter we will explore the trend for binary thinking and polarised arguments that fuels the tribalism we see on different platforms, and how this is increasingly creeping into the discourse between professionals and even in academia. In doing so we will attempt to plot a path back from the edge of the abyss and outline what steps we can take to combat binary thinking in our own environment to safeguard real debate.

THE FALLACY OF BINARY THINKING...

As the saying goes, the problem with binary thinking is that it is always one thing or another. Everything is framed as an either/or scenario. Things are presented is terms of right versus wrong. Good versus bad. Left versus right. We seem to need to paint one party as the hero and so the other must be the villain. The unstated assumption is that there are in essence only two viewpoints or conceivable options available to us.

As I have shared with practitioners in different disciplines, if you are seeking certainty, or thinking in terms of right versus wrong, then working with humans is not for you. There is no such clear delineation with complex adaptive biological systems. Each human we encounter presents a unique puzzle. By extension, there are a host of different and equally valid perspectives on any given problem, and a variety of workable solutions. To repeat, we are dealing with complex adaptive biological systems – with a mind attached. As such, all is *spectral*. In other words, properties and individual responses exist on a continuum. It is rarely the case that we are dealing in binary outcomes.

"You cannot find formulas in human affairs that will determine the outcome in every particular case"

– Noam Chomsky

Binary thinking is at the heart of polarised debate. Polarisation is both cause and effect of the tribalism we see in various fields, as is increasingly evident in the interactions we see on different platforms.

THE MADNESS OF CROWDS...

In the previous chapter we introduced the 'wisdom of crowds' phenomenon, whereby the aggregation of independent judgements from individuals within a group can provide better prediction than the opinion of a single expert. It is worth reinforcing that this process is distinct to finding consensus: the strength of this method is that it takes an average of all of the disparate individual inputs, rather than the group coalescing around a singular viewpoint.

We also highlighted that group dynamics, and phenomena such as herding and socialisation, can exert a strong influence on the judgements and behaviours of individuals who are part of the group. These forces can serve to undermine the independence and diversity of thought, thereby negating what underpins the wisdom of the collective judgement of the crowd. Essentially, we respond and behave differently when part of a collective, in comparison to when we are left to our own devices.

"A person is smart. People are dumb, panicky dangerous animals and you know it"

– 'Kay', played by actor Tommy Lee Jones in 1997 film 'Men in Black'

What we term 'group think' is often divorced from reason. There are numerous instances of collective thought and behaviour that is objectively irrational. Being part of a crowd offers fertile ground for dogma and world views that would otherwise not stand up to scrutiny. When a particular version of reality is communally agreed upon and reinforced, this lends strength to the collective delusion and adds to our sense of subjective 'truth'. All of this serves to further bond us to the group, given the reassurance and sense of conviction that sharing in collective delusion and solidarity with the group provides.

Mob mentality finds its ultimate expression in the acts of aggression and even violence that humans can be moved to commit when part of a group. Communal influences can override our ability to reason. Such forces may even lead us to take part in irrational behaviours and act in a way that we would not sanction otherwise.

COMFORT IN CERTAINTY AND STRENGTH IN NUMBERS...

As humans we have a yearning for things to be straightforward. We crave certainty so it is disquieting when we are faced with navigating complex issues. We warm to easy answers, however facile they may be. Humans flock in numbers towards those who profess to know; we are impressed by the conviction of those who make their claims with absolute certainty. We derive comfort in those who project this illusion of certainty, and feel a sense of safety in numbers when surrounded by those who share this illusion with us.

It is both striking and on the surface quite baffling how quick we are to jump into one camp or another on any particular topic. Part of what makes aligning to a particular camp or school of thought so beguiling is the sense of security and belonging that comes with it.

"An imagined community is a community of people who don't really know each other, but imagine that they do"

— Yuval Noah Harari [39]

Groups of individuals who feel they share the same superficial interests and habits of thought consider themselves part of the same enlightened tribe. Being part of this 'imagined community' provides a sense of safety and certainty, and helps define an individual's subjective sense of self, both on a professional and personal level.

"The pull of us versus-them thinking is strong even when the arbitrariness of social boundaries is utterly transparent"

– Robert Sapolsky [40]

Once we assign a label to ourselves, and then to others, our attitudes and behaviours inevitably become shaped in accordance with the tribal lines that we have drawn.

MODERN TRIBES...

Tribal behaviour is very much in evidence within the factions that have become increasingly prevalent in our respective fields. Tribalism fuels polarisation within any society, whether we are talking about practitioners in a particular discipline or the academic community. In a circular fashion, this polarisation then serves to create further distance between respective tribes and factions.

Polarised views and entrenched positions create a distance between partisan groups that is very difficult to overcome. Once established, there is increasingly little meaningful (or civil) engagement between factions. The exchanges we see on contentious topics are often not really debates at all, but rather an exercise in mudslinging aimed at the opposing camp.

Interestingly, this scenario occurs regardless of whether our opinion on specific issues is in fact consistent with the actual views of others within the group we identify with (or the views of individual members of the groups we view as being 'the opposition'). This contradiction has been noted in the literature and has led authors on the topic to emphasise the distinction between 'issue-based ideology' and 'identity-based ideology'.

Social identity has an emotional rather than objective or rational basis. Tribalism, and the notion of *us* and *them* that comes with the social identify conferred by being part of a group, has a biological basis which has roots in our evolution as a social species. The animosity that frequently accompanies exchanges between groups of humans on contentious topics in essence shares the same basis as the territorial and aggressive behaviour towards outsider groups that we observe in primates [40].

Given the biological origins, this makes it somewhat inevitable that identifying as part of a particular tribe, even one as tenuous as a particular school of thought, thereby impacts our thinking and behaviour on an unconscious and emotional level, regardless of the fact it is not rational.

EMOTIVE EFFECTS OF SOCIAL IDENTITY...

As we have alluded to, identifying with a particular school of thought provides a sense of social identity. The elements that define social identity include not only a sense of inclusion and belonging to our chosen group, but equally important is that this is to the exclusion of others.

"Modern human societies rely... on cultural kin selection... This malleable, rather than genetically fixed, path of identity formation also drives people to adopt arbitrary markers that enable them to spot their cultural kin in an ocean of strangers"

– Robert Sapolsky [40]

The particular group we identify with profoundly shapes how we behave towards others and also how we entertain new information based on the source. What is striking is that this is often entirely independent of any consideration of the calibre of the information presented. Essentially, it is less about considering the merits of the respective positions on an issue, and far more about staunchly defending the dogma and stated position of our imagined community of choice.

The sense of allegiance and group identity is a big part of what drives our opposition to contrary views, particularly when voiced by those we associate as being 'the opposition'. The source of kinship and connection we feel to our chosen group or imagined community is after all emotional, rather than rational. This goes a long way to explaining the emotionally reactive behaviour that individuals demonstrate in relation to group status and their conduct towards others who they deem to be in opposition.

"'In groups' are implicitly judged to be superior to 'out groups', and the judgement is seated in the connection between the group status and the self concept rather than any objective facts"

— Lilliana Mason [41]

When we are part of a tribe, our views of the opposing camp and their views, both on an individual and group level, is largely a projection, distorted beyond all recognition so that it bears little relation to the individuals concerned. This hostility is aimed at a label ('the opposition'). All that seems to matter is that it is framed as the 'opposing view' so by extension we reflexively and staunchly oppose it, without any consideration of its merits. Once again the manner in which we respond to others according to the label we have assigned them is rooted in emotion and devoid of any objective assessment. We largely refuse to entertain arguments or points of view regardless of their merit simply because of our assumed dislike and declared opposition to the group that the individual represents.

In a later chapter we will introduce the idea that there are a number of recurring cognitive distortions that our negative thought patterns have in common. It is interesting to note many of the same cognitive distortions are evident in how we label others, entertain diverging views, and make judgements about the source.

TRIBES OF THE SCIENTIFIC AND PROFESSIONAL COMMUNITIES...

The growing polarisation and tribalism in society is most often studied in the realms of politics and religion. However, this is also increasingly evident within academia and even in the scientific community (the social sciences are naturally prone to this, but sadly the hard sciences are also not exempt). What is all the more troubling is that we have started to observe these trends in the behaviours and exchanges between groups of professionals in different fields.

To use the example of sport, tribalism and polarized debate are becoming ever more prevalent in the fields of sports science and medicine, and related professional fields or 'industries' (notably the new religion of nutrition). Authorities in different fields (often self-proclaimed) seem to constantly spew forth evangelical proclamations, push their ideology and promote others who espouse their doctrine, and decry those who express contrary views. Sadly, it appears there are no shortage of young zealots eager to answer the call to join the modern crusades conducted on a social media battlefield.

Often what lures us into identifying with a particular group is that they espouse a world view we find appealing. As I have written about previously, academics and professionals alike are incredibly quick to suspend critical thinking when the particular doctrine speaks to our bias or something we desire to be true. Regardless of education or status, professionals in different fields and academics are as prone to motivated reasoning as anybody. Indeed greater knowledge merely seems to make us more adept at rationalising the position we have assumed and inventively spin doctoring whatever new information is presented.

Having opted to align with a chosen group on the strength of the apparent superiority of their position, you might expect that we would hold our chosen brethren to a higher standard given the enlightened status ascribed to them. Yet we actually observe the opposite. Strangely we find ourselves adopting the role of apologist, and engaging in mental acrobatics to justify and rationalise even the most outrageous statements from members of our own tribe.

"Highly politicized people are willing to interpret even extreme remarks from their own political tribe in a generous and forgiving light while reading the remarks of those in any opposing camp in as negative and hostile light as possible"

– Douglas Murray, in 'The Madness of Crowds' [42]

It is striking that we show no such tolerance to far milder views expressed by those outside our imagined community. Indeed, there is a tendency for overreaction that sometimes verges on the hysterical. Once again, we increasing see this in the debates between academics and professionals in different fields of sport performance and sports injury. Proponents of a particular school of thought are quick to distance themselves from others who align with the opposing 'team'. This 'us versus them' mentality is increasingly evident in the public interactions between those who advocate different viewpoints. Antipathy and even outright animosity is shown towards others in the field who hold contrary views.

As a result of the encroaching tribalism in the scientific community and within professional realms, there is increasingly less real engagement in the public discourse, particularly in the case of social media platforms. One side does not entertain the substance of what is being said by the other, and what is heard is distorted and misinterpreted in a way that further fuels the discord and animosity. Increasingly we are seeing esteemed figures in academic and professional fields publicly vilify the opposing camp, both on a group and individual level, and ridiculing any contrary views expressed.

THE MODERN BATTLEGROUND...

If we accept that social dynamics play a significant role in this context, it follows that social media provides a natural platform to connect other members of the camp we identify with. By extension, social media has also become a place where we do battle with those we consider to hold opposing views.

"Social media turns out to be a superlative way to embed new dogmas and crush contrary opinion just when you needed to listen to them most"

– Douglas Murray, in 'The Madness of Crowds' [42]

Events such as seminars and clinics also serve as social gatherings, and a forum for like-minded individuals to promote a particular ideology or dogma. On occasion it can appear that gaining support for a doctrine is the primary objective, rather than any real pretence of sharing ideas or debating different viewpoints.

I recently attended a 'conference' that became such a social gathering for those who share the same bias and alignment in their narrow viewpoint. Over the two days of the event for the most part the selection of presenters and the content delivered was skewed to promote a distorted and polarised view of a complex subject matter, largely to the delight of the audience (with very few but noteworthy exceptions). The lack of balance and moderation was such that the event had the feel of a recruiting drive for a cult, rather than a conference or scientific forum to debate ideas.

TENUOUS CONNECTIONS...

Among the masses who make up the audience for these displays, it is increasingly common to adopt an entrenched position without any real basis or intellectual attachment.

Aligning with a camp is part of how we differentiate ourselves from others. As we have spoken about, this is to the exclusion of those we deem to be 'other', and with this comes resistance to information we perceive to be conflicting.

Those who are quick to claim allegiance with a label, camp, or school of thought do not necessarily possess a coherent opinion or considered view, beyond parroting the party line. The staunchest acolytes are frequently not prepared for follow up questions. When cross-examined they often fail to demonstrate any real depth of understanding on the topic.

Nevertheless we find hordes of eager recruits to the cause on whatever contested issue might be trending, without troubling themselves to read up on the substance behind the doctrine they have signed up to. Beyond the buzz words, many members of the mob only pretend at a working understanding.

THE INERTIA OF STRONGLY HELD POSITIONS...

Our resistance to changing our minds comes not only from our allegiances to imaginary tribes, but also from the simple inertia of having adopted an entrenched view in our own minds. In the start-up world the maxim 'strong opinions, weakly held' has become popular as a proposed solution to this tendency. There are also flaws to this approach, but the general idea of not becoming too attached to our views nevertheless has merit.

In other words, we should leave room for doubt, and thereby retain our ability to change our minds. Inevitably there is a tension between having the necessary conviction to act, whilst remaining open to diverging viewpoints and new data that might lead us to alternative conclusions over time. If we become attached to a particular idea or whatever we deem to be the best system of operating this naturally makes us more resistant to allowing our ideas and practices to evolve.

"Goals can direct motivated reasoning to produce systematically biased beliefs"

– Nicholas Epley and Thomas Gilovich [43]

Allegiance to an idea or viewpoint in effect serves to distort our thinking in similar ways to membership of a group. The term *motivated reasoning* describes how we have a tendency to construct sometimes elaborate but nevertheless reasoned arguments in order to at whatever our prior happens to be [43]. In other words, rather than our positions being the result of deductive reasoning, we begin with our preferred conclusion and purposefully work back from there. Essentially this is a circular process, whereby we reverse engineer our reasoning to provide the justification for the conclusion that we favoured ahead of time. Having done so, our well-crafted rationale can be used as a shield against contrary views.

The inertia of our existing views and the herding mentality that we are prone to as humans often coincide with each other. Having adopted a viewpoint, it is natural for us to gravitate towards others who express similar views. In this way, attachment to our viewpoint and allegiance to the imagined community who share our views become superimposed, which compounds the barriers to entertaining contrary views thereafter.

FACING OBJECTIVE REALITY...

It is rare for us to even to acknowledge the assumptions that form the bedrock of our often tenuous mental models of the world, let alone question them. Upon closer inspection many conventions in practice amount to little more than systems we have dreamed up and orders we have imagined. As with the bonds that bind imaginary tribes, many of the essential 'truths' we hold so dear are fabrications. Returning to the notion of motivated reasoning, we should allow for the possibility that the rationale that we cite to support our position might be nothing more than a carefully crafted post-rationalisation of whatever viewpoint we adopted in the first instance.

"As far as the laws of mathematics refer to reality, they are not certain, and as far as they are certain, they do not refer to reality"

— Albert Einstein

The perhaps unwelcome reality is that there are very few absolutes, particularly when dealing with complex adaptive systems. We are dealing in probabilities, with few certainties. There are very few rules that apply universally to all situations and to all individuals. Those who deal in absolutes are at best deluded. When confronted by 'authorities' who project certainty and speak in absolute terms, this alone should give us pause.

"One thing that being a scientist has taught me is that you can never be certain about anything... You iterate towards the truth. You don't know it."

— James Maxwell

TOGETHER ALONE...

As noted earlier, identifying with a group, school of thought, imagined community, or tribe is at the root of polarisation. In order to escape the unconscious effects on our cognitions and behaviour we effectively need to abandon our 'in-group' status. As long as we associate or identify with a group, we will exercise less scrutiny in relation to other group members, effectively giving them a pass and rationalising any position they take, no matter how outrageous. We will also fail to fully entertain the merits of alternative views and arguments made by members of other groups. Only once we have abandoned this status and severed the bonds will we be free of the clouding emotions and cognitive distortions that inevitably accompanies social identity, given its biological origins.

As I have noted previously, it is hard to escape the tendency to gravitate towards like-minded individuals who share our biases. It is beguilingly easy to find ourselves in an echo chamber where we are surrounded by those expressing the same views that we hold. Ultimately we must step out of the echo chamber if we are to seek enlightenment.

In order to take this necessary step, we must be ready to stand alone and be uncomfortable. We must resist any and all inclinations to align or identify with any and all groups or schools of thought. It has been said that leadership can be a lonely place. Nevertheless for those of us who wish to lead effectively, and indeed those who simply wish to navigate the complexities of the world we operate in, eschewing tribal allegiance and social identity is the price that must be paid for freedom and independence of thought.

As noted by Douglas Murray and other commentators, the rules and consensus viewpoints in the present era are increasingly not arrived at in a rational way, but are essentially determined by mob stampedes. We need to remind ourselves that it is possible to hold more than one view in our head at the same time. Indeed doing so is absolutely necessary if we are to derive an independent viewpoint. To triangulate a balanced viewpoint requires that we entertain multiple sources and differing opinions. By definition, we must consider diverging viewpoints in order to arrive at a sensible position somewhere in between.

"Intelligent individuals learn from every thing and every one; average people, from their experiences. The stupid already have all the answers

— Socrates

A friend and colleague named Angus Ross, who is one of the great free thinkers I have come across on my travels in elite sport around the world, is shamelessly non-exclusive in his intelligence gathering. Angus is agnostic in how he arrives at a position on a particular issue and also where he seeks information. As Angus has told me, he is prepared to learn from everybody. What is all the more remarkable is that this also extends to those who Angus does not necessarily agree with, or even feel any affinity towards. This is rare wisdom and demonstrates the merits of being agile in our thinking so that we are able to objectively entertain information in a way that is independent of whatever feelings we might have towards the source.

From a wider perspective it is possible, and in fact highly likely, that we will not agree 100% with others on a particular topic. We can agree to differ, and it is still possible to have respect for others even if our thinking on a given topic does not align. Moreover, we should allow that those who we dislike might nevertheless have something to say that is of merit.

In the previous chapter, we cited the author Adam Grant [38] who highlighted the necessity of dissent in separating a collective from a cult. Indeed the degree to which we encourage, entertain, and respond favourably to dissent is arguably the biggest factor in shaping the nature of the environment we have stewardship over, and how the collective functions under our watch.

QUELLING THE RIGHTEOUS INDIGNATION...

We are perhaps in the age of the hysterical reaction. It is quite extraordinary how easily what are often seemingly quite innocuous comments or stated opinions can spark outrage. The swift pile-on (often on social media) to condemn and attack the source of the offending remarks is also somewhat bewildering and at times quite frightening to behold. The rise of the phenomenon of being 'triggered' is perhaps the best illustration of the distress increasingly easily provoked among individuals and challenges presently faced by organisations.

As noted in the previous chapter, if you possess delicate sensibilities that are so easily offended then competitive sport is perhaps not the place for you. As an athlete, thin skin and emotional reactivity are liabilities that will be exploited ruthlessly. For coaches, practitioners, and support staff alike, the heightened emotions and propensity for clashing personalities that are a ubiquitous feature of performance sport and the crucible of competition similarly leave little room for easily bruised egos.

Beyond sport, it has been noted that graduates from the 'i-Generation' (those born in the years since 1995 and the dawn of the internet) are struggling to adapt as they enter the workforce in different industries (and causing some consternation in the process). Commentators are tracing these issues back to the climate that has been created in college and university settings, as administrators have become hyper vigilant to anything that might offend. We have perhaps become too indulgent of hypersensitivity. The overzealous attempts to neutralise any real or imagined causes of offence might paradoxically be the cause of much of the newfound fragility and collective hysteria [44].

Beyond generational issues, if we find ourselves 'triggered' with so little provocation surely this should make us pause and reflect. The standard response of organisations at present seems to be to target the source and implement measures addressing (or outlawing) the topic that provoked the outrage. Whilst this might be the stock response at present it does not seem to be proving very effective. Continually indulging what is often based on subjective and even spurious causes of distress and offence does not appear a sound strategy.

From a people management perspective, when individuals are triggered so readily and somewhat irrespective of circumstances, it is worth considering that this may be more about the person constantly taking offence than the other individuals expressing the offending opinions. We might therefore pre-empt these issues in how we screen potential applicants when recruiting. In our efforts to address these issues we can also counsel those on staff to be mindful of their own cognitions shaping their emotional responses, and help them better manage the cognitive distortions that are the cause of much of the distress. We will explore these themes at length in a later chapter.

SOME PRACTICAL SOLUTIONS...

As we have already noted, it is important in our role as leader that we are independent of any particular cause. It is possible to maintain a set of core values and principles and yet remain agnostic in our methods and flexible in our models of thinking. It follows we should similarly strive to foster independent thought and critical thinking among staff. Beyond broadening their perspectives, this would serve the overriding aim of creating a working environment based on a meritocracy of ideas and free thinking.

To that end, as leaders and managers we should also stipulate that staff and particularly new staff relinquish any blind allegiance they might have to a school of thought or fixed way of thinking and operating. Exercising critical thinking requires that we first entertain differing viewpoints. Without such a readiness among members of the team this is where things are liable to fall down at the first hurdle.

For both ourselves and our staff we should seek to actively combat the tendency for how we entertain views expressed to be unduly influenced by our preconceived notions about the source. Developing the discipline to deliberately and consciously engage with the substance of what is being said by those who hold alternate viewpoints, regardless of what group they might belong to, should therefore be a priority. Simply making members of the team aware of our unconscious bias against opposing camps is a first step to becoming mindful of this tendency, and helping us to avoid a knee jerk reaction and the default response to dismiss and discredit contrary views.

From an operations point of view, we can take practical steps to combat the tendency for cliques or factions to form within our own staff. To a large part, this is built upon the assumption and assertion of mutual respect. This does mean working on a good faith basis, whereby it is assumed that there are good intentions behind whatever contrary views are expressed, even if it might be upsetting or discomfiting to us to hear. It should be recognised as a demonstration of respect to be honest and direct in our feedback. This respect should be reciprocated in how feedback is received and interpreted. Collectively we can also adopt a code of conduct, whereby all staff members undertake that any views we might express about a colleague should be expressed to them directly and in person.

IN CLOSING...

The fallacy of binary thinking is all too prevalent in the Information Age, and this is one of the great ironies of the era. These trends are exemplified in the interactions and conduct we see on social media. The forces of polarisation are to be resisted at all costs if we are to achieve real engagement between factions and genuine debate.

It is crucial that we recognise that aligning with a group will ultimately restrict our thinking and narrow our frame of reference. We must resist the lure of false certainty, the reassurance of safety in numbers, and illusory sense of community that comes with claiming allegiance to a particular camp.

To seek enlightenment requires that we first step out of the echo chamber. In order to triangulate an independent and considered viewpoint we must be ready to entertain diverging points of view.

In doing so we must remain mindful in how we entertain and critically appraise information from various sources. This applies especially when we encounter ideas or perspectives that deviate from our prior learning. Much like an athlete, we must develop our agility in how we deal with diverging views and sources.

Equally, we should not give a pass and suspend critical thinking when we encounter something that speaks to our bias or something we wish to be true. We should apply the same scrutiny regardless of the appeal of the message. There is very little that we should swallow whole.

Conversely, there is generally some nugget or element of what is being presented that we can learn from and find value, even if we do not have an affinity for the speaker or the particular camp that they represent. This ability to objectively entertain the information presented independently of our subjective feelings towards the source represents a higher order skill, largely because this is not natural or intuitive for most humans.

REFLECTING AND CONNECTING THE DOTS...

Does what is presented in this chapter reflect your own observations on recent trends within your particular sector, and more globally?

Upon reading this chapter do you recognise these tendencies or habits of thought in yourself?

What groups or schools of thinking do you identify with, and how would you say this influences how you perceive those who represent other camps or contrary viewpoints?

What practical steps can you take to be aware of unconscious biases and remain mindful to retain the ability to entertain diverging viewpoints independently of the source?

To what extent do you feel you are receptive to entertaining new data that might conflict with your prior views?

How would you say your views and how you practice has evolved over time? In general do you think you are open to changing your mind?

How often do you re-examine bedrock assumptions and critically evaluate the reasoning behind your positions on particular topics?

What barriers do feel you might have to overcome in order to objectively audit your philosophy and practice, and challenge your own assumptions?

What countermeasures do you employ or might you introduce in future, in order to avoid finding yourself in an echo chamber?

Part Two: Leading and Coaching Others

If we accept that coaches are de facto leaders, and leadership has a significant element of coaching, then we need to understand what attributes and aptitudes are necessary to operate as a coach.

By extension those who lead and manage others similarly need to understand the fundamental principles that govern the practice of coaching humans.

At the outset we also stated that coaching represents a blend of physics and philosophy. It follows that establishing the laws of motion in relation to coaching humans and exploring the key tenets of coaching philosophy are necessary steps in our quest...

Traits of Elite Coaches and High Performing Practitioners

In order to model our approach it is useful we explore some of the traits that differentiate the best coaches and practitioners in their fields. One disclaimer before we start is that this chapter is based on observational study. To some degree the themes we explore reflect wisdom shared by prominent individuals via different forums and media. However, I unapologetically give more weight to traits and behaviours that I have directly observed. I have been fortunate to interact with a representative sample of these exceptional individuals across multiple sports in various contexts; this has provided the opportunity to see how they approach their work with 'live' athletes in different scenarios, as opposed to how individuals claim they act and operate in practice. The themes we explore are therefore more a product of this direct observation, rather than simply distilling what has been presented elsewhere.

CURIOUS SCEPTICS ...

One striking attribute of the best coaches and practitioners I have encountered is that they manage to blend boundless curiosity with a very healthy dose of scepticism. The insatiable curiosity these individuals possess leads them into diverse realms as they seek to discover and explore what is not known. The ongoing search for answers and continual drive to discover further helps to fuel a commitment to lifelong learning, which is another characteristic that is commonly cited with pioneering individuals in different fields.

A notable distinction with these individuals is that this curiosity is however tempered with scepticism and a propensity for critical thinking; this is a potent combination as it allows them to take nothing at face value. This unique blend of qualities allows these individuals to avoid chasing novelty for its own sake, and falling prey to the fads that afflict others in their respective fields. In essence, the stance they adopt is that every idea merits consideration, but nothing should be swallowed whole.

VISION AND FREEDOM OF THOUGHT...

A trait that the best have in common is a predisposition to take their own path. Part of what makes these individuals exceptional is an extraordinary ability to see things differently.

The type of vision that the exceptional few possess is not shaped or unduly influenced by the consensus viewpoint. The mental models that these individuals deploy to make sense of the world (and the sport) are thus not constrained by the dominant narrative or conventional wisdom of how things work. Being able to perceive the problem differently, and without the distortion of convention, opens up the possibility of new solutions.

Freedom of thought requires a certain level of bravery. What allows these individuals to fully explore these alternate views and deploy alternative mental models is that their vision is combined with the requisite conviction and obstinacy to entertain ideas that differ to the consensus position, even in the face of scorn.

NON-CONFORMITY...

Taking the path less travelled requires a propensity to resist the urge to follow the herd and societal pressures to conform. A first step is a willingness to defy the accepted view on the given problem, and go against the conventional wisdom of how things work in order to conceive different approaches to the problem and novel solutions.

The best instinctively rebel against herding mentality and 'sameness'; they are discomfited when they find themselves among the crowd.

"Whenever you find yourself on the side of the majority it is time to pause and reflect

— Mark Twain

Whilst on the surface it may appear similar, there are fundamental differences between this type of non-conformity and simply being a contrarian. The exceptional few do not take the opposing side merely to be perverse; when they do so it is because the alternative position has real merit.

All the same, these individuals do possess the mental agility to entertain multiple and diverging viewpoints in their head at the same time. Being adept at 'what if' thought experiments allows them to explore differing arguments and propositions. Hence when they ultimately adopt a position you can be assured they have fully explored the alternate positions, and have an intimate understanding of the supporting arguments and rationale.

ZERO F***S GIVEN...

A trait that differentiates the best is that they dare to stand apart from the crowd. They are not unduly troubled by the prospect of being ridiculed for adopting a position that contradicts the majority view. These individuals intuitively understand that what we take to be the wisdom of the crowd can just as often be crowd madness.

Part of what permits this freedom of thought and action is that these individuals are uniquely immune to peer-pressure. The best are uncommonly secure in their own skin (at least in a professional context), and as such do not feel the same imperative to not seek the approval of their peers or those in authority. Being free of the need or desire for affirmation that tends to handicap most mortals goes a long way to explain the extraordinary immunity to peer pressure that these individuals exhibit. Certainly external validation is not a major consideration or driver for how the enlightened few choose to practice.

The missing element that explains the rest is that the best are clear on what and who they are doing this for. In particular they are clear that it is not to impress authorities in the field or their peers; after all if you are the best, by definition you have very few peers. Rather what drives them is the satisfaction that comes from making a difference to those they serve. The opinions of those who are removed from this process are not relevant, regardless of their status.

DIVERGENT THINKING...

The exceptional few perceive truths that others do not. A major part of this is the propensity to look beyond the obvious and grasp things that are counter-intuitive.

"If you think the same as everybody else you will take the same action as everybody else. If you take the same actions as everybody else you will have same performance as everybody else. By definition this cannot result in above average results

— Howard Marks

What Howards Marks describes as 'second order thinking' is the ability to not only think differently, but also to think *better* than the crowd. Adopting a different view and course of action is merely the first step; ultimately you must be proven to be right.

The divergent thinking shown by exceptional individuals in the field of investing has parallels to coaching. This is what allows the best coaches to perceive extraordinary potential in an athlete when others do not, or when the consensus view has written the athlete off. More importantly they possess the confidence to go out on a limb and demonstrate the uncommon courage to back these assertions with action. It is this conviction that permits the athletes in their charge to make exponential improvements and ultimately achieve remarkable things.

A good example from track and field athletics is the exceptional jumps coach Fuzz Caan, who staunchly backed his athlete Robbie Grabarz (rated 85th in the world at the time), even supporting him with financial assistance independently when the national body withdrew his funding the year prior to a home Olympic Games. With Fuzz's support Robbie Grabarz won the Olympic silver medal in the high jump event at London 2012.

Once again what makes the best exceptional is that they are able to not only think differently to the crowd, but also think better than the crowd. What also bears repeating is that they further possess the courage of their convictions to put money down and stake their reputation on this judgement to translate this into action.

DEFIANCE...

I was interested and surprised to hear a former navy seal (and trainer of navy seals) state that one of the distinguishing traits of special forces operatives is that they bring a healthy disrespect for authority when they enter as recruits. Whilst this is tempered and harnessed with training, effective leaders in these elite squadrons nevertheless retain the capacity and willingness to bend rules, according to what is demanded by the situation.

Willingness to defy rules and conventions is likewise a trait that differentiates the best leaders, coaches, and professionals in their fields. Rather than being a slave to authority, they are willing to bend rules to do what needs to be done. A common observation is that these individuals do not ask for (or require) permission.

Once again, part of what makes the best practitioners exceptional is the clarity that they act in the best interests of those they serve (which in the case of sport is the athlete). Ultimately they obey their own moral compass. As such they do not blindly follow dictates from above or act with unquestioning loyalty to the particular organisation that employs them. This profound sense of service and duty of care means that they are willing to defy authority and conventions in order to do what they deem to be morally right and in the best interests of the athlete(s). Moreover they accept any repercussions for doing so.

RELENTLESS IN THE PURSUIT...

A trait that I have repeatedly observed with the best coaches and support staff is their insatiable pursuit of better. They share a general contempt for mediocrity. Part of what separates these individuals is that they are accordingly unwavering in the standards they demand of themselves and others. In essence, the best never lower their expectations. Effectively this forces the athletes and staff around them to rise to their level (or make their exit), rather than the other way round.

What is also remarkable is that these individuals constantly strive for excellence regardless of tenure or what has been achieved previously. What explains this extraordinary longevity is that they remain enamoured with the puzzle itself and fully immersed in the process of solving it. Essentially, reaching the destination was never the major source of satisfaction; it is the process of getting there where these individuals derive the most meaning and genuine enjoyment.

GRACE UNDER PRESSURE...

A final trait of the best coaches and practitioners is that they are unfazed by the spectacle. How these individuals conduct themselves and behave towards other humans remains impressively consistent, regardless of the spotlight and profile that accompanies working in professional sport and involvement at high profile sporting events.

What makes these individuals particularly remarkable is that they are able to maintain a level of equanimity, even in the crucible that is major competition. Despite being utterly committed to the pursuit, the exceptional few nevertheless possess a rare ability to retain some perspective. In doing so they are a reassuring presence and provide a source of calm and strength for the athletes, during what can otherwise be an overwhelming experience.

Amidst all the drama and emotion, the exceptional few are able to maintain sufficient separation that they do not lose their sense of self.

IN CLOSING...

Aside from the more obvious elements of drive and commitment to excellence, a strong sense of self, independence, moral fibre, courage, perspective, and empathy are all recurring themes when I reflect on my experiences with the exceptional coaches and practitioners I have been fortunate to spend time with and work alongside.

The apparent importance of such character traits harks back to the contention I have made a number of times that to be a good coach (or practitioner) you must first be a good human. It would seem to follow that to be an exceptional coach of humans, you must be an exceptional human.

REFLECTING AND CONNECTING THE DOTS...

Do the themes presented in the chapter resonate with you?

What is your own experience? Do you observe the traits and points of difference described in this chapter among leaders in your field that you have encountered or worked alongside?

What steps might you take to foster the traits that you identify with?

Rejecting the Industry

Practitioners across different domains will be familiar with their field of practice being referred to as an 'industry'. This trend has even crept into the realm of sport. We frequently hear mention of the strength and conditioning industry, the sports physiotherapy industry, even the sports coaching industry. In this chapter we consider the trend of framing our professions in this way, and explore why an 'industry approach' might be problematic when our work primarily involves developing and interacting with humans. From these discussions we will attempt to plot a path back to focusing on cultivating our craft and examine whether resisting an 'industry' mindset might help restore meaning in our chosen profession.

SCALABLE PRACTICE FOR INDUSTRIAL OUTPUT...

On the one hand the desire for practice to be scalable is understandable. Coming up with a reproducible system of working and creating a consistent 'client experience' on the surface would appear to have some merit. From an operational or procedural point of view there is clearly merit to being systematic in our approach. For example, a checklist approach has been used to great effect in fields such as medicine, as has been famously championed by Atul Gawande [45] in surgery, who also advocated this approach in other domains.

However, there are some important distinctions to be made here. The first, as I have made the case previously [46], is that it is possible to be *systematic* in our approach without restricting ourselves to a *system* of operating. It is equally crucial to differentiate between standard procedural tasks versus more complex exploration, discovery, and problem solving endeavours. The former lends itself to standardisation, the latter does not.

Despite such apparently benign aspirations, I would contend that in referring to our field of practice as an 'industry' we have unwittingly created major problems. As we will explore, these problems are manifested in numerous ways.

FLAWS IN THE INDUSTRY APPROACH...

By definition, the term 'industry' immediately conjures the notion of mass production and output on an industrial scale. We immediately think of 'service delivery' in terms of automation and a generic one-size fits all approach designed for the masses.

An illustrative example is the 'strength and conditioning industry', particularly as it exists in the United States (funnily enough, the genesis of this chapter came following a visit to the US in 2017). This 'industry' mindset can be seen in the drive for replication, standardisation, and reducing practice to a 'system' designed for mass consumption and franchising.

A 'model of practice' or a 'training system' to some degree implies a machine-type approach, whereby there is a direct, reliable, and repeatable relationship in which input A leads to output B. By definition, this assumes a level of consistency and predictability, both between individuals and within the same individual over time.

Unfortunately, neither consistency nor predictability are generally features associated with biological systems. By their nature, biological systems are dynamic, and subject to a host of different influences at any given time. As such, outcomes when dealing with biological systems are both nonlinear and unpredictable. Working with humans adds further layers of complexity, as we are now dealing with biological systems with a mind attached.

The basis for an industry approach is therefore inherently flawed when we are dealing with humans. Even in a relatively homogeneous population such as elite athletes you still find a great deal of diversity. Moreover variability is an inherent feature, even when dealing with the same individual at different points in time.

THE GHOST IN THE MACHINE...

Dealing with sentient beings such as humans greatly adds to the variability that is inherent with complex adaptive biological systems. How an intervention is anticipated and appraised affects how it is perceived and experienced by the individual, and in turn the stress response and adaptation that is elicited by a given stimulus. Numerous psycho-social factors, both within the environment where the intervention is carried out and beyond, can all influence the time course, magnitude and direction of outcomes.

"It's not just the external reality; it's the meaning you attach to it"

— Robert M. Sapolsky

In other words, the same intervention performed in exactly the same manner can be anticipated, perceived or experienced in a different way, and as a result we can see a different outcome. Indeed, the same intervention performed with the same individual at different time points, or against a different backdrop in terms of lifestyle factors or other psychological or emotional aspects entirely unrelated to the intervention, might also lead to a divergence in outcomes.

As we consider these points we can immediately see that this scenario does not lend itself to a standard system of operating. Whilst we have used examples from athlete preparation this equally applies to any intervention involving humans, regardless of the domain.

SOLUTIONS WITHOUT QUESTIONS...

Staying in sport, but moving onto the sport science and technology realms, commercial interests are a major driver for what becomes standard 'industry practice' employed by practitioners. We are seeing a growing array of off-the-shelf 'performance solutions' promoted by the manufacturer for a variety of applications. There are numerous examples of this in sports coaching, training, and sports injury.

The motivation for the use of these tools in practice is typically driven by marketing. Beyond the allure of shiny new toys with flashing lights, the biggest hook is that these products are positioned and promoted in a way that exploits respective practitioners' biases and insecurities. Often these tools are purchased and employed simply out of desire to keep up with our competitors, rather than with any specific purpose or to fulfil any particular need. After all, it is hard to position ourselves as 'industry leading' without 'state-of-the-art' equipment.

A consequence of the uptake and application of such tools and technology being driven in this way is that 'performance solutions' are increasingly employed without any consideration of what the question might be.

To be clear, the problem here is not the technology, or those who manufacture them (after all, they genuinely do work in an industry). The tools are not to blame. Rather the issue is what motivates our choice to employ these tools and the purpose (or lack thereof) behind their use in practice.

A corollary of this trend is the push for standardised interventions, which by definition are not tailored to meet the specific needs of the situation at hand. This generic approach inherently fails to give appropriate consideration to the unique requirements of the individual, or the specifics of the problem we are here to help to solve. Yet once again, such systems of operating are promoted as 'industry leading'.

A DOT-TO-DOT APPROACH TO A NONLINEAR PROCESS...

Returning to another example within the realm of sport, the strength and conditioning 'industry' has given us heavily promoted 'training systems' and 'must-have' equipment with the latest technology as 'training solutions', sometimes in combination. In the sports injury realm we further see trademarked protocols for injury screening (complete with certifications and an accompanying set of equipment available for purchase) and endorsed 'prehabilitation' schemes. Amidst all this it seems natural that we are now starting to see 'plug-and-play' approaches in the sports coaching 'industry'.

Beyond the issues we just discussed with respect to data and how it is applied, when we venture into coaching human movement, whether for exercise therapy or in a training or coaching context, we need to recognise and understand the intricacies of motor control and the complexities of the processes involved in both executing motor skills and acquiring them.

As famously noted by Nikolai Bernstein, in reality no two repetitions of a given movement are identical. Variability is an inherent feature, even for the same task performed under similar conditions by the same individual.

Motor learning and skill acquisition are also by their nature entirely nonlinear processes. The trajectory for changes and improvements does not trace a neat line. Rather, things can seem to vacillate in an erratic manner; there are periods where progress plateaus, and performance might decline at one time and then lurch forwards thereafter. Moreover, the trajectory and time-course for this progression is highly individual, and as such can vary markedly between individual performers within a group.

Once again, plug-and-play coaching options, involving the reliance on a singular method of instruction or packaged programme for intervention, are clearly not fit for purpose when working with performers who happen to be individual humans, given all the variability and intricacy this encompasses.

Beyond sport, there are parallels here to all domains that involve working with humans. In particular these themes apply to our attempts to guide actions and alter the behaviours of individuals. Most of us readily acknowledge that a one-fits-all approach is not appropriate, yet in practice we are not necessarily adept at evaluating what is required in a given situation, proceeding on a case by case basis, or accounting for the differing timeframe and trajectory in each instance.

Whilst transformational leadership might be what we aspire to in our capacity as leaders and managers, the reality of delivering this is far more intricate and nuanced. Rather than an industrial approach, this is more akin to bespoke tailoring, and as such is a craft that requires considerable investment of time and consideration.

OUR 'PERSONAL BRAND' IN THE INDUSTRY...

The notion that we are operating within an 'industry' inevitably leads us to consider our own brand identity. The idea of our personal brand has become ubiquitous, particularly in the social media era. Almost inevitably this leads to marketing our personal brand – i.e. self-promotion. After all we must build our personal brand awareness. In this way we can add to our status in 'the industry', and the perceived value attached to it.

Since we have come to accept our field as an industry, it should not be a surprise that we see 'start ups' aggressively market themselves as they attempt to disrupt the marketplace. Take a tour of social media and you will find a legion of 'virtual experts' vying to establish their brand.

Social media provides a virtual platform to parade our wares and extol our own expertise. Indeed, in the Information Age virtual expertise and 'online presence' are becoming valued in a similar way as actual applied knowledge and real-life experience. There are a number of notable examples of individuals being recruited into senior roles based on the name they have created on these platforms and the perceived credibility this has afforded them, with astonishingly little regard for any demonstrated competence with live humans in a real world athletic setting.

'THE INDUSTRY' SPAWNS GURUS...

The areas of continuing education and professional development, which we might assume are borne of some degree of altruism and desire to impart knowledge, likewise provide fertile soil for those with an 'industry' frame of mind.

We find that the premise and value proposition associated with workshops and resources are increasingly manufactured. Often, it is quite thinly veiled that the primary aim is selling rather than providing education per se.

Examples of this include practical workshops instructing techniques or using technology in order to create demand for a product. These events also provide a vehicle for indoctrinating those who attend in the value proposition and marketing for said product (and of course directly selling it).

An illustrative example from the sports injury realm is *kinesio tape*, which spawned a spin-off industry for workshops delivering training on how to best use this magical tape, whilst 'educating' practitioners attending on the full gamut of the miraculous advertised benefits (despite the lack of evidence pertaining to its efficacy [47]). This case is all the more pertinent given recent events whereby a number of the marketing claims made by the manufacturer have since been disproven, prompting a lawsuit for false advertising.

One way the industry mindset can be observed is in the scrabble to attain (or self-proclaim) the status of 'authority in the field' or 'industry leader'. The whole premise for this dubious practice is unsound, as it implies some sort of monopoly on knowledge. In the words of Richard Feynman, there is no 'authority' who possesses the right to proclaim what is a good idea. Or as the lyric goes (for fans of Sting and The Police), 'there is no monopoly on common sense'.

PROFESSION VERSUS INDUSTRY...

Describing our respective field as an industry alludes to the commercial interests that come with working in a professional capacity. It is true that these are occupations for which we get paid; it follows that making money becomes part of what motivates us to practice. However, the danger here is that in defining what we do in this way, we lose sight of the more honourable definitions of a profession.

Let us assume what originally motivated us to take the path into our chosen profession was something more meaningful, as opposed to being driven primarily by the desire for commercial success (making money) or ego (making our name in the industry).

There is nothing wrong with getting paid. Indeed we should operate with the expectation that we will be compensated for our time in a way that is commensurate with the expertise and value we provide. However, financial compensation should be a by-product, not the primary motivator that determines our approach and drives our behaviour.

On a fundamental level, the transactional mindset that comes with framing our practice in this way is also not appropriate to professions that are meant to be about service to others. When we work with an individual performer, ultimately our aim is autonomy; we are aiming to provide the individual with the tools or to fix what is currently troubling them in order that they can perform and manage without us. In essence, we should be seeking to make ourselves redundant, not fostering dependence in an effort to secure repeat business.

This is of course particularly pertinent to sport. When coaches and practitioners choose to view our respective field as an industry we inadvertently rob ourselves of the original sense of calling or vocation. In particular, any onus on cultivating our craft is quickly lost when we succumb to an industry mindset.

The solution here is to return to viewing our field of practice as a profession, and reject the assertion that it is an industry. Altering our mindset in this way might help us to resist our practice becoming driven by commercial interests. Reinstating the profession will also allow us to reject the gurus and virtual experts with their claims that are divorced from any value offered. This would certainly help reduce such conduct that devalues the service provided by other practitioners in the field and ultimately undermines the integrity of our profession.

On a similar note, rather than self-promotion, for professionals in the digital era it remains possible to be circumspect and share only what might provide value to others. We can still inform and educate on what we offer, and provide opportunities to demonstrate the value. This way we allow the proposition to sell itself.

ELUCIDATING THE QUESTION...

As we have explored, framing our profession as an industry encourages a standard mode of practice and pre-packaged solutions. In this scenario, given the process is predetermined and the solution is preconceived, there is really no impetus or inclination to invest much time or attention in assessing the human in front of us or hearing what they have to say.

This alone constitutes a major failing in our duty to the individual.

I was very fortunate to work alongside Dr Gerry Ramogida for a period of time. Gerry is an excellent and highly acclaimed performance therapist who works with a number of high profile professional teams and athletes. Gerry purposely allocates extra time for his initial appointment with a new client, as this allows for a more thorough patient history. Something that Gerry shared which stayed with me is that the simple act of listening to the individual, permitting them to tell the story of what has been bothering them whilst he actively pays attention to what they have to say, is one of the biggest ways he can serve them as a therapist. To paraphrase the philosophy that Gerry has adopted, 'if you just let them speak you will find out what is going on with them'.

Within the context of sport, from a performance or injury perspective each athlete presents a different puzzle. Moreover, even for the same individual this is a puzzle that will change over time. This is particularly the case when dealing with an injury or underlying pathology (and this will apply to the majority of athletes at different points in time). Logically, failing to take the time to establish the unique features of the puzzle in front of us before we try to solve it does not make a lot of sense.

When we are involved in leading, educating, managing, developing, or healing humans, the task we face is not one of manufacturing or mass production. Rather than a focus on replication, we should be aiming for customisation. Irrespective of what role or sector we are operating in, working with humans comprises a problem solving process that represents an ongoing journey of exploration. We should therefore be striving for excellence in problem-solving and seeking to engage with each individual we encounter. In contrast, adopting a standardised approach or system of operating can easily lead to becoming an automaton in how we practice.

THE ILLOGIC OF BEING DATA-DRIVEN...

In the digital era there is a great onus on being 'data driven' across all domains. The drive to be objective and quantify input and output is eminently understandable. The well-worn phrase that gets thrown around is 'how can you manage something if you don't measure it?'.

We do however need to be very careful about what metrics we use as a proxy for the thing we are attempting to evaluate. There is inevitably a separation between the measure we can objectively quantify and the complex entity that it represents. We need to be very confident about the specificity and sensitivity of the particular measure in relation to what we are seeking to evaluate, to avoid false positives (detecting something that isn't there) and false negatives (failing to detect something that is there). On a more fundamental level, complex phenomena defy simple measurement.

"Not everything that can be counted counts, and not everything that counts can be counted"

– William Bruce Cameron [48]

I have publicly argued that the present onus on being 'data-driven' is by definition illogical. The advent of *big data* is making this all the more problematic. The data are not sentient, so it is nonsensical that they be granted the role of driving our decisions and behaviours. Proclaiming being data-driven in our practice as a badge of honour to signal how advanced we are is frankly bizarre behaviour. Any meaning is borne out of our interpretation of the data. Accordingly, being *data-informed* seems a more worthy (and logical) proposition.

"The numbers have no way of speaking for themselves. We speak for them. We imbue them with meaning"

– Nate Silver [27]

Similarly, the use of metrics that is prevalent in all sectors becomes problematic if we do not understand the nuances (and paradoxical effects) of their application. By extension we need to be very considered in our interpretation when choosing to act based on the data. This necessarily includes deciding what weight we assign to particular metrics when making decisions. A first step is to understand the limitations and uncertainty involved with any metric we choose to employ. We then need to take these considerations into account in how we interpret and apply the data in our decision making process.

"A large portion of what we manage *can't* be measured, and not realising this has unintended consequences. The problem comes when people think that data paints a full picture, leading them to ignore what they can't see"

– Ed Catmull (President of Pixar and Disney Animation) in *Creativity Inc.* [49]

As leaders and managers we further need to be very mindful in what we communicate to those we lead when it comes to what metrics we are using to evaluate them. The *observer effect* derived from the field of physics is relevant here.

In essence, to measure something is to change it. This applies all the more when working with sentient beings; when we select a metric and assign importance to it, this inevitably influences subsequent behaviour.

THE DISTRACTION OF METRICS...

"The world cannot be understood without numbers. But the world cannot be understood with numbers alone."

– Hans Rosling

To be clear, use of data should be a fundamental part of what informs our decision-making, and we should absolutely seek to collect quality data to support this process. Equally, professional sports provide a host of examples of the unintended consequences that come when we let data alone drive our judgements. The burgeoning use of data and increasing attention given to an ever growing array of performance metrics is changing how teams play. Moneyball [50] famously brought data analytics in sport to mass consciousness, and general managers in many professional team sports now use data analytics extensively when recruiting athletes.

The use of data to recruit athletes in professional sport seems benign and largely positive. However, as coaches seek to leverage data this is serving to influence the tactics employed by teams, and in turn technical development among players to some extent. In professional sports it is becoming abundantly evident (ironically from trends in data) that the actions of players are also being shaped by the metrics the coaching staff are looking at. As specific aspects of players' performance are being evaluated (and rewarded) based on selected metrics, this inevitably drives how they subsequently operate on the field, on the court, or on the ice.

"When a measure becomes a target, it ceases to be a good measure"

– Marilyn Stathern

As we stated earlier, to measure something is to change it. Moreover, *Goodhart's Law* (this time from the field of economics) describes how the act of (publicly) assigning importance to a metric inevitably changes behaviour in a way that the metric no longer provides valid insights into independent and freely chosen behaviour (given that that the metric itself has now become the driver for behaviour).

A generic example is the standardised assessment employed in education: given the stakes involved students are steered to direct their efforts to preparing for the test, rather than learning the material to understand it. As a result test scores reflect students' ability to successfully prepare for the test, rather than necessarily their understanding of the material or their ability to apply it. This is something of an issue as learning for understanding was the original purpose and is the central premise of education. Making the measure the target, by assigning a high degree of importance in terms of future prospects, negates its ability to evaluate what we were originally seeking to measure, and alters behaviour in ways that are contrary to our original purpose.

"Let the main thing stay the main thing"

– Brendan Venter

A similar scenario can be observed in sport, and more specifically within the area of strength and conditioning. When particular assessments are employed to evaluate the progress of the athlete, and thereby the effectiveness of the training programme, naturally this leads practitioners to train the athlete to score well on the assessments, as opposed to preparing them to compete in the sport. Similarly, the currently popular practice of *velocity-based training*, whereby athletes are given feedback on bar velocity following each repetition, predictably prompts athletes to chase numbers, with little regard for how they are performing the movement. Indeed *chasing numbers* is an apt description of the many scenarios where an emphasis on metrics adversely affects the quality of the output, and distracts from, or even displaces, the original purpose of the endeavour.

There are also numerous examples from a host of domains that demonstrate how humans (and other sentient beings) find ways to *game* the chosen the metric. The metric itself drives their behaviour to gain greater rewards, rather than simply engaging in the original task. One such example was the introduction of GPS monitoring in team sports, whereby players are evaluated based on metrics such as total distance covered in a game, which led some players to run around pointlessly during breaks in play simply to drive their total distance numbers up.

Incentivising work with performance based metrics further changes the source of motivation. What we are seeking to foster and preserve is intrinsic motivation derived from the work itself and the inherent satisfaction of doing good work. In turn, this is associated with a feeling of purpose and a sense of meaning in our work. When we start to employ metrics in an attempt to shape reward desired behaviours by definition we introduce extrinsic motivation, which is fickle, and this is to the detriment of the intrinsic motivation that we seek.

Once again, the industry approach of incentivising performance with rewards (or punishment) based on metrics inevitably tends towards a transactional mindset. Inducing such a mindset is poison to any sense of purpose and robs the endeavour of its original meaning. Moreover this is not conducive to loyalty or attachment to the team or organisation.

EXERCISING JUDGEMENT VERSUS DRIVE FOR OPTIMISATION...

As we alluded to in an earlier section, when we select a metric and attach importance to it, naturally this will lead us to optimise for that metric, and thereby the metric starts to drive our behaviour rather than the task itself. At a surface level, optimising performance would seem to be a good thing. However, human performance is a complex phenomenon. The drive for optimisation and efficiency is worthwhile and makes sense when it comes to procedures and operations, which once again lend themselves to standardisation and evaluation. More complex endeavours with humans are far less amenable to this. When we attempt to employ this approach it follows we run into trouble.

Simple systems are easy to optimise. Complex systems are not. Our attempts to optimise complex systems inevitably lead us to oversimplify and we substitute performance for more simple and easier to quantify metrics. In different realms of human performance we select key performance indicators. Indicators of performance are separate from performance itself, particularly when it comes to human performance. Once again, when we select key performance indicators, naturally there is a tendency to optimise for those metrics. In doing so, behaviours become driven by optimising for the key performance indicator metric, rather than performance itself. In this drive to employ metrics and optimise clearly we have lost our original purpose. When dealing with complex phenomena such as human performance it follows we need to temper the industry drive for optimisation.

We can avoid these issues when our use of data and optimisation efforts are tempered with critical thinking. Exercising professional judgement would seem to be a much better approach when we are dealing with complex adaptive systems such as humans, rather than solely relying upon a metrics and a standard operating system independently of critical thinking and professional judgement. Professional judgement is oddly becoming largely forgotten in the era of big data, and the present drive to optimise and operate in a *data driven* manner.

A rare exception in the realm of sport is the *professional judgement and decision making* framework proposed by Martindale and Collins [51]. This framework was designed as a tool to assess applied practice of support staff and evaluate the effectiveness of their input and intervention (as opposed to relying on standardised evaluation). Equally this is something of an oasis in the sea of data-driven, metrics-based assessment of output that is so prevalent in professional sports.

IN CLOSING – THERE IS NO SECRET SAUCE...

Working with humans is complex. Whilst we have used the lens of sport to expose the various issues with adopting an industry approach to practice, this equally applies to professions beyond sport (including those we tend to conceive of as industries). Automation and the growing use of algorithms and artificial intelligence is removing much of the operational and procedural work that lends itself to standardisation and a single system approach. When it comes to the knowledge work and human interaction-based roles that represent the sustainable professions and growth areas across sectors, I contend we should be thinking as professionals who work with humans, rather than adopting an industrial approach in how we work.

A revelation from my travels working with elite athletes, coaches, and practitioners across the world: there is no secret sauce. It is not about finding a magical formula that we can trademark and franchise to build our empire.

In fact, what separates elite coaches and practitioners are their higher order skills that allow them to better explore and solve problems, not their use of some unique method or tool. What we require is critical thinking and clinical reasoning, not some magic bullet or trademark approach.

It is not about attracting customers by proclaiming we have the solution. We must take the time to figure out what the problem is before we can even consider formulating what approach we might take to tackle it. We should view our practice in terms of bespoke tailoring not mass production.

Whatever the advertised benefits, a preconceived notion of the solution can blind us to the problem. Buying into a particular method or fixed way of operating similarly constrains our ability to be agile and adaptable. Once again, the differentiating factors are the higher order skills that allow us to evaluate and discern the puzzle to be solved, adapt our approach to the individual and the scenario in front of us, and innovate to create a custom solution tailored to the unique problem.

Reinstating our field of practice as a profession, rather than succumbing to 'industry' thinking, offers a path back to sanity. We can restore a mindset of cultivating our craft and refocus on the higher order skills we require for the space we operate in. Once we turn minds away from chasing fame and fortune we can similarly return our focus to the individual in front of us and how we might best serve them.

REFLECTING AND CONNECTING THE DOTS...

Do you feel the term industry applies in your particular sector?

What is the convention within the field you operate?

Would you say that how the realm in which you work is framed influences working practices?

Is there a particular drive for standardisation, replication, and scalable output?

Are those you work with encouraged to adopt a particular system of operating?

What is your view on how these issues shape professional conduct?

How is data employed in your particular area?

Where do metrics feature in how work performance is assessed presently? Do you feel this influences motivation or working practices?

To what degree are strategy and decisions shaped by judgement versus driven by data? Do you feel the balance is appropriate?

Based on this chapter do you feel there is a need to reinstate the profession within your area?

Do you feel there is sufficient onus on craft, customisation, and professional judgement?

Emotional Aptitude for Leaders and Coaches

Emotion has traditionally been viewed as something to be suppressed, particularly when acting in a professional capacity. The logic goes that as leaders and people in positions of authority we should be detached and act 'without emotion'. If somebody is described as 'emotional' generally this is construed as a bad thing; when we become 'emotional' the implication is that we are no longer being rational or we are not capable of reason. Conventional wisdom further advocates that we should avoid an emotional response, or making emotional decisions. In contrast to these established views, more recent study in this area demonstrates that emotion is in fact integral to reasoning, decision making, guiding our behaviour, and relating to others. Emotional intelligence is accordingly becoming recognised as being at least as important as more established forms of intelligence. Indeed we increasingly hear commentators proclaim that 'EQ trumps IQ'. With this chapter we delve into the role of emotion in organisational leadership, coaching, and our work with humans in general, and explore what aptitudes we need to possess in this area as leaders, coaches, and practitioners.

DEFINING EMOTIONAL INTELLIGENCE...

"Emotional aptitude is a meta ability"

— Daniel Goleman [52]

Emotional intelligence is a blanket term that encompasses a host of aptitudes. What we are speaking about is our ability to discern, express, and understand emotions; and in turn, regulate how we respond to them. Moreover emotional aptitude pertains not only to navigating the emotions of others, but also being cognisant of our own emotional state. This awareness represents the first step to regulating our emotions, cognitions, and behaviours accordingly.

In his pioneering book that brought the topic to a wider audience [52], Daniel Goleman outlines five domains of emotional intelligence. The first is awareness of our own emotions (in the moment). The second pertains to our ability to manage our emotions. The third aspect relates to how we motivate ourselves. The fourth domain of emotional intelligence is the ability to discern the emotions in others. The final domain concerns fostering and managing relationships.

Clearly then, emotional intelligence encompasses intra-personal and inter-personal elements. The meta-abilities that comprise emotional aptitude are central to our ability to understand ourselves, regulate our own behaviour, and relate to others. It is easy to see how each of these respective elements is relevant to our ability to lead and work collaboratively with others.

As we will see in the context of sport, the element of emotion in athlete preparation is manifested in a host of different ways. As leaders, coaches, and practitioners the various aspects of emotional aptitude similarly relate to all aspects of our work with the humans we serve.

EMOTIONAL INTELLIGENCE IN SPORT...

Sport has a unique propensity to ignite passions and stir emotions. Working in the domain of sport thereby provides a fertile environment for each of the respective elements of emotional intelligence.

What has been termed 'emotional competence' is thus increasingly considered essential for sports coaches [53]. Being good with humans is clearly a critical attribute for coaches, practitioners, and any member of support staff who interacts with athletes. Elite sport coaches intuitively understand this. Interviews with a sample of elite coaches identified nine psychological attributes that they deemed to be critical to coaching effectiveness: three of the nine related to emotional intelligence [54].

Equally, measures of emotional intelligence among athletes further show a relationship with how they perform in competition [55]. The propensity of the performer to manage their own emotions and relate to others thus represent critical factors in terms of their ability to perform, and also their physical health and psychological and emotional wellbeing. Emotional aptitude has a major bearing on the psychological and physiological stressors imposed on the individual, both within the daily work environment and beyond. Moreover these abilities are also implicated in the coping skills and social support structure the performer is able to bring to bear to mitigate these stressors [56].

The health of the performer's relationship with the coach (or manager) is a primary factor that governs the psycho-social and physiological stressors they experience [57]. As such, the coach-athlete relationship and the dynamics of the daily environment under the stewardship of the coach are strongly associated with athlete health and wellbeing.

The athlete's physiological stress response to training is impacted by the motivational climate under the stewardship of the coaching staff, as this impacts how they appraise and experience training [58]. It is easy to see how this cumulative stress may affect the athlete over time. Moreover, the motivational climate created by the sport coach has implications beyond the practice environment. An investigation of student athletes demonstrated that the motivational climate in their respective sport further related to recorded measures of life stress, academic performance, and engagement [59]. This relationship may be positive, in the case of a supportive and task-focussed environment; however, an ego-involved and dysfunctional environment is associated with adverse effects on life stress, academic performance, and engagement.

As coaches and leaders we have a high degree of influence on the environment we create for those we serve. Wittingly or unwittingly, we have a great deal of power over the performer's emotional state. Our interactions with each individual have a pronounced effect on their psychological and emotional state, and this manifests itself in the psycho-physiological stresses they experience even when they are not with us [58]. In the context of sport, how an athlete perceives the quality of the relationship with the coach shows a demonstrated link to their likelihood of burnout [60]. Emotional aptitude comes into play in how we lead, coach, and prepare athletes to perform. Given the stakes involved, clearly we need to explore the topic of emotion more deeply in relation to its role in human performance.

EMOTIONS CONNECTING BODY AND MIND…

The term 'embodied cognition' has been used to describe how body and mind interact to determine how we think, what we feel, and in turn how we act. Embodied cognition captures how our thoughts and what we perceive combines a host of sensory inputs from multiple sources, both internal and external to the body [61]. When we think and prepare to act we integrate sensory information from the environment with information derived via sensations from our own body.

Emotions are experienced as 'somatic sensations'. In other words, they are manifested bodily. In this way emotions serve to mediate the bi-directional link between body and mind.

A related term that has emerged is 'motor cognition' [62]. Part of how what guides our actions and ongoing strategy during activity is by monitoring changes in what we feel in our body as we move, along with relevant cues from our environment (including other actors, such as an opponent to use an example from sport). This concept emphasises the interconnected nature of cognition, perception, and action. Once again, emotions are a key feature of this connection.

Emotions serve to provide the impulse to act. Emotion is a driver to how we move; conversely, how we move is manifested in our emotions. The posture, facial expressions, and bodily movements we adopt are both a reflection and a driver of our emotional state. Put another way, motion and emotion are inextricably linked.

Our ability to navigate and work effectively with our emotions is accordingly integral to functioning effectively, in terms of both mind and body. As our emotions contribute to the bodily sensations we experience at any given time, the ability to understand what lies beneath and identify the underlying emotions will help us to read the bodily cues we use in thought and deed. This relates to how we conduct ourselves as leaders, coaches, and practitioners, in the same way as it applies to the athletes we serve.

Being aware of the interconnected nature of cognition, perception, and action – and how emotion is a thread that runs through each of these aspects – is also critical to our ability to evaluate the actions of others. Coaches who know their athletes are often able to intuit when something is amiss, simply by watching them move [63]. Considering all of these elements similarly helps us to interpret actions in various ways, including getting to the root cause for the particular behaviour or responses we are seeing in a given situation.

EMOTION IN JUDGEMENT AND DECISION MAKING...

As has been stated by researchers on the topic, emotion and decision making go hand in hand [64]. Emotion serves an integral role in our judgements and decision making. Emotions are central to how we imbue information with meaning in order to make choices. This is applies to human movement, and the term *embodied choices* has been proposed to describe the process of choosing between available actions in the moment [65].

Thus emotions inform our judgements and motivate our choices. When the input from emotion is removed, we are essentially robbed of our ability to make effective decisions in the moment. Emotions are also central to how we reflect on past decisions, in turn helping to shape our future choices.

"Emotions powerfully, predictably, and pervasively influence decision making"

— Lerner & colleagues, 2015 [64]

What is certainly true is that our mood state affects (pun intended) how we perceive the world and those around us. Our emotional state not only provides motivational drive that influences our decisions, but can also alter our cognitive process when making judgements. For instance, when we are happy we may not engage in the cognitive heavy lifting, but rather rely on more superficial heuristics or rule of thumb based judgements. Conversely, when we are in a different emotional state we may be more inclined to be more deliberate in our thinking and process things more deeply.

We should of course differentiate between emotions that directly relate to the choice or decision at hand, and incidental emotions that arise from unrelated matters, but are nevertheless present and part of the emotional landscape when choices are made. It appears that both integral and incidental emotions have a bearing on our judgement and decision making process [66]. The notion that our judgement and decisions may be unduly influenced by extraneous events and emotions is something of a concern. Clearly this is not conducive to being consistent in our actions and interactions with others, which we generally deem to be important in a leadership role or a position of authority.

It is also worth making the distinction between emotion and mood. The original emotion is transient, whereas mood persists. As such, persistent feelings that we would describe as our mood or emotional state are more likely to be fuelled by our thoughts and ruminations, rather than simply an extension of the original fleeting emotion.

The mood or emotional state that influences our decision making and cognitive processing is not necessarily the product of the original emotions themselves, but rather the thoughts that accompany them and the secondary feelings which are elicited. Thus how we appraise and process our emotional responses has a major bearing on our mood state.

The term used to describe this is 'ruminative cognition', which encompasses the thoughts inspired by our emotions and past, present, and future situations. Our expectations and societal norms influence how we view our emotions as appropriate or otherwise. Often it is how we feel about our emotions due to the stigma attached that is the source of much of our anxiety. The ruminations that follow the inciting event are certainly considerably longer lasting, and typically more distracting, than the original emotion itself.

Once again our mood may be largely incidental to whatever scenario we happen to be facing; yet it has the potential to influence our feelings about the situation, and in turn colour our judgement in a way that may alter the decisions and actions we take. Clearly it will serve us to make use of the emotional aptitudes that enable us to moderate how our emotions influence our thought process and decision making.

Being cognisant of our emotional state at the time and mindful of our mood permits us to weigh these considerations accordingly in how we integrate our feelings on the situation, and ultimately decide how to proceed. Simply having an awareness of our decision making process, our present mood, and how those two things may interact, can help mitigate the adverse effects of our mood and incidental emotions, in terms of unconsciously biasing our decisions.

REGULATING OUR EMOTIONS...

Emotion helps steer our behaviour: as noted previously, emotion represents an impulse to act. How we choose to heed this impulse is a key tenet of emotion regulation. This encompasses the ability to discern our emotional state and interpret our emotional responses, and in turn exercise some control over how we act on these impulses. What occurs between the external event and our subsequent actions is central to our ability to harness our emotions in ways that serve us.

"Between stimulus and response there is a space. In that space is our power to choose our response. In our response lies our growth and our freedom"

— Viktor E. Frankl [67]

If we are to work in synergy with our emotions, there are some related 'meta-abilities' we need to master. The first step is to be conscious of our emotions. Possessing self-awareness and emotional literacy means being able to accurately identify our emotions. This also entails the reflection that allows us to make sense of our emotions and determine the origins of what we are feeling. From here we can develop our ability to modulate our emotional state, recognising the role of cognition, and acknowledging when our emotional responses and ruminations are maladaptive. Ultimately this provides the path to regulate how our emotional responses to outside events influence our behaviour. Emotional regulation is therefore underpinned by these various elements of intra-personal intelligence concerned with how we are able to discern, interpret, and process our emotions.

"Emotion regulation can thus serve to influence the type (i.e., which emotion one has), intensity (i.e., how intense the emotion is), time course (i.e., when the emotion starts and how long it lasts), and quality (i.e., how the emotion is experienced or expressed) of the emotion.."

– Peña-Sarrionandia and colleagues [68]

In relation to emotional regulation, the term 'emotional reactivity' describes instances where we react in the moment with unchecked behaviour that is directly triggered by our emotional response to the external event. Returning to the wisdom of Viktor Frankl, avoiding such an involuntary 'knee jerk' reaction requires us to create some separation between our emotional response to external stimuli and the behaviour that follows. In this way we can conserve our capacity to appraise the situation and exert some rational influence in how we respond amidst the maelstrom of our emotions.

In a similar fashion, emotional resiliency necessitates being able to return to some sort of equilibrium, so we can restore our capacity to be objective and rational in the wake of challenging situations. Being able to observe ourselves with a degree of objectivity helps us to retain a level of equanimity. Ultimately this allows us to retain our ability to deal with external events, and buffer our behaviour towards others from being unduly influenced by surrounding events. Bringing the discussion back to the realm of coaching, these aptitudes are crucial to avoid outside events in our life impacting how we conduct ourselves and interact with others.

SOCIAL INTELLIGENCE...

A potential downside to self-monitoring and reflection is that constant inwardly directed attention might conceivably make us somewhat self-absorbed. Clearly it is imperative that we remain similarly attentive to these emotional signals in those around us. On one hand, it is true that our propensity to entertain and accept our own emotions makes us more receptive to dealing with the emotions of others. Equally, we need to attend to social cues and to the feelings of others, in order to avoid neglecting the critical social elements of emotional intelligence.

Emotional connection is central to social intelligence and being able to form and maintain the social bonds that underpin cooperation [69]. If we are to respond appropriately in real-time, it is crucial that we are attentive not only to the words of others, but also to non-verbal cues and related signals. Beyond words and facial expressions, once again we infer the emotions of others from their bodily movements [63]. Our ability to read and interpret these signals is a critical skill built upon tacit knowledge that is generally acquired in childhood and adolescence. These acquired aptitudes enable us to relate to others, and to foster and maintain healthy relationships.

There are a number of different implications of this social intelligence aspect of emotional aptitude from a coaching viewpoint. The first is the realisation that even when we say nothing our emotions are likely to be communicated to our athletes [70]. The other salient point is that we need to be vigilant to the expressions of emotion and associated non-verbal cues from our athletes. Once again, we must be aware in order to be responsive to the athlete's emotional state. Like much of coaching this is largely a matter of paying attention.

EMOTION IN COACHING AND LEADERSHIP...

The ability of leaders to regulate and harness their emotions is demonstrated to relate to how they perform in a leadership capacity [71]. Emotional intelligence in leadership and management is identified as a critical factor for organisational success in a variety of fields, from business to medicine [72]. It is likewise acknowledged that 'emotional competence' is fundamental to coaching athletes [53]. Emotion-related aspects feature prominently in the attributes identified as underpinning coaching effectiveness [54], and this finding can be applied across domains. Both leadership and coaching are collaborative endeavours, so this would seem to follow.

The various tenets of emotional intelligence are integral to being able to engage with and motivate others. It is demonstrated that emotional intelligence factors underpin effective interpersonal relations in various contexts and social settings [73]. Empathy, and the ability to adopt and appreciate the perspective of the other person, determine our ability to engage with others and build rapport. From a people management perspective, being attuned to the emotional states of others, and able to express our own emotions, are central to effective communication and our ability to influence groups and individuals. Each of these respective elements are central to organisational leadership, and indeed leadership in any context.

Beyond the ability to interact with others, working with our emotions effectively is crucial to our judgement and making wise decisions in a leadership capacity, and this applies to practice across sectors. For instance, emotional competence has been identified as critical for effective decision making among health professionals in various disciplines [74].

In the context of sport, building and maintaining our relationship with individual athletes necessitates managing ourselves and our interactions with others, both in the day to day environment and in the crucible of competition. It is important to acknowledge that the emotions we express as coaches with our words, expressions, or body language have a demonstrable effect on the athletes concerned [70]. This can have either a positive or negative impact, depending on the emotions involved and the context.

"Stress is contagious, and if as coaches we wish to build low stress environments, perhaps as a first step we need to develop our own capacity to deal with stress"

– John Kiely [75]

When we lack self-awareness, or fail to regulate our emotional state and what emotions we express, there is a high likelihood of 'contagion' [76]. Emotions such as anxiety and anger tend to be highly communicable and thereby impact those around us. In the context of sport this affects the climate within the training environment, and has a direct and indirect impact upon the physiological and psychological stresses experienced by the athletes.

Having an appreciation of the potential impact of our emotions on our behaviours, and the knock on effects on those around us, in itself is helpful. Simply being mindful of the consequences supports our emotion regulation efforts. That said, the objective is not to act without emotion. As we have explored, emotion is integral to much of what we do as leaders and coaches. When we try to suppress our emotions, this actually proves detrimental for our leadership performance [71]. Rather, the challenge is to engage with our emotions in ways that better serve us.

Part of how we resolve this challenge is to differentiate between the emotions directly elicited by external events, and the indirect emotions prompted by our thoughts about the event and the other humans involved. It is generally more useful to respond to the situation itself, rather than our reaction to the situation and our judgements about the parties involved.

Effective emotion regulation appears to be more of a case of what strategies we use to manage situations, where we steer our attention, and how we appraise both the scenarios we face and what we feel in the moment. In this way, there are essentially four avenues we can exploit to regulate our emotions effectively: **situation**, **attention**, **appraisal**, and **response**.

As noted previously, leaders and coaches similarly need to be attentive and attuned to the emotional state of the group and each individual at any given time. Being aware can allow us to intuit the other person's state and how they are likely to respond, take appropriate action if necessary, and adapt our interactions accordingly. Ultimately it is a shared responsibility for all support staff who come into regular contact with the athlete to pay attention and be attuned, particularly under conditions of heightened stress, such as during the approach to major competition.

Emotional intelligence serves to buffer the effects of acute stress [77]. From this perspective emotional intelligence can be viewed as protective for leaders and coaches, particularly for those who work in high stress environments, such as elite and professional sport. Emotional intelligence is also linked to more adaptive responses to stress [77]. These abilities are thus related to the ability to manage the emotional labour involved in leading and coaching in a way that guards against burnout [78].

HARNESSING EMOTION IN LEARNING AND PRACTICE...

Emotion is central to multiple facets of the learning process. Emotion shapes what and how we perceive, and where we direct our attention. Emotion similarly has a role in harnessing working memory and allocation of cognitive resources [79]. Furthermore, emotion is integral to the curiosity, confidence, motivation, and reward aspects that are fundamental to learning. The myriad roles played by emotion thus include our drive to learn, our approach to the learning process, allocation of attention and working memory, and our capacity to sustain learning over time.

Emotion has a potent effect when it comes to directing attention and mobilising working memory capacity [79]. In turn, retention after the event is related to the background emotions, or 'emotional landscape', associated with the learning activity. Emotions not only provide the context, but also mark the occurrence or observation as significant in our minds.

It follows that we can apply 'affective practice design' by using emotional constraints to optimise conditions for skill acquisition [80]. Emotion is one of the ways we can increase motivation and make practice more engaging. For instance, we can employ imaginary competition scenarios during the learning task to simulate competition constraints and conditions in practice. Aside from greater engagement, this is also likely to aid retention, as the experience of practice in the mind of the athlete becomes richer as a result.

The experience of competition is laden with emotion; however, what is less often recognised is that emotion is similarly a feature of the practice environment. Periods of learning (or relearning) are associated with more variable motor performance in practice (and competition), and so more intense and wide-ranging emotions are elicited at those times. Learning new or different ways of performing an action inevitably involves some degree of struggle. Depending on the athlete's disposition, moving from the familiar to the unfamiliar and uncertain can be very challenging. This is especially true for experienced performers, given the inherent difficulty of making alterations to established movement patterns and strategies.

One way we can account for the elements of emotional and psychological load in the planning process is by incorporating these parameters in the periodised plan. In this way be can be systematic in how we introduce novelty, regulate amount of instruction, and manipulate difficulty and degree of psychological challenge in practice during respective phases of training.

We can also periodise these elements according to the competition schedule (and academic calendar in the case of student athletes). This is a theme of the '5A model' for technical refinement proposed by Carson and Collins [81] (Analysis, Awareness, Adjustment, (Re)Automisation, Assurance). Essentially, this model proposes that we plan a period of consolidation prior to key competitions, whereby we permit the athlete to practice without further manipulation and with minimal coaching intervention. This affords a high degree of perceived control so that performance is more stable and the athlete is more assured when they come to compete.

Ultimately, the performer will be required to perform under the full spectrum of emotions at various times. It follows that if we want practice and training to be representative of competition conditions we must account for emotion. We should therefore seek to expose performers to the array of emotions that they are likely to encounter during competition in a systematic way during practice and training.

We can also manipulate challenge and perceived 'threat' conditions during practice for the specific purpose of developing tolerance and coping strategies. With the performer's consent we can devise situations that are likely triggers for emotional reactivity, in order to develop related abilities in an environment of relative psychological safety. In doing so, we can also take advantage of opportunities for the performer to rebound in the aftermath and ultimately develop resiliency. In a similar way we can work through and utilise the lessons from challenging experiences in competition, using the practice environment to trial solutions and countermeasures.

The emotional landscape during practice and competition is of course not always positive or necessarily beneficial. One of the pitfalls of the recognition that comes from achieving success is that the performer persona can easily become intertwined with the individual's identity. A typical consequence is that the performer adopts a conservative and risk averse mindset as they seek to protect this status. Competition and even practice itself can become laden with perceived risks and associated negative emotions, as they labour under the weight of real and perceived expectations. This 'ego involvement' and outcome focus puts a great deal of strain on the individual over time, and accordingly is associated with risks of athlete burnout [82].

STRATEGIES AND COUNTERMEASURES...

As leaders and coaches clearly we have a stake in helping the performer to express the qualities we worked so hard to help them develop. To use sport as our example, it is the collective responsibility of the coaching staff to equip the athlete to perform under the stress of competition. As leaders and coaches in other domains we can similarly help those we serve to better manage their emotional state and perform under pressure.

Emotional intelligence is related to general subjective wellbeing in humans [83], and also serves to buffer the impact on our wellbeing during times of stress. By extension, there is a positive relationship between emotional intelligence and competitive performance [55]. Athletes who rate higher in emotional intelligence report less stress and negative emotions, both in general and during competition specifically.

Enabling the performer to better harness their emotions would therefore seem a worthy goal from the perspective of both performance and general wellbeing. As part of this quest, a helpful mental skill for performer to learn is being able to 'get out of their head'. From a sports performance viewpoint, it is important to avoid the distraction and potential disruption of motor skill execution that comes with excessively inwards focussed attention, particularly for athletes who have a disposition that tends towards introspection [84]. However, this scenario applies more widely at different times, even for outwardly confident individuals, especially when they are challenged to perform under high stakes conditions.

I vividly remember counselling an athlete on the need to 'stay out of her head' on race day a few years ago, and her turning to me with a concerned and exasperated expression and asking 'how do I do that?'. Whilst I was able to suggest some things, at the time I felt the answer I gave was incomplete, and I have continued to mull over the question over the years since that conversation.

Given how our cognitions, perceptions, and actions interact to determine our state, one way we can assist is to encourage the performer to develop some form of mind-body practice. At the very least, engaging in these activities can provide a period of respite and allow them to 'get out of their head'. These respective practices can serve as a reset, mitigating the impact of whatever emotional turbulence they might be experiencing.

Whilst traditionally viewed as 'alternative', over recent years mind-body practice has become more widely accepted, with high performers in all walks of life (including high powered business types) adopting a regular practice of some sort. The specific application of mindfulness practice to performance sport is likewise increasingly acknowledged. These practices are becoming a standard part of the mental skills tool kit to help performers cope with stressors and to confer protection against the negative performance effects associated with excessive rumination and anxiety [85].

The newfound acceptance of mind-body practice is in part due to the growing volume of data supporting its efficacy. Mindfulness practice, which may take many forms, is specifically demonstrated to serve a beneficial effect on emotion regulation [86]. Brain imaging studies have demonstrated that even a short term mediation training intervention (8 weeks) can favourably alter neural activity observed when presented with stimuli designed to provoke an emotional response [87].

Beyond the mystique, part of the benefit of 'mindfulness' practices is simply providing something to harness our attention and divert it towards a different focus. A related strategy is to steer the performer to focus their attention outwards towards their environment, essentially immersing themselves in their surroundings. For instance, simply taking some time to walk in nature is advocated as a mindfulness practice.

The act of (mindfully) engaging in performing a sequence of movements can similarly serve as a meditation. The mind-body connection is evident in the way that we can alter our mental state simply by the postures we adopt with our body [88]. Yoga is accordingly starting to be specifically employed a therapeutic intervention to help develop self regulation and emotional resilience [89]. As an aside, I employ derivatives of yoga exercise extensively in my work with athletes; I am however careful to avoid using the term yoga, or the specific names of the 'poses', and I certainly avoid referring to them as poses, as the baggage associated with these labels can be an unnecessary barrier.

Tuning into the body and scanning for tension is another practice that performers can employ to manage physical manifestations of emotional stress [90]. There are similarly self active relaxation practices, which permit the individual to release points of tension to calm the agitation felt in the body and in turn settle the mind [91]. Simply focusing on breathing patterns can similarly alter our state.

FOSTERING EMOTION REGULATION...

Beyond mindfulness practices, we can also help those we serve to develop specific strategies and 'emotional skills' to better cope with stressors, and in doing so improve their ability to manage themselves and perform under conditions of pressure. Developing resilience is the topic of a later chapter, so for now let us just consider how we can help the performer to develop habits that might assist them.

One example where we can have a positive influence is by helping the performer to switch mode from ruminating to acting [92]. Switching from inwardly focussed attention on our own nagging thoughts, or 'ruminative cognition', requires a strategy to direct our attention elsewhere. A related objective is to lower the volume of the internal chatter. We can find ways to help the performer to quieten the commentary of the narrator within their own head, accepting that we are unlikely to silence it entirely. These practices also serve to anchor the performer in the present, rather than ruminating on past events, or speculating on what might happen in the future.

In a similar vein, maintaining focus on the task, and resisting the distraction of surrounding concerns and externalities, is in itself a highly effective emotion regulation strategy. Simply directing the focus towards salient information and encouraging the performer to tune into the process helps to keep things in the present tense, thus steering them away from speculating about future outcomes and ego-involved consequences. This simple strategy is demonstrated to mitigate stress responses among athletes [82].

Much of the performer's unease or disquiet comes from stepping into the unknown and the uncertainty regarding the outcome. Amidst this uncertainty we can find assurance by latching onto something familiar. In the context of sport the athlete's warm up routine can serves this purpose, so that over time it attains the power of ritual. Engaging in the routine of the warm up not only provides the performer with something they can immerse themselves in, but the act of repeating a sequence of steps that they have performed innumerable times in itself provides reassurance, and helps switch them into performance mode.

Equally it is critical that we encourage the performer to give themselves permission to feel emotion. Rather than avoidance, we can counsel the athlete to acknowledge and accept whatever emotions they feel in response to external events. An important message is that what they are feeling is a natural and an appropriate response. It is necessary to take away the stigma and any surrounding anxiety that it is somehow wrong to be feeling what they are feeling. In doing so, we liberate them from any fears or concerns that they are somehow weaker or lesser for it. Emotion is an essential part of how we experience sport, and performing on the biggest stage naturally invokes the highest intensity of emotion; indeed this is part of what first drew us to it. Simply reminding and reassuring the performer of this is often helpful in terms of how they respond to whatever emotions they are feeling, and goes a long way to reducing the tendency to ruminate.

A final tried and tested strategy that we can leverage is termed 'reappraisal'. This relates to how we appraise the situation we face, and also how we perceive the feelings or sensations we are experiencing [93].

A countermeasure that we can use to alter the psychological and emotional response to stressors essentially involves helping the individual to reframe how they appraise the activity or event [94]. Specifically, we can choose to perceive a particular scenario as a threat and something to be anxious about, or an opportunity and a challenge to be embraced [95]. Ultimately this is a matter of perception, which means it is modifiable.

We can also reframe our interpretation of what we are feeling [96]. The experience of being fearful or agitated has much the same somatic sensations as excitement. Rather than urging the performer to calm down we can work with the intensity of what they are feeling. In other words we can switch mode to a similarly intense but positive alternative emotional state. Sensations that were previously perceived as anxiety or fear can be reinterpreted, so that the feeling becomes one of excitement [97]. Another way we can alter our mode is making the switch from feeling anxious and averse, to being curious and eager for what is to come.

IN CLOSING...

Emotion is an integral and essential part of being human. As humans who work with humans, regardless of what discipline we work in, we often find ourselves operating in a de facto coaching role and this involves navigating the emotions of those we are responsible for. Our effectiveness as leaders, coaches, and practitioners ultimately rests upon our ability to foster and maintain good relations with the humans we work with, and manage relationships with both colleagues and those we lead.

The critical role of emotional intelligence is now recognised and acknowledged in all realms of business and leadership. Emotional intelligence is however something of a nebulous term, as it encompasses a number of discrete elements. In order to get any clarity, it is important that we understand each of the respective elements that comprise 'emotional intelligence'. There is a need to be specific when we speak about such a complex topic and to be clear on what particular aspect we are referring to.

As always there is a danger of lapsing into buzz words and superficialities. We can observe many in leadership positions paying lip service to emotional intelligence. As with respect and integrity, claiming to be emotionally intelligent is missing the point. It is self-evident when somebody possesses emotional intelligence and demonstrates these aptitudes in different scenarios. Much like claiming to have integrity, those who proclaim themselves to possess emotional intelligence often prove to be lacking in this regard.

In the context of leadership, coaching, and practice in sport, there is a need to acknowledge the profound influence we have on the emotional state of the athletes in our care. This is enacted in our stewardship over the daily training environment, through our direct and indirect interactions with athletes and support staff, and how we express our own emotions both verbally and non-verbally. This equally applies to other sectors: when others look to us for leadership we need to be aware of what we express and signal in our body language, and their potential impact on others' frame of mind. It is important that we understand that we hold positions of great influence, and we need to be highly mindful of the scope to influence others (both positively and negatively) this confers.

Fostering emotional aptitude in those we serve I would argue also falls squarely in our domain as coaches of humans. Indeed, the performance environment provides the richest context for learning, with abundant opportunity to exercise emotional aptitude and bring relevant aspects to the performer's awareness. It would seem remiss to miss such opportunities to develop and trial different strategies. Similarly we can help to guide and consolidate learning through reflection and debrief following exposure to high stakes situations and emotionally charged experiences.

If we strive to be effective as leaders, coaches, and practitioners, then fostering and maintaining a quality relationship with those under our care and the humans we operate alongside is an integral part of this. From each of these perspectives it is incumbent upon us to invest the time, attention, and mental resources to develop our own emotional aptitude. When we unpack the host of meta-abilities this encompasses we start to appreciate the size of the task we face. Practically, this entails being more self-aware of our emotional state, engaging in reflection to understand our own emotions, regulating how our emotions impact our thinking and behaviour, and being more attuned to the emotions of others so that we can better relate to them and adapt our interactions and behaviour accordingly.

Whilst such lofty aspirations may appear unattainable, we are not aiming for perfection, but rather for improvement! We are human and inevitably on occasion we will get it wrong. Equally being aware of the various facets of dealing with emotion will help us to get it wrong less often. As long as we remain committed to the pursuit we can be assured of doing better over time.

REFLECTING AND CONNNECTING THE DOTS...

Do you have any examples within your own context of leaders or colleagues who were 'emotionally tone deaf'? How did this impact their effectiveness and affect those around them?

In a similar vein, have you encountered individuals in leadership or management positions who paid lip service to emotional intelligence, yet this was not reflected in their actions and behaviours?

What opportunities do you envision in your work with others to better leverage the element of emotion across the respective areas described (decision-making, teaching and learning, leading, communication)?

How would rate yourself in each of the five domains of emotional intelligence (identifying your own emotions, emotion regulation, self motivation, awareness of others' emotions, managing relationships), and the respective intrapersonal and interpersonal elements?

How 'emotionally reactive' do you think you are (i.e. how readily is your emotional state perturbed by external events)? Do you feel this helps or harms you, both professionally and from a personal perspective?

What practices do you engage in outside of the work environment that provide a psychological and emotional 'reset'?

Do you see merit in exploring some sort of regular practice (or expanding what you do already) to serve this purpose, based on the evidence and rationale presented in this chapter?

Introducing 'Agency' in Coaching and Leadership

Agency is a central but arguably under-recognised concept for coaching and leadership in general. As we are talking about choices, actions, and outcomes, agency naturally leads us to the notion of volition. Bringing these concepts to the attention of those we are coaching allows us to shine a torch on the crucial point that they themselves have an active and integral part to play. If what we are seeking is for those we lead to take responsibility, assume the authority to make decisions, and to act independently when the situation demands it, then instilling a sense of agency represents a crucial first step. In the chapter that follows we peel back the layers of agency using examples from athlete preparation. We will also explore what agency means (and what it doesn't mean) with regards to how we lead and manage others.

AGENCY AND VOLITION...

Sense of agency refers to the experience and perception that we have control over own actions and the outcomes that result [98]. We can further unpack agency as the sense that we are free to make our own choices, the feeling that we are in control of our actions, and in turn perceiving that we are able to exert some control over the outcomes that follow [99].

Given that agency relates to our perceived capability to make something happen, it involves not only the choice to act, but also the ensuing actions. In this way, sense of agency is closely linked to *volition*. Volition pertains to the initiation and control of action [100]. With volition comes the sense that our actions are voluntary and intentional, rather than beyond our control, or involuntary. Volition also encompasses our capability to control the quality of our actions, or in other words how they are executed. Each of these aspects are highly relevant to the domain of sport, but they are equally applicable to professional practice across all realms.

Possessing a sense of agency permits us to feel that through our choices and our actions we are able to exert influence over external events. Agency is thus central to how we perceive our interactions with the outside world. In essence, agency is integral to the notion that we have some degree of control over our situation, our standing in the world, and our future direction.

CONTROL, CONFIDENCE, AND COPING...

Whilst we might assume that a sense of agency is implied in the work we do and what we ask of others, equally we might pause to consider whether we have mentioned or alluded to the elements of choice and free will. From a leadership and coaching perspective there is merit in making agency and volition explicit, and bringing these principles to the awareness of those we serve.

Instilling a sense of agency promotes a feeling of control over the present situation, and the notion that the individual is able to influence both the process and outcomes over the longer term. Developing a strong sense of agency is therefore very powerful, and accordingly shows positive links to health status and perceived quality of life [98].

Heightened awareness of the elements of agency and volition further facilitates a sense of *self-efficacy*, or in other words, the degree to which we are confident in our ability to handle whatever scenarios we encounter within a particular domain or context.

This link between agency, sense of control, and perceived capability is significant. If our sense of self-efficacy is lacking, naturally we will have doubts over our ability to cope in different situations and handle unforeseen events. Such doubts are a common source of anxiety among performers: feeling we are not in control or have no power over the outcome in a given scenarios is clearly troubling. From both coaching and leadership perspectives it follows we should seek to promote a sense of self-efficacy, not least to combat the anxiety that is increasingly prevalent among performers and young people in general. Emphasising agency offers an important route towards this outcome.

The experience of feeling in control in a particular situation has multiple facets. Agency, and the sense that we have the power to choose the appropriate actions we take is clearly an important element. Likewise, volition comes into play in our sense that we have the capability to execute the particular actions required to achieve the desired outcome, or in other words the feeling that 'I can do this'. The final (and most intractable) element is our sense that our actions will have the intended outcome.

Matching the intentions of our actions with their effects constitutes an ongoing learning process, given there are various elements involved in the outcome, not all of which are within our control. When our experience of the outcome is consistent with our expectations and our intentions, this strengthens our sense of agency [101]. Conversely, when the outcome of our actions is not what was expected, this gives us pause and our sense of control over the situation can be temporarily weakened as we are prompted to re-evaluate. Whilst this can be a disorientating process at times, if it is managed properly with time the learning provided overall adds to our sense of agency, and builds confidence that we are able to cope with any given scenario, even when something unexpected happens.

The notion that we have agency and volition in the present situation and over our future direction applies to all things. In the context of sport, this starts with the sport(s) the athlete selects to participate in, the coach they choose to work with, the team or squad they opt to join, and the degree to which they choose to invest in the process, both in general, and on a day to day and moment to moment basis. In addition to these decisions and choices, they have power over the quality of the actions they take, and thereby further influence over their outcomes.

REALISATION OF CHOICE...

As we move away from dictatorial management styles, and our view of leadership and coaching evolves, the central role of the performer in the process becomes more apparent. In the case of sport, the athlete is not simply a passive actor in the process; they are not simply a passive recipient of instruction or coaching. This is equally the case in other sectors, particularly as we move towards a knowledge economy.

Each individual has free will. Whilst there will naturally be some constraints, each actor has some degree of independence in how they operate within the day to day environment and in the crucible of competition (or the 'performance environment' in whatever domain they work in). In turn, irrespective of the parameters or orders they are following, each individual has the ultimate responsibility. The individual has the final choice in what actions they take and how they execute those actions is also down to them. It follows that the individual must accept their share of the responsibility for the final outcome and whatever consequences might result.

It is of course true that individuals in different realms are often subject to a host of influences, expectations, and perceived obligations when they make choices. Nevertheless the power to choose still resides with them. In certain circumstances it may be the case that the athlete has opted, consciously or unconsciously, to abdicate responsibility to a parent, advisor, or an agent. Even so it is necessary is bring to the individual's attention that it remains their choice to proceed in this way. Given that they were party to events, and so everything leading up to the present situation was de facto by their consent, there needs to a reckoning with the fact that they are in the present position effectively by their own choosing, and they have voluntarily taken the actions they have taken.

Once again, agency provides the means to get the athlete out of a victim mindset. Clearly we need to overcome and escape the perception whereby everything that befalls the individual in their life is attributed to external circumstance and forces outside of their control. This scenario can be described as *learned helplessness*, and is the opposite to a sense of agency.

The *binding* between action and outcome is easier to perceive when the outcome follows the voluntary action in a timely manner [102]. When there is a delay, as in physical preparation whereby changes and improvements in capacity become apparent over time, it is more difficult to perceive this cause and effect connection and so we may not have the same sense of agency in these situations. Another example would be overuse injuries, as the onset of symptoms is insidious and so there does not appear to be a particular triggering event. This scenario will be familiar to those who have suffered episodes of back pain: pain simply emerges apparently out of nowhere, or is triggered by something innocuous like reaching down to pick up a pencil.

In the absence of timely feedback in such cases, connecting the voluntary behaviours that were ultimately responsible for the eventual outcome may require outside input to help trace the line of causation. In some instances this may require going back over a period of months or even years. The obverse is also of course true with the absence of observable change. On occasion it is necessary to connect the dots between the performer's behaviours and the resultant lack of improvement observed over time. As the saying goes, 'don't complain about the results you didn't get from the work you didn't do'.

The suggestion that our present circumstances are the product of our choices can be confronting, particularly when negative events have befallen us. When we find ourselves in a situation that does not serve us it is very difficult to acknowledge our role in the chain of events that led up to it. Whilst it may seem uncharitable to point this out, equally it is necessary to face this reality. Confronting the truth of our own involvement is what sets us free. This is the crucial first step that allows us to arrive at the realisation that by extension it remains within our power to change our present circumstances and take a different path moving forwards.

"Mongo only pawn in Game of Life..."

— 'Mongo' (actor Alex Karras) in 1974 classic 'Blazing Saddles'

It is also important to confront and combat the notion that when things go awry we need outside intervention to resolve the situation. Once again, abdicating responsibility and deferring to others to get us out of sticky situations ultimately does nothing to help us become better equipped to navigate such circumstances moving forwards.

Indeed even when unknowable external events do befall us, we should recognise that we still have agency over our emotional response in these circumstances. We remain in control over how we perceive such events, how we interpret the situation, and how we choose to respond.

"You have a choice..."

— Dan Pfaff

It is sometimes the case that the choices we face are unpalatable. Over the course of a career, performers may be confronted with difficult choices in determining their future direction, particularly regarding relationships with coaches and other members of their team. The decision to change coach, switch therapy provider, or move to a different team are undoubtedly among the most harrowing choices athletes have to make. Equally, choosing to take no action is still a choice and that too has consequences.

AGENCY AND ACCOUNTABILITY...

As noted in the previous section, experiencing the outcomes that are consequent to our decisions and actions is fundamental to the discovery process that drives learning, helps calibrate our expectations, and serves to guide future behaviours. However this does assume that we make the connection within our own minds. A crucial aspect of agency is recognising the link between our chosen actions and what outcomes occur as a result (both positive and negative). In that sense, agency leads us to acknowledge our responsibility for our actions and their consequences.

There is an interesting cognitive bias that is often evident in how we attribute outcomes to our own actions. Specifically, there is a 'self-serving' bias, whereby we tend to more readily attribute positive outcomes to our choices and actions [102]. In contrast, we are typically slower to acknowledge that negative outcomes are similarly a result of our choices and freely chosen actions.

It is worth noting that such attribution biases are as prevalent among leaders and coaches as they are with performers. A rugby coach I worked with early in my career, who ironically was otherwise a very poor example of a head coach, offered the wisdom that when a team is winning the coaching staff get entirely too much credit, and when the team is losing they take entirely too much blame.

This is something of a universal theme. When things go well, we are happy to claim responsibility and take the credit. Conversely, when things go awry, we are strangely tempted to absolve ourselves of any fault, and either blame others or events outside of our control. At times we can indulge in some impressive mental acrobatics and inventive post-rationalisation to deny our own involvement in adverse outcomes and dodge our share of the responsibility when things go wrong.

"Let us not confuse rationalizing with rational — the two are almost always exact opposites"

— Nassim Nicholas Taleb [103]

Not least to counter this tendency, agency and volition represent critical concepts to introduce early in the process, and reinforce regularly thereafter. It is important for each individual to acknowledge the fact that their own choices play a significant role in determining their reality. Whatever decisions we make and actions we take (or choose not to take), the final outcome is determined in a large part by our choices and the quality of our actions.

It is particularly critical to highlight agency and accountability in scenarios with negative outcomes. Moreover, as coaches and leaders we need to model this accountability with our own actions. It is important for the athlete to see that we are the first to put our hand up and accept responsibility for our choices and actions when things go wrong. Clearly we are not infallible and we should get past any urge we might have to appear otherwise. My experiences having publicly acknowledged my own error or declared an adverse outcome to be my fault is that far from being diminished in the eyes of the athlete or staff member, if anything the admission and the fact that I openly took responsibility strengthened the connection and trust.

Equally it is incumbent on all members of the team to call out behaviour that is contrary to taking responsibility for choices and actions. As the coach I cannot let things slide and give athletes or colleagues a pass when they attempt to deny responsibility or distance themselves from adverse outcomes. To change our future behaviour and make better decisions moving forwards, this first requires us to take responsibility for past choices and our role in events, especially in cases where the outcome was not positive.

Failing to acknowledge fault, or take responsibility even when challenged to do so, constitutes a huge red flag. Unless the individual is able to overcome this quickly, as coaches there is little we can do to help and arguably our involvement should probably end soon thereafter.

FOSTERING A SENSE OF AGENCY IN PRACTICE...

The most straightforward strategy for ensuring that agency becomes a central feature in the daily environment is to bring awareness to the element of choice that exists in much of what individuals do. We can and should emphasise each of the respective areas that are under the volition of the individual and the power this has over the outcome.

In the context of coaching or preparing performers, committing to an intervention or to making a change does not represent a single choice, but in fact comprises a series of choices. Regardless of what input and direction we provide, how each individual opts to engage with the process, how they choose to operate, and the quality of their actions day to day are up to the individual performer. This point matters because these freely chosen actions over time go a long way to determining the outcome for each individual. If the individual acknowledges that investing in the process constitutes a series of choices that only they can make and the quality of their actions are also up them, then the supervision we provide is no longer about ensuring compliance but rather facilitating the process and supporting the performer.

Beyond making these points explicit and continuing to highlight them, there are some other tactics we can utilise to encourage and emphasise a sense of agency in the day to day environment. Given that a sense of agency comes from not just choosing but also doing, it follows there is merit in giving individuals the opportunity to perform and carry out tasks independently. Permitting opportunities to act with some independence, make mistakes, and learn from their errors with our guidance offers the best route to practical learning. Moreover with time this will instil the necessary sense of self efficacy to make each individual a confident and capable operator, and eventually a coach to others.

There is also scope for us to incorporate some element of choice in terms of what tasks are tackled and in what order. To use an example from sport and athlete preparation, we can provide a limited selection of pre-determined options, and permit the athlete to choose between them. Simply allowing the choice between two or more pre-set alternatives is demonstrated to increase perceived sense of agency and feelings of control over outcomes [104]. It appears that this small allowance of limited choice is sufficient for the individual to feel they have a more active role in the process. Such feelings of control and sense of agency may increase when provided with a greater number of alternatives to choose from.

An extension of this approach is the practice (termed *flexible nonlinear periodisation*) of allowing athletes to select which of the workouts provided for the week they will perform on the respective training day [105]. Note that the athlete still performs the same workouts prescribed during the course of the week; they are simply permitted to select the order, choosing from the available sessions on the scheduled training days. All of the workouts are ultimately completed by the end of the week, it is only the order that may vary. An extension of this approach, which has been given the grand term *auto-regulation*, further permits the athlete to progress at their own pace and self-select the loads they attempt on any given workout, based on what they perceive they are capable of on that particular day [106].

PROVIDING CHOICE VERSUS CEDING AUTHORITY...

Staying on the theme of developing individuals, an important distinction is that the previous example whereby individuals are able to select from pre-set options falls some way short of what is advocated by academic constructs, such as *self determination theory*. We can once again illustrate this point with an example from athlete preparation in sport. Young athletes in particular should absolutely be afforded the opportunity for free play and unstructured informal practice. However, the purpose of supervised sessions is to enlist the expertise of the coach, so that the athlete receives appropriate direction, instruction, training provision, and opportunity to learn under guidance.

At one point in my career I served as coaching director for a programme providing physical and athletic preparation to youth sports athletes. The director of the programme, who was no longer involved in coaching, became enamoured with self determination theory, and encouraged the coaches who worked with the programme under my direction to adopt this approach when delivering supervised sessions. As is often the case with the social sciences, there was a gap here between academic theory and the realities of the practical setting.

In the context of supervised practices, the training environment, and the structure and content of the session are necessarily the domain of the coaching staff. Autonomy is the end goal when it comes to athletes' structured practice or formal preparation, not the starting point. The athlete, and parents in the case of young athletes, certainly still have agency and volition under these conditions. They choose which coach or team to enlist with from the available options locally. They choose to attend each practice or training session, and the athlete continuously chooses how they engage with the training provided. The athlete further has volition over the quality of the actions they perform within the constraints of the training prescribed. But having agency does not extend to determining practice.

A very experienced (and highly successful) national performance director I worked with shared the wisdom that programmes should be *athlete-centred*, but made the important distinction that this should not be confused with *athlete-led*. My experience delivering a programme for youth athletes with back pain once again illustrates this point. At the end of the eight week programme we asked the kids their favourite and least favourite activities, and also what they needed to carry on working on to help continue to relieve symptoms and improve function. Almost without exception, the activities that the kids listed as their least favourite were the same ones that they then (somewhat grudgingly) acknowledged they needed to continue focussing on.

In my experience it is highly improbable to expect that young athletes will independently opt to engage in activities that they struggle with, and the data would seem to corroborate this contention. Studies examining performers' practice habits report that the majority choose to practice what they are already good at and neglect the skills and elements that are weaker. The main finding is that these choices are what differentiated the higher-grade players. High performers distinguish themselves by freely choosing to invest the time practising their weaker skills, rather than working on their strengths as is observed with lesser performers [107]. So it turns out there are good reasons why we as leaders and coaches should determine how training is conducted, especially in the case of less experienced performers.

Over time we should permit increasing opportunity to choose within the supervised training environment, and allow the individual to make more important decisions when it comes to their preparation. As time passes we might see a progression from the coach having 100% control over the plan, to increasing the degree of input from the performer, then transitioning to work collaboratively to devise the plan, and finally arriving at a situation where the performer steers the ship and the coach adopts what is essentially a consulting role.

The critical point here is that the individual needs to first spend time in a structured environment in order to ultimately earn this right to greater input. It is only having attained the necessary level of understanding under the guidance of suitably qualified and experienced coaches that we can expect the performer to arrive at a stage where they are able to make informed decisions.

The reader should note that the progression described tends to be a multi-year process with senior athletes. The idea that this level of autonomy should be automatically given to every teenager is stretching credulity, to say the least. In the first instance (and likely for some time to come) there needs to be a grown-up in charge; and that grown-up should be a suitably qualified and experienced coach. The same principles and considerations equally apply in other sectors.

IN SUMMARY...

Agency is integral to our quest to learn and grow as humans. The concept of agency emphasises the active role of the individual in both the process and the outcome. Heightened awareness of agency promotes self-efficacy and ultimately develops a sense of autonomy. Equally important, with agency comes accountability.

How we evaluate outcomes, and what we attribute them to, are critical aspects to emphasise on an ongoing basis. Agency and accountability should be standard themes in the daily environment that we create. At development level particularly, it is critical to regularly highlight to the athlete (or team member) that they are here by their own volition. It merits emphasising that whatever actions they take are quite voluntary. Essentially, whatever they do, and how they do it, is ultimately by their own choosing. These themes are critical to the development of the individual, both as a performer in whatever sector they operate and as a human.

Something that needs to be made explicit early in the process, and reinforced regularly thereafter, is the direct relationship that exists between our voluntary behaviours and their outcomes. Whatever situation we find ourselves in is a result of our choices and actions. Whilst this may seem to be stating the obvious, it bears highlighting the each individual has volition, and our choices and actions have consequences. We should readily take our share of the responsibility when things go wrong, just as we are quick to accept credit for the wins. It does not serve ourselves or others when we permit those in our charge to blame others or abdicate this responsibility.

Finally, a sense of agency can be incorporated within the daily environment with opportunities to auto-regulate, affording choice in the selection of tasks, and autonomy in how they are tackled. This is not the same as abdicating responsibility entirely and allowing the individual to call the shots. Over time our aim is that each individual attains the necessary understanding and earns the right to increasing responsibility and direction over the process. However, autonomy is the ultimate destination and should be arrived at by degrees; it will be a journey to arrive at this outcome, and the time course will be determined as appropriate to each individual.

REFLECTING AND CONNECTING THE DOTS...

Did the themes presented in this chapter resonate with you?

What is your view? Are agency and volition concepts that we can assume people are already aware of, or do you think there is merit in highlighting these elements?

To what extent would you say agency and volition are implied or explicit in day to day operations within the environment in which you operate?

Do you feel there is any particular need or merit in bringing these themes to the attention of your colleagues, or those who report to you?

What strategies do you feel might help leverage these concepts to assist members of staff to assume greater responsibility and accept greater accountability?

What are your reflections in relation to your own practice when leading and coaching others? Do you feel there are opportunities to integrate these ideas, or does your present leadership style and coaching practice adequately account for these concepts?

What opportunities are there to incorporate some element of choice in the context in which you operate?

Do you have a strategy to develop autonomy in those you are responsible for? What timelines are involved in this process?

Part Three: Lessons from Preparing Athletes to Perform

Moving beyond principles, it is instructive to explore the methodology and mechanics of the coaching process and interventions employed with athletes.

Delving into the process of preparing athletes to perform in the crucible of competition allows us to discover applications for human performance in other realms.

We can employ this understanding to find a path to endure and ultimately excel in our chosen field.

First Do No Harm: Iatrogenics in Coaching and Practice

Iatrogenics is a term most commonly used in medicine. As attested by the Hippocratic Oath (and the premise 'First Do No Harm'), a concept which is ingrained within the medical profession is that any intervention may pose risks and cause unforeseen consequences. It is somewhat strange that this guiding principle does not seem to have transferred across to other sectors. For instance, in sport the idea that we may either not be helping or through our involvement inadvertently making the individual worse off does not necessarily occur to coaches and practitioners. In this post we explore how iatrogenics applies to our intervention and practice in sport as an exemplar for how it might apply in other contexts. We will also examine the case for weighing potential risks against prospective benefits before we intervene.

IATROGENICS DEFINED...

 "Practice two things in your dealings with disease: either help or do not harm the patient"

— Hippocratic corpus, "Of the Epidemics"

The central theme of iatrogenics is that when we intervene there is the potential that we could cause harm. In the realm of medicine it is easy to see how invasive surgical procedures or prescribing medication involves some level of risk of an adverse outcome. It is clear how there might be the potential for 'complications' or 'side effects' caused by the intervention itself, and unrelated to the condition it originally sought to treat. There can also be unanticipated consequences medical intervention, including disruption to natural processes and normal function, or knock on effects such as secondary conditions elicited by the intervention itself.

Beyond medicine there is a need to recognise that essentially any intervention involving humans carries some potential for unforeseen consequences. The consequences might include direct negative impact, akin to the complications or side effects in the medical example, or there might be secondary issues that occur as an unintended consequence. In either case there is some possibility that our interventions might have adverse outcomes.

The concept of iatrogenics has important implications for our practice and what deliberations we engage in when deciding on a course of action. The most important corollary of the concept of iatrogenics is that we need to consider this potential for unforeseen risks and unintended consequences before proceeding with an intervention involving others.

IMPLICATIONS FOR COACHING AND PRACTICE...

My experiences from working with athletes and within organisations would suggest that as leaders, coaches, and practitioners we do not routinely consider the scope for iatrogenic risks of our input and intervention with the humans we work with. More often we simply proceed without hesitation. We may not necessarily give any real thought to the consequences, or weigh the potential risks versus probable benefits.

Perhaps more troubling is that we often do not consider iatrogenics as an explanation when the outcome is not what was intended. We have a tendency to look elsewhere for the reasons why the individual's performance or condition either failed to improve or became worse following our intervention. This is perhaps an extension of the attribution bias discussed in the previous chapter. Equally, such blindness to iatrogenic risk might also be due to a simple lack of awareness.

IATROGENICS IN SPORT...

Iatrogenics is most often discussed in relation to medicine and in this context we are referring to harmful effects on health (i.e. morbidity and mortality). When we apply this principle in the realm of sport the application of iatrogenics goes beyond the conventional and relatively narrow medical definition. When discussing iatrogenics with respect to our work with athletes we should consider not just physical health (for instance injury status), but also performance. Furthermore, it merits considering these aspects from both mental and physical perspectives.

An illustrative example of iatrogenics in sport is the well-publicised case of a biochemist who held the role of sport scientist with one of the premier Australian football league (Aussie rules) teams. The individual in question administered a supplement program to players containing prohibited substances, leading to the 38 players who consented to receiving the supplements (including injections, intravenous fluids, and tablets) being sanctioned for anti-doping rule violations. Thirty-four players from the squad were subsequently banned from playing for two years. The sport scientist in question was given a lifetime ban, and the club and coaching staff were sanctioned with fines and bans for failing in their duty of care to the players.

Those who operate in others sectors might question the extent to which iatrogenics applies in the context of their work. It is true that there is typically far less scope for the health of individuals to be placed in direct danger within the working environment, with the notable exception of military personnel and the emergency services, who are rightly recognised as 'tactical athletes'. However, despite the lack of obvious direct risk of physical harm, work-related stress represents a notable iatrogenic risk to health in all sectors. The potential impact on individuals' psychological and emotional wellbeing can be significant, which in turn affects physical health.

IATROGENICS IN COACHING...

Leaders and managers in all sectors will be well aware of the weight that the authority to 'hire and fire' carries. Sport coaches at professional and elite level similarly wield a great deal of power over the athletes for whom they are responsible. At elite and professional levels of sport, our actions as coaches and practitioners impact not only the athlete's athletic career, but also potentially their livelihood. To some degree this applies to competitive sports at all levels. The powers of the coach often include selecting which athletes get to compete, which may in turn impact opportunities to earn a college scholarship, or even influencing decisions on who gets a professional contract.

Our decisions and actions have consequences for those who operate under our authority, and as such there are inevitably iatrogenic risks involved in coaching and leadership. In view of the position of authority and associated level of influence, our conduct also inevitably has some effect on each individual and on the group as a whole.

Leadership style and communication provided by the coaches are two elements that are repeatedly highlighted in interviews with elite athletes as contributing (positively or negatively) to team effectiveness [108]. In part, this is mediated through the environment we create both day to day and in the performance arena. The lead coach, and the wider coaching staff, can exert potent adverse effects in demotivating athletes within the group [109]. As coaches our interactions with others, not least how we engage with each individual directly, can impact not only their performance, but also their general wellbeing [57]. Examples of iatrogenic effects in this context include reports of the major role of coaches' conduct in relation to negative team dynamics and even athlete burnout [60].

Beyond the decisions we make, the actions we take, and how we conduct ourselves, there is also the potential for the instruction and input we provide as coaches to have adverse effects on performance and even health. The technical instruction we provide can conceivably lead to mechanically disadvantageous execution of athletic movements and sport skills, which will clearly not be optimal for performance, and may also predispose the athlete to potential acute injury or overuse injuries over time. A potential iatrogenic 'coach effect' that is more insidious concerns the excessive provision of feedback and 'over-coaching' with respect to instruction and input, which may ultimately impair performance and the athlete's ability to execute under competition conditions.

IATROGENIC EFFECTS OF TRAINING ADMINISTERED...

Returning to medicine, the administration of medication has a dose-response effect. A minimum effective dose is that which is required to elicit some positive effect, whereas excessive doses are harmful and can even be fatal. Between the minimal effective dose and the minimal harmful dose there is an optimal range that elicits the greatest degree of benefit. The respective dosages involved are however specific to the individual, based on their size and particular physiological makeup. Each of these dose-response characteristics equally apply to physical preparation and training prescription for athletes. Interestingly, the dose-response relationship of athletes is different to other mortals (even trained individuals) [110], illustrating that athletes represent a 'special population'.

It is easy to conceive how inappropriate provision or excessive exposure to training might have harmful effects on the athlete, rather than preparing them to perform as intended. Over-training or unexplained under-performance syndrome is one such phenomenon, whereby performance and health are adversely affected for an extended period as a result of the training performed by the athlete. This phenomenon is not restricted to athletics. The same elements of how hard to push and for how long equally apply to managing high performers in other sectors, in order to avoid exceeding their limits to the extent that they are unable to bounce back following a period of rest.

Improperly administered or inappropriate training prescription equally poses iatrogenic risks to the athlete. Injuries sustained as a result of the training provided would clearly fit the definition of iatrogenics. One such example I recall from my time in Scotland was a head strength coach's experimentation with *German volume training* practices (10 sets of 10 reps), and high repetition olympic lifting for 'conditioning', which led to an epidemic of sports hernias within the professional rugby union squad he was responsible for. As in many such instances, the practitioner involved received no sanction, despite the harm done to the athletes and the negative consequences for their professional playing careers.

What dose elicits the optimal positive response (versus causing harm) is specific to each individual. The trajectory and time course for improvements in capacity and capability are similarly highly individual. These principles equally apply to all areas of human performance beyond the realm of sport.

Conversely, with insufficient dosages (or ineffectual physical preparation) we can also place athletes at risk of injury in competition by failing to adequately prepare them for the expected rigours involved. This similarly applies to education and how we train and develop individuals as they enter the working environment or transition into new roles. Failing to adequately prepare individuals for what is to come might not predispose them to physical injury as in sport, but it does carry some degree of iatrogenic risk and potential for negative consequences, which will be manifested in other ways.

IATROGENICS IN 'LOAD MANAGEMENT'...

As described with the dose-response relationship, individual tolerance to workload and in turn what dosage is optimal varies widely between individuals. Moreover this tends to change *within* the same individual at different time points. Practices in sport that impose arbitrary limits on athletes' workloads thereby confer an iatrogenic risk by ignoring this fundamental principle of individuality. In effect this may render some individuals within the group *more* susceptible to injury when they come to perform in competition, by failing to expose them to the requisite dosage of training as appropriate to each athlete.

The other aspect of load management that poses iatrogenic risk is the practice of artificially restricting the degree of variation in workloads employed during training and practices within narrow bounds. This neglects the need of a biological system to be exposed to variable conditions in order to adapt. Once again, failing to allow the stimulus to provide the adaptation that will confer protection ultimately renders athletes more susceptible to injury, as they have not been adequately prepared for the fluctuations in physical stresses that they will be exposed to when they compete.

These restrictive practices are most widespread in team sports, largely driven by marketing to promote the use of the technology employed to quantify workload, and facile reasoning on the part of authorities in the area. Whilst such methods became hugely popular and prevalent by speaking to the particular biases and desires of different practitioner groups, there has recently been a backlash, as the flaws in the original data presented to justify the approach and the rationale employed have been exposed.

Presuming to know the limits of tolerance, or indeed the limits of human potential, for a group of individuals ignores not only individuality, but also *epigenetics* and the very nature of the complex adaptive biological systems we are dealing with.

By definition, workload monitoring on a group level and associated practices relies on the assumption that tolerance is predictable, universal, and uniform. Dealing with each of these assumptions in turn, it is very hard to forecast how an individual will respond to a given training stimulus (i.e. it is unpredictable). Tolerance is also not in fact universal between individuals; as we have noted it varies widely. Finally, tolerance is not uniform within a given individual but fluctuates according to a host of factors. What we do know is that imposing restrictions on overall load and fluctuations in load is likely to lead to maladaptive outcomes by depriving the system of the stressors and variability it requires to become resilient to these elements.

Let us zoom out from sport for a moment to consider the lessons and how these examples might apply to human performance in other sectors. The major implication is that there is potential for our well intentioned attempts to protect and safeguard to have paradoxical negative effects by making individuals less resilient. When we impose arbitrary limits or constraints on what performers are exposed to within our controlled environment we can unwittingly reduce their ability to withstand unexpected events and render them less able to cope with shocks or fluctuations in demands imposed. This not only applies within a professional setting but also to life beyond the working environment.

IATROGENIC RISKS OF RECOVERY MODALITIES...

Another example of interventions that seek to counter or attenuate the body's natural adaptive processes is the routine use of passive recovery modalities designed to reduce inflammation. Examples of these modalities include cryotherapy and non-steroidal anti-inflammatory drugs (NSAIDs), such as ibuprofen. These modalities have become routinely employed in all sports during competitions and regular training. I was working in professional rugby during the era when ice baths became popularised and each of the clubs promptly adopted their customary use not only after games but also daily training sessions.

As in the previous example of restrictive workload management practices, empirical study has caught up to these trends and the data have begun to demonstrate a lack of benefit in many instances. There are also paradoxical negative effects in some cases [111].

We might argue that if the effect is neutral (i.e. no apparent harm) then we could conceivably continue with these practices. As long as we feel it is worth the time and effort invested, it could be argued that if the athletes concerned believe it helps there might be some benefit due to placebo effects [112]. The use of ice baths and related modalities following matches or competition is such an example where the perceived benefit versus neutral or minimal risk might make it worthwhile.

Conversely, there are instances where these interventions have caused direct harm – such as well publicised cases of professional athletes suffering ice damage to the skin from cryogenic chambers, causing them to miss practices and games. Recovery modalities may also have an adverse effects on function over time, particularly in the case of strength training [113]. For instance, the potential to blunt training responses and suppress adaptation should raise major questions about their routine use during training [114]. Given that our objective is to support the athlete's preparation and ultimately make them better able to perform, knowingly employing interventions that have the potential to compromise training adaptations and attenuate performance changes over time is clearly not obeying the 'either help or do not harm' principle.

There are examples of various analgesics including paracetamol, aspirin, and the aforementioned NSAIDs (such as ibuprofen) being routinely administered to athletes during competition particularly [115]. This routine use of different analgesics is intended to serve a variety of purposes. One is prophylactic use to guard against inflammation caused by muscle damage that will likely be sustained when competing. These pharmaceuticals are also used for their proposed ergogenic (performance supporting) effects, on the basis that reducing symptoms of soreness occurring during the competition might facilitate greater output [116]. Finally, as in the above example, analgesics may be routinely administered following competition with the intention of reducing soreness and inflammation, and thereby accelerating recovery.

However, as in the case of other passive recovery modalities, there is growing evidence to suggest that the use of these pharmaceuticals may impair the physiological adaptation to training and thereby impair performance over time [117, 118]. The data regarding acute benefits to performance are also highly equivocal [119]. More importantly, as with any medication, there needs to be a clear understanding of side effects and health risks associated with their use, both in the immediate term and over time. For instance, a fun fact for male athletes is that routine use of ibuprofen may alter testicular physiology (and not in a good way) [120].

Adopting the *first do no harm* principle, the potential for serious health risks should make us very reluctant to adopt the use of pharmaceuticals for recovery or as an ergogenic aid, whatever the supposed benefit. Clearly athletes must be informed of all potential risks before they provide their consent, but from a duty of care viewpoint the degree of risk tolerance should also reflect the population we are dealing with. For instance, there is no reasonable case to be made for the use of pharmaceuticals for such purposes with young athletes. Accordingly it is highly concerning that reports from major competitions in sports such as (soccer) football suggest the use of medication at elite youth level is almost as prevalent as reported in senior professional football.

There are similarly examples in other sectors and aspects of our life where practices and activities that are meant to be complementary and supportive can end up distracting or even detracting from the central purpose. Beyond sport, the use of analgesic medication for recovery in particular has parallels to the predilection towards medication that is prevalent in some western societies – notably in the United States. Once again, this also extends to children and adolescents. This represents an excellent example of significant iatrogenic risks that are customarily overlooked.

REHABILITATION AND RETURN TO SPORT FOLLOWING INJURY...

There is an apparent 'therapist effect' that helps to determine whether an individual will ultimately make a successful return to pre-injury levels of participation following injury [121]. Given the uncertainty, it is somewhat inevitable that there will be errors when we are seeking to push the envelope and accelerate the process in a time-pressured scenario as is commonly the case in elite sport. It is a trial and error process to establish present tolerance, and ongoing trial and error is similarly required to probe the boundaries of what the athlete is able to tolerate over time. Equally, being attentive to symptoms and responsive to adverse reactions is central to successfully navigating this process. It is crucial that we heed the warning when minor setbacks occur, so that we mitigate the inherent iatrogenic risk and avoid causing any significant damage or adverse impact on the overall outcome.

Similar pressures can lead to athletes returning to practices or competition prematurely. Whilst these influences must be acknowledged, known risks should nevertheless be mitigated as far as possible. A recent investigation indicated that the majority of the athletes studied had not met minimum standards on return to sport assessments when they were released by their treating practitioner to resume participating [122]. This would seem inexcusable. Achieving acceptable scores on a battery of assessments is certainly far from a guarantee that the athlete will make a successful return; equally, failing to achieve minimum standards represents a total failure to mitigate known and foreseeable risks.

Conversely, and arguably more commonly, a different type of negative *practitioner effect* involves being over-protective. Whilst it might be done with the best of intentions, ultra-conservative practitioners can effectively deprive the athlete of the stimulus they require to support and direct the healing process. Excessive caution can similarly prevent the athlete from attaining the requisite level of conditioning, restoring capacity, reacquiring capability, and recovering the confidence to return to performing.

A notable finding with traumatic injuries such as knee ligament rupture is that the recovery of function at six months post-surgery is indicative of the outcome at 12 and 24 months, and in turn has a major bearing on the probability of a successful return [123]. My experience is that in private practice especially the treating practitioner too often does not allow injured athletes to engage in the necessary remedial work during the critical periods in the weeks and months following the injury. As a result of these restrictive practices athletes become de-trained, so that their capacity and tolerance to load is severely impaired. At best this serves to delay their recovery and return. At worst such intervention can put the individual in a hole that they never climb out of, so that they ultimately fail to return to their previous level or cease participating in the sport entirely.

Returning to practitioner conduct, beyond what treatment is undertaken and what exercise is prescribed, a critical part of managing the rehabilitation and return to sport process is accounting for the athlete's psychological needs. There is a fine line between being supportive versus becoming a crutch in ways that present a problem further down the line. Naturally, the athlete is in a vulnerable place in the early phases of their recovery and it is easy for them to form a strong attachment to the practitioner providing care. As such, part of the duty of care of the treating practitioner is to reduce this attachment over time and mitigate the iatrogenic risk of fostering dependency. This becomes particularly important as the athlete progresses in their rehabilitation and starts to look towards returning to performing. A practical solution is to hand over the reins to another practitioner or coach to manage the preparations to return to performing to help ensure their continuing involvement does not become a barrier to the athlete returning to being independent.

How we behave and what we communicate, both in terms of both instruction and general tone, are similarly crucial when dealing with athletes who are returning from injury. Injured athletes are highly prone to getting 'in their heads', and this is manifested in hyper awareness of the injured area during activity and a tendency to try to consciously control athletic and skill movements which should be relatively automated [124]. Therapists and coaches who work with injured athletes can inadvertently compound these issues with excessive instruction, causing them to overthink things to an even greater degree.

What is communicated both verbally and via the general demeanour of the therapist, coach, or support staff member can similarly exacerbate the doubt and amplify the anxiety that injured athletes will naturally be experiencing. *Kinesiophobia* (fear or apprehension of movement, due to the possibility of pain or discomfort) is a common issue following serious injury, as it is with recurrent and chronic overuse injuries. Clearly this has implications for the athlete's willingness to engage in activity and may also be manifested in how they move following the injury [125]. How well we are able to guard against this creeping anxiety and aversion is thus linked to the likelihood of a successful outcome [126]. In relation to iatrogenic risk, kinesiophobia can be somewhat contagious – and sadly my experience is that all too often athletes catch it from their therapy provider. Learned helplessness is a related phenomenon that can impair recovery following traumatic injury [127], and once again the treating practitioner may unwittingly be a contributing factor.

Beyond the realms of sport and injury, *stress contagion* is similarly a real phenomenon. Just as another person's excitement can infectious, when we display signs of stress and anxiety this is similarly transmitted to those around us. Anybody who has spent time in the company of high anxiety individuals can attest to this. As in the example of an athlete returning from significant injury, those who are in a vulnerable place can be particularly affected. As a social species, stressful experiences and the emotional state of an individual are transmitted to those around them via social interaction. What we express and signal with our behaviour can thus affect (or infect) others. As stress contagion has a neurobiological basis, this is not only manifested in the observer's psychological state but also causes measureable physiological changes [76].

Thus iatrogenic risks even extend to our social interactions. From a human performance viewpoint and other perspectives, each individual within the team should be aware of their social responsibility and the potential impact of their behaviour on other team members (particularly those who may be vulnerable). When we are in a position of authority our conduct becomes all the more critical under stressful conditions. As far as possible we should therefore strive to resist being unduly affected by the situation, given the impact our behaviour may have on those who are looking to us for leadership.

IN SUMMARY...

This may have been a confronting topic for some readers. However, if we are to embrace our role as coaches of humans then on a fundamental level we must reckon with the fact that we work in service of others and this engenders certain responsibilities. Part of our duty of care is to understand these obligations and the potential consequences when we exercise our prerogative to intervene. This necessarily involves considering the possibility of adverse outcomes or unanticipated knock on effects.

How we conduct ourselves affects others in direct and indirect ways, both through the environment we create and via our interactions with each individual concerned. Based on the examples in this chapter iatrogenic risk clearly applies to leadership in sport, and for the coaches and practitioners responsible for providing support and care to athletes. Equally there are parallels and corresponding risks within the context of leadership and management in various realms.

Something that applies irrespective of the sector (and regardless of what we intend) is the potential for our intervention to have paradoxical negative effects. Rather than facilitating the work of those under our authority, our involvement equally has the potential to stifle creativity, innovation, and problem-solving. The coaching intervention or input we provide similarly has the potential to have a negative effects on the individual's performance, both in the short term and over time.

The purpose of introducing the concept of iatrogenics and exploring how it applies to sport and professional practice in others sectors is not to instil anxiety or to inhibit how we operate. The main take home message here is simply that we should engage in some deliberation before we proceed to act, and make the necessary allowances in how we deliver interventions and in turn how we evaluate the outcome.

By definition, in sport the outcome is always uncertain and this equally applies to all sectors that involve humans. Being successful in how we operate thus requires that we acknowledge and embrace the uncertainty. We must bear some degree of risk, and we need to give consideration to all sources of risk when deciding how to tackle the problem at hand.

Inevitably we are dealing with incomplete information. Besides this, given the circumstances and the fact we are dealing with humans, not everything is knowable. Given the constraints we are effectively dealing in best guesses. We cannot foresee the outcome with perfect clarity and on occasion we will be faced with outcomes that we did not anticipate. Equally, we do have an obligation to mitigate the risks as far as possible; and we should consider our own actions and conduct as part of the iatrogenic risks we are seeking to mitigate.

REFLECTING AND CONNECTING THE DOTS

What were your immediate thoughts when reading this chapter?

Does the idea of iatrogenic risk resonate with you? Can you recall any instances whereby your intervention had unforeseen consequences?

To what extent do the various examples of iatrogenic risks in sport relate to your particular discipline or sector? Do you think there are many parallels to the context in which you operate?

What is the general level of awareness of these concepts? Do you feel that your colleagues generally subscribe to the principle of 'first do no harm'?

Based on the information presented, what steps might you implement to mitigate potential iatrogenic risks moving forwards?

The Why, What, and How of Coaching Intervention

There are a few fundamental questions when we are considering initiating some sort of intervention in our role as 'coach', beginning with 'why?', and then 'what?', and finally 'how?'. This is pertinent to all practitioners in sport, given that coaching is an observable part of the daily working environment. Whatever our discipline, we find ourselves directing the athlete on where and how we want them to move, and giving instruction on how to perform whatever exercises we prescribe for our various purposes. More broadly, coaching humans is a somewhat universal feature of the work undertaken by professionals in all fields. It would serve us all to become cognisant of the underlying principles that govern coaching intervention and skill acquisition, so that we are proficient when we find ourselves coaching others to do things in a new or different way.

During the course of this chapter we will get into some specifics of coaching athletic movement to explore and illustrate key themes, so I ask the reader to bear with me as we draw these strands together and relate this information to coaching humans more generally. In this opening part of this chapter in three parts, we consider the 'why' behind coaching intervention.

BEFORE WE DO ANYTHING – STARTING WITH WHY...

My former colleague Dr Gerry Ramogida, who at the time of writing serves as performance therapist for the Golden State Warriors and the Seattle Seahawks, shares some great wisdom on what governs his approach when treating athletes. He said: "before I do anything, I first ask myself 'why?'". Gerry's words equally apply to coaching. If we cannot answer such a fundamental question at the outset then we should perhaps go away and figure it out before we proceed any further. I contend that we would all do well to apply this premise when considering any intervention.

As a natural follow-up to 'why am I doing this', the next question we should pose is 'what exactly am I aiming to achieve by doing this?'. In our quest to be intentional in our approach and concise in our delivery, we must first be clear on what functions we are looking to fulfil and what objectives we are looking to meet.

COACHING FOR LEARNING...

Fundamentally, when we discuss coaching in essence what we are talking about is learning. This might constitute learning something new. Alternatively it might involve learning how to do a previously learned or familiar action in a different manner.

So let us consider two scenarios:

Scenario #1 is that you are provided with the solutions to memorise (essentially a cheat sheet).

Scenario #2 is that you work through each problem, reason it through, figure it out (all with appropriate guidance), and finally arrive at the solutions.

Which of these two scenarios would you expect to provide the most effective learning? More specifically, which is more likely to result in superior recall and understanding?

The process of working through the task and coming up with solutions clearly has an element of trial and error. The learner's exploration of the task that includes trialling different solutions is in fact an integral and essential part of the learning process [128]. To paraphrase a friend and peer in the field, whether they get it right or they get it wrong, either way a lesson is learned and the new information is 'in the vault'.

Given that this process of trial and error has inherent value, it would seem remiss to skip this step. To use the example of sport, as coaches we should be at pains not to deny athletes the opportunity for experimentation to triangulate their approach. Failing to provide some opportunity to attempt different solutions simply to expedite the process does not serve us in the long run. Yet we see this all in the time when we instruct others. This applies especially when practitioners instruct athletes on how they want them to move.

To continue this theme during the course of providing instruction we have a tendency to leap in at the first opportunity and immediately intervene when the performer' first attempt is not 'correct'. To relate this to sport, all too often practitioners insist that the athlete replicates what we deem to be 'correct' form from the outset.

AM I ADDING VALUE?

Part of being a coach, and something that is an essential part of the process for any professional striving for continuous improvement, is asking ourselves the hard questions. Exercising this discipline is likewise fundamental tenet of *reflective practice*. To that end, a crucial question we need to consider at the outset, and revisit throughout the coaching process that follows, is whether we are truly adding value to the learning process or making a meaningful difference to the performance outcome.

In this vein, there are some specific questions we need to ask ourselves in our role as 'coach'. For instance, a critical question is: 'am I effecting change?'. Is the change positive? Is the change robust? In other words is the intervention 'sticking'? Does my input have any foreseeable adverse side effects? Is the performer able to adapt? The solution we have cultivated might look good, but is the performer capable of coming up with alternative solutions when faced with different scenarios?

On a fundamental level, it is important for us to entertain the notion that our input may not be entirely helpful. We should allow for the possibility that our presence and involvement may not be assisting the athlete's learning process. As noted in the previous chapter, we should consider the potential iatrogenic risks of our intervention. This includes the possibility that our ongoing involvement might be interfering in the process.

Such a realisation raises further questions: are we inadvertently adding noise? Is our input distracting the athlete from attending to other salient information and intrinsic feedback as they practice? Might we be impeding the performer from exploring potentially viable solutions? Finally, is our involvement serving to foster dependence?

Despite our best intentions we need to consider that we might be getting in the way.

Dependency is a major side effect that we need to keep in mind during the coaching process. The most revealing test of our coaching is what happens when we are not there. Is the positive change we are effecting dependent on us being there? If that is the case, then by definition we have created dependency. The objective should be creating autonomy not automatons. Paradoxically, our ultimate aim as coaches should be to make ourselves redundant.

THE NECESSITY OF COACHING INPUT...

There is presently a school of thought in the field of sport and athletic preparation that contends our role as coaches is merely to facilitate the environment to allow the learner to spontaneously 'self organise'. As it happens, this view does somewhat misrepresent the skill acquisition and motor control literature. In any case, the story goes that when left to their own devices, the individual will be able to explore the task, and the constraints of the task and environment will steer them to adopt and refine movement strategies that are appropriate for their own capabilities. This is essentially a bastardised version of a paradigm variously described as 'ecological dynamics' and the 'constraints led approach', and borrows heavily from dynamical systems theory [129].

Whilst appealing in theory, in practice it is a stretch to think that a performer will self-organise in a perfect fashion and spontaneously adopt the most mechanically optimal technique of their own accord. In some ways, this reminds me of the *infinite monkey theorem* (I will let the reader google that one).

To illustrate this point, take a stroll down to any nearby routes popular with recreational runners and marvel at the running techniques on display. In doing so, you may gain some insight into the reasons behind the high injury rates among recreational runners. These individuals might have cobbled together a strategy and movement pattern that is more or less a viable approximation of running, but it certainly is far from optimal from a mechanical effectiveness and efficiency viewpoint.

What is also evident at junior levels of sport is that a growing number of the athletes we encounter are presenting with a glaring need for guidance and remedial work. This mirrors a wider trend in society as modern lifestyles become increasingly sedentary, with the result that the level of fundamental movement skill mastery among children and adolescents continues to decline [130]. For instance, an investigation of 12- and 13-year olds reported that only 1 in 10 (11%) demonstrated mastery or advanced skill proficiency in all nine fundamental skills assessed [131]. These fundamental skills comprised run, skip, jump, throw, catch, striking a ball with a bat, kicking a ball, etc., and so are highly relevant to athletic and sport skills. Such findings are replicated in various parts of the world, so it is no longer safe to assume young athletes will have acquired the basics as part of their normal development. Practitioners who work in sport can therefore expect that their role in this space will only expand moving forwards.

From these observations we can conclude that self-organisation is clearly an imperfect process. When we watch sport at various levels the movement mechanics that athletes spontaneously adopt, acquire, and adapt over time are frequently suboptimal, albeit they may get away with this (at least for a time).

Stepping back from the competing theories, we should acknowledge that from the outset more pragmatic authors described the learning process as 'guided exploration' [132]. What this points to is that there is a need for a guide.

In the context of sport, it would seem to be a dereliction of duty to stand by and watch athletes continually operate in a manner that is mechanically unsound and injurious. Equally, how the athlete has operated to date might have been adequate to reach their present level of performance, but in order to continue to improve and make the step up to higher levels of performance often requires revisiting and remodelling their approach.

Clearly we have a role to play as coaches within our particular domain. Performers at all levels can benefit from guidance and coaching input when it is appropriate and delivered effectively. We just need to be clear on the scope of what our role might be in this space and what specific functions we are seeking to fulfil.

OUR ROLE(S) IN THE PROCESS...

Following on from some wisdom that Dan Pfaff shared on this topic, our guiding purpose as coaches (and practitioners in sport) is to ensure the effectiveness of the strategies employed by the individual and strive to enhance their efficiency on an ongoing basis. In sport, coaches can use the lenses of mechanical effectiveness and efficiency to best serve the athlete, both in terms of enhancing performance and from the perspective of mitigating injury risk.

To that end, I would contend that a key part of our role from the outset is to help the individual concerned understand the physics of what they are trying to do. Given that learning is central to coaching movement then our role here is that of a teacher. Providing the athlete with clarity on the fundamental physics at play is critical to help inform the athlete's attempts to come up with effective movement solutions that align with the physics involved. Once again, there are 'physics' or laws of nature that govern processes in all domains, so this approach equally applies beyond sport.

Once we have armed the individual with this understanding, our main function is then that of a guide. We are there to help steer attention to salient features of the task, help them to conceptualise the task and to conceive potential solutions, and provide feedback to help them refine those solutions.

An insightful comment from Dale Stevenson, coach of current world champion shot putter Tom Walsh, was that he decided he needed to get really good at asking the right questions. Dale considers that a major part of his role as a coach of an already accomplished athlete is 'probing' to stimulate the ongoing discovery and learning process over time. From this perspective, coaching represents a shared endeavour in which each individual makes a significant contribution.

Borrowing from dynamical systems theory, on occasion our role as coaches is to provide the nudge that dislodges the individual from their existing strategy for the purposes of freeing them up to move onto alternative solutions that might be more effective or efficient. Let us use the analogy of a pinball game. Sometimes the ball becomes stuck in a shallow well, so we give the system a nudge or shunt to dislodge the ball, making it free to roll and perhaps find more favourable locations.

SECURING AGREEMENT ON THE NEED FOR INTERVENTION...

Now that we have some clarity on the terms of reference for the coaching endeavour, the preliminary step when seeking to initiate any prospective intervention is to first communicate to the individual concerned why we feel there is a need to make a change. In the context of performance sport, there is a particular need to make the case when what we are proposing is markedly different from how the athlete has operated (with some degree of success) to date. Oddly many practitioners fail to consider this first step and simply proceed without first attempting to get the athlete on board with the change they are advocating. Funnily enough this is not conducive to eliciting commitment and engagement on the part of the athlete during the process that follows.

One of the more intelligent frameworks to guide our approach to instigating and executing a coaching intervention is the '5A model of technical refinement' outlined by two applied sport psychologists named Howie Carson and Dave Collins [133]. This framework was devised for sport but has application to coaching in all domains. The first step is *analysis*, which comprises detailed evaluation and exploration of the evidence. This is our opportunity to communicate why we think there is need for change, and suggest what direction the proposed change should take, based on the evidence presented.

Having provided the opportunity to contemplate the proposition, the coach can engage the individual in weighing the pros and cons of making the change. From there we can discuss what form the intervention might take, and the likely timeframes involved. Returning to sport, once the athlete has indicated their support and affirmed their intention to make a change, the athlete and coach can jointly participate in the process of identifying the new technical model that will best fit the athlete and resolve the existing issues that have been identified. In this way, the performer is enlisted as an active participant in the process from the outset. The sense of ownership this brings is important in fuelling commitment during the process that follows.

IN SUMMARY...

For practitioners and professionals alike, we have multiple parts to play in our capacity as de facto coaches of humans. At various points we assume the roles of teacher, inquisitor, guide and facilitator. It is critical to be clear on our purpose and always mindful of the danger that inadvertently we might become an obstacle, a crutch, or a constraint on the process. Clearly there is more here than meets the eye when it comes to coaching to elicit change. The next part deals with the 'what' in relation to coaching and considers the process by which we devise the content and substance of what we are aiming to convey as coaches.

ONTO THE WHAT...

Within our respective realms we find ourselves directing others on what we would like them to do and in what manner. In other words, we coach them. In the opening part of this chapter we delved into the why, as we attempted to elucidate what our role is and defined what objectives we should be seeking to fulfil when instigating a coaching intervention. And so we move onto the 'what', in relation to what makes for an effective intervention.

As we delve into discussions on coaching athletes to illustrate the key themes, we must first reckon with the fact that 'athletic movement' and indeed 'performance' are somewhat nebulous. In any given sport, athletic performance encompasses a variety of different actions, takes multiple forms, and is expressed in a range of different scenarios. The expression part in the context of competition in turn comprises a host of perceptual-motor skills that athletes must acquire and refine in order to train and compete successfully in their sport.

To help unpack 'athletic movement', we can begin with an inclusive list of fundamental motor skills that are common to sports, such as gait/locomotion, jump/land, squat, lunge, balance, throw, catch, push, pull, twist/rotate, and pivot. Essentially athletic movement skills are the composite of these component skills in some combination, with various permutations that are expressed in the context of the sport. These variations and combinations are refined in training and expressed in competition [46].

Irrespective of the domain it is helpful for those in a coaching role to identify the critical competencies for a performer. From this starting point, we can devise a framework to undertake a 'needs analysis' for each individual. An inclusive list of key component skills and competencies thus serves as a reference to evaluate the present capabilities of the individual performer against. In this way we have a basis to identify areas for development and also to inform coaching interventions.

FINDING THE PATH...

Learning and skill acquisition are nonlinear processes, and this is particularly the case with motor skills [134]. The timelines and trajectories involved can also vary considerably according to the individual. Reflecting the nature of what we are dealing with, the processes of instruction and coaching can also be considered to be nonlinear and will be similarly depend upon the individual.

Accordingly the path that the coaching intervention takes will tend to be different in each instance. Each individual represents a different puzzle to solve. Indeed the same individual may present as a different puzzle at various time points in their career. As coaches we can therefore expect it to be a different journey in each instance. Our task is to find the best path for each individual as we figure out the puzzle with them. Returning to the idea of 'guided exploration', our role is to provide guidance as the performer feels their way and works through what is essentially a problem-solving exercise.

"Principles are few. The man who grasps principles can successfully select his own methods..."

– Ralph Waldo Emerson

It should now become clear that coaching is not about trying to find the full-proof system, 'best method', or magical cue. We should rather strive to acquire a sound grasp of governing principles. We then apply these principles in a way that is appropriate to our chosen domain, and reflects the context and particulars of the situation. To paraphrase Ralph Waldo Emerson, if we grasp the principles and have a solid appraisal of what the individual in front of us requires, we can select methods accordingly.

SOME ASSUMPTIONS...

As we scrutinise traditional approaches to instruction, it seems that there are certain assumptions which underpin what is commonly practiced when coaching others.

Firstly, it is strongly implied that there exists a stereotypical 'ideal' way of doing things, and by extension that this should serve as our template when instructing and coaching others. Oddly, it is rare for us to question the notion that there is one 'correct' method or textbook way of executing a given skill. Is the idea of a single universal solution that is applicable to all individuals really plausible?

Perhaps we might allow that the best way will differ somewhat according to the individual. However, this still assumes that there is only one 'best way'. Should we really only coach one solution for an activity that will be performed in different conditions and scenarios?

Conventional wisdom in relation to coaching and skill acquisition also leads us to believe that with learning things become more grooved, so that motor performance becomes more consistent and less variable. By extension, it is assumed that skilled performers can be expected to show very little variability in their motor patterns, as the motor skill becomes more automatic and reproducible. But is that actually the case?

ON CLOSER INSPECTION...

When we closely observe highly skilled performers executing the 'same' closed skill it becomes apparent that successive repetitions of the movements are never actually identical. This phenomenon was famously termed 'repetition without repetition' in the pioneering contributions to the literature by Nikolai Bernstein [135], which was borne out of his observations of skilled blacksmiths at work.

Skilled performers, be they sportspeople, performing artists, or craftsmen, are able to produce a highly stable outcome (successful performance) via a multitude of different actions. These different actions range from subtle variations of the primary solution to entirely novel improvised solutions. This diversity between performers and the variations we observe in the actions they perform in different scenarios are features of skilled performers. So we can reject the assumption that there is single universal correct solution.

These realisations have led some to propose the notion of 'good' variability that is flexible and adaptive versus 'bad' variability that leads to adverse outcomes or is unsustainable for other reasons, such as predisposing to injury. This is an oversimplification, but the mere fact that variability is becoming acknowledged as integral to skilled performance and skill practice nevertheless constitutes a major step forwards. In any case, we can safely refute the notion that skilled performance does not exhibit variability. It is the performance *outcome* that is consistent, not the performance itself.

LEARNING IN PRACTICE...

"Practice is a form of exploratory behaviour, a continually evolving search for task solutions"

— Newell & McDonald [136]

There are some key elements in this description of the practice of acquiring and refining skills that merit attention. The first is that exploring the problem is essential and integral to the process. By extension, the performer should be afforded an opportunity to explore the boundaries when executing the task, and to engage in some trial and error as they practice. In the context of elite sport, on occasion athletes can conceive extraordinary solutions that defy conventions, in keeping with their extraordinary capabilities. It is important to allow this possibility with star performers in all domains.

A second important theme is that solutions are *continually evolving*. It is also worth noting here that we are talking about solutions plural. To that end, we should allow and encourage the performer to trial multiple solutions or 'families of solutions', and to keep doing so as time progresses.

There is generally more than one way to do something. Due to the dynamic nature of the performance environment the individual will be faced with different constraints and scenarios that will necessitate being creative and adaptable to achieve the same outcome via different means. Returning to sport, if we limit an athlete to one solution during practice, even if it a really good solution, we are not adequately preparing them to perform under the different constraints and conditions they will encounter in competition.

STABILITY AND FLEXIBILITY...

One of the hallmarks of expert performers is *meta-stability*, meaning the ability to successfully complete the given task under different constraints and in different scenarios [137]. It follows that we should be seeking to develop not only the ability to produce a stable performance outcome, but also the adaptability to demonstrate flexibility in how that outcome is arrived at [137]. Skilled performers are equipped with multiple options, termed 'multi-stability'. In essence, they are able to bring different solutions to the same problem.

"...not fixed into a rigidly stable solution, but can adapt movement coordination patterns in a functional way, as a function of system degeneracy... perceptual motor systems are stable when needed, and flexible when relevant"

— Seifert and colleagues [138]

Defining skilled performance in this way contrasts to the traditional view of skill or expertise as simply the ability to repeat a single stereotyped, choreographed, and well-rehearsed 'textbook' action. Neurobiological systems, that is brain and body, have in-built 'redundancy'. This is reflected in how we execute different tasks, including motor tasks. The fundamental property of redundancy, or 'motor abundance' [139], gives rise to the concept of 'equivalence', whereby multiple solutions or 'families' of solutions can be employed to achieve an equivalent (i.e. successful) performance outcome via different routes.

A major benefit of possessing a bigger bandwidth for solutions is that we can maintain performance under a range of different task conditions. Having a repertoire of solutions provides us with 'work around' options to ensure that we can get the job done regardless of the circumstances. With flexibility comes adaptability and the ability to improvise when faced with unexpected constraints or obstacles.

Accordingly, part of practice in athletics and the performing arts is ensuring that performance and execution of athletic skills is robust to 'perturbations' – i.e. performers are able to execute successfully under different conditions and find a way. By extension, when developing performers in different domains, we should seek to expose them to various challenges that force them to come up with alternative solutions, so that they are ultimately able to perform successfully whatever the scenario they are faced with.

PHYSICS TRANSCENDS PHILOSOPHY…

In learning and coaching there are few universal rules. The exception is that the physics of motion apply universally to all performers, regardless of their capabilities and the peculiarities of the performance environment or sport. The conversations that allow the coach and performer to have clarity and a shared understanding of the 'performance problem' and the potential solutions should thus be grounded in physics.

"Laws of physics define behavior of the neuromotor system at any level"

– Mark L. Latash [139]

Newtonian laws of motion govern terrestrial motion and as such have universal application to all sports and performing arts. Accordingly, these physical laws seem a good starting point for discussions on fundamentals of the performance model for an athletic skill as it pertains to the individual.

For practitioners in sport we must recognise that physics equally applies to our practice, irrespective of the discipline we happen to work in. Physics has zero regard for our philosophy, coaching model, chosen sport, status in the field, or reputation. Be assured: if you attempt to violate the laws of physics, physics will violate you. By extension, there are similarly fundamental physics and laws of nature within any domain that professionals ignore at their peril.

"Laws of nature have no pity and no exceptions"

– Mark L. Latash [140]

Returning to our '5A model of technical refinement' [81], having identified and committed to the need to make a change, the discussion between the coach and the individual on the specific nature of the technical refinement to be made should necessarily centre on the universal laws of physics and motion as they apply in the context of the performance arena. Bringing the discussion back to sport, no athlete can claim that they are not subject to physics, so this provides stable and irrefutable ground for the discussion.

I invite the reader to bear physics and the laws of motion in mind; this will be important as you read the following section that takes a deeper dive in the context of performance sport…

ALIGNING AIMS AND OUTCOMES…

Achieving one aim should not be to the detriment of another. We should be at great pains to ensure that the foreseeable outcome of our intervention has merit from all perspectives.

We can illustrate this in the context of sport. As the authors of a recent publication pointed out, efforts to devise 'safer' movement strategies do not necessarily acknowledge the impact the particular intervention might have on athletes' performance [141]. If what we are instructing athletes has the potential to impair their ability to perform this would seem pertinent information to disclose. Certainly this is something that as coaches we need to take into account.

Inevitably if the strategies and interventions advocated are not congruent with performance outcomes this presents a problem. We cannot realistically expect athletes to comply with something that negatively impacts their ability to move and perform as required by their sport. Returning to iatrogenics, from a coaching standpoint we cannot endorse something that harms athletes' performance.

An illustrative example comes from a couple of prominent publications in the ACL injury prevention literature which have proven very influential among physiotherapists and those involved in the sports injury prevention realm.

See if you can follow the logic. Concerning biomechanical risk for ACL injury, it was identified that a more lateral foot placement when changing direction creates a greater moment arm for forces acting on the lower limb in general and the knee in particular. Similarly, if more force is applied at the foot then larger forces are transmitted through the *kinetic chain* of the lower limb, conceivably increasing the strain on joint structures and thereby the potential for injury. This reasoning was the basis for prominent voices in the injury prevention field to advocate a two-fold strategy for 'safer' change of direction. Firstly, foot placement should be more *narrow* – i.e. the base of support should be positioned more directly underneath the athlete's centre of mass, thus reducing the mechanical moment arm for abduction forces at the knee [142]. The second recommendation was that athletes should employ 'softer' foot contacts when changing direction to reduce the strain imposed [143].

Clearly, these recommendations are well meaning, and on the surface the reasoning might appear sound. Sadly, it does also violate the physics of what we are trying to do.

Any change in velocity is determined by the magnitude and direction of the impulse of force applied by the athlete to the ground in relation to their own body. The magnitude part is relative to the mass of the athlete's body. Given that change of direction activities are typically executed whilst in motion, we further need to consider not only the athlete's mass (and inertia) but also their momentum. Essentially, when in motion the greater the change of direction or the higher our speed as we execute the change of direction, the larger the magnitude of impulse of force we need to apply to the ground in the appropriate direction for there to be any deviation in our path of travel.

What all this means is that advocating a soft foot contact when attempting to change direction contradicts the physics of what the task of changing direction demands. Our body has inertia (and if we are heavier our inertia is greater), so we need to apply large amounts of force in order to overcome this inertia to generate movement. This is even more so when we are in motion, as we need to overcome our own momentum – which means the magnitude of forces required are higher still. Failing to apply sufficient force means that we either remain where we are (when stationary), or carry on in the direction we are going when in motion.

It is a similar case with the narrow foot placement part of the recommendation; that too fails to adhere to the laws of motion. By definition, if we want to move in a lateral direction we have to position the foot that pushes against the ground outside of our centre of mass in order to propel ourselves towards the intended direction of travel (once again, creating leverage). If our feet remain underneath us, we will basically continue to travel in approximately the same direction as we are already going.

What this demonstrates is that each part of the dual-pronged strategy advocated for safer change of direction (i.e. more narrow foot placement, soft foot contact) violate the physics of what the task of changing direction requires. In effect, the implication is that the act of changing direction is in itself dangerous, and so what would be 'safer' is to continue running in roughly the same direction. Indeed, to make it safer still, we should encourage athletes to slow down by employing gentler foot contacts.

Oddly enough, studies that have attempted to implement these technique modifications with athletes have failed to elicit any observable changes in their movement mechanics following the intervention [144]. It is almost as if athletes are intuitively resistant to adopting changes that negatively impact performance and their ability to execute the tasks required by the sport. Strange, no?

If we to take this risk management approach to its logical conclusion, really in order to be most safe we should recommend that the athlete just sits down... on the bench. After all, if they are not in the action, they can't get hurt.

In fact, maybe they should sit in the stand... although not too far up in the stands, lest they fall down.

We can see similar misalignment and confused messages in all domains, due to the somewhat conflicting priorities that exist between different departments or working groups within an organisation. Once again, reconciling these differences and aligning the messages we give to the performer is greatly aided if all parties are clear on the essential physics that govern the performance outcome.

EFFECTIVENESS AND EFFICIENCY...

As illustrated in the previous example, we cannot lose sight of the effectiveness of the strategy or solutions we are advocating. Our proposed intervention must remain true to the essence of the task and the performance objective. For instance, the task when changing direction is straightforward: the shortest distance between two points is a straight line, so that should be our intended path, and our objective is to cover this distance in the shortest time possible.

It seems timely to return to the wisdom shared by Dan Pfaff that as coaches we should continually strive to improve effectiveness and efficiency. In sport we can demonstrate that more mechanically sound technique enhances work economy and thereby improves endurance performance [145]. Employing more mechanically effective and efficient movement strategies further serves to reduce the stress placed on the system [146]. As an aside, what this emphasises is the missing biomechanical link in the resilience to training load discussion in sport. Those athletes who move in a more mechanically efficient way incur less stress and are therefore better able to tolerate higher workloads without undue risk of overuse injury [146]. In the context of sport, when we use the lens of mechanical effectiveness and efficiency we are thus able to unite both performance and injury risk management objectives.

Whilst this discussion has largely centred on sport, there is one very important take away for would-be coaches in all domains. When we achieve alignment on all relevant aims with our coaching intervention (and respect the physics of the task), we increase the likelihood of the individual adopting the sought after change and assimilating it into how they operate in future.

IN CLOSING...

When devising a coaching intervention we should be governed by the essential physics of the task and the natural laws of the performance environment. From this starting point, all parties involved should collectively seek to ensure that all relevant aims, outcomes, and messages are aligned. In a sporting context, it seems logical that physics and laws of motion should govern our approach when coaching athletic movement. Sadly, common practice in the realms of sports science, sports medicine, and sports coaching is sometimes more driven by convention and dogma than we like to believe. We cannot assume that what is advocated or presently employed in practice necessarily considers or adheres to the fundamental physics of the task. This should serve as a cautionary tale for professionals in other domains.

ONTO THE 'HOW'...

In the opening of this chapter we delved into the 'why', and sought to elucidate what roles we have to play as coaches of humans. We then got into the 'what', and proposed that the lenses of mechanical effectiveness and efficiency might help unite aims and outcomes when devising an intervention. To complete the final piece in the puzzle we now get onto the 'how'.

Acquiring a new skill, or making a change to an existing skill, necessitates a degree of awareness on the part of the performer. To change how another individual executes a particular action further relies upon our ability to communicate the ideas, concepts, and specific elements of the skill we want the performer to assimilate. In this chapter we thus seek to guide how we might deliver the 'what' that we outlined previously, and ultimately fulfil the roles we identified in the opening of the chapter.

FIRST LET'S BE CLEAR...

Intention is a powerful tool when learning a skill or making a change in how we do things. However, in order for an individual to act with intention they must first be clear both on the task and the desired outcome. From the outset our guiding purpose is thus to provide absolute clarity on the nature of the task. This applies both when a new task is introduced for the first time or when adopting a technical refinement to an existing skill that is nevertheless a new way of doing things for the performer. In either case, to be successful the individual we are coaching must be clear on what specifically they are trying to do.

When instructing the performer on a given task we should seek to provide the salient details or 'task-relevant' information. The performer should understand the essential physics involved, and what specific objectives they are striving to achieve when executing the task. Finally, everybody concerned needs to be very clear on what constitutes a successful outcome.

If we want it to be clear and explicit what we want the athlete to do there is also a need to monitor what message has been received. Inevitably there is always some distortion. My experience is there is often some discrepancy between what we have said and what has been heard by the other person. It is generally unsafe to assume that the message was received in full, and until we ask it is also unclear which part they might have latched onto.

Verifying what message has been received at regular intervals is thus an integral part of our coaching process, so that we know what exactly the performer has understood from what we have just told them. This is something for us to continually monitor so that we can manage the distortion as we go along.

IN OTHER WORDS...

One of the fun parts of coaching is that each person's mind operates in a different way. What keeps things interesting is that the same way of explaining a task or prompting somebody on how to perform does not work for everybody. To illustrate this with an example from sport, the same way of cueing a movement does not produce the desired outcome with all athletes. Our standard way of instructing a skill might have worked in many instances previously, yet we will still encounter individuals for whom the same combination of words fails entirely to get the message across. It is always entertaining to marvel at the strange and bizarre responses our words can sometimes elicit.

Practitioners in sport often fall into the trap of assuming that there exists a single 'best cue'. There are even attempts within organisations to seek consensus on an agreed upon 'best way' of coaching a particular exercise or movement drill, for the sake of consistency or standardisation. The reality is that there is no magical cue and no single best way to coach a movement. This principles applies across domains when working with humans.

"Cues are like clothes: try it on for size; if it doesn't fit, discard it and try something else"

— Dan Pfaff

There are a host of different ways to impart the information that the performer requires in order to grasp the essence of the task and figure out how to perform it successfully. As coaches we need to be ready to explain or describe things in a variety of different ways, and to employ a range of modes and media to help convey the salient details to the learner.

When it comes to practical skills, some of the modes for imparting the necessary information may be non-verbal. For instance, in a sporting context, simply demonstrating the skill can allow the athlete to model their movement from what we have shown them. In a similar way, we can employ training partners who are proficient with the movement to model the desired skill, or alternatively use video of a skilled performer who exhibits the particular technical quality we are seeking. As coaches we can even employ simple gestures and sounds without any words necessarily being involved.

Beyond providing a conceptual understanding, what we are seeking is for the performer to attain a sensory blueprint or 'embodied understanding' of the particular skill. Ultimately this can only be developed by the learner engaging in the task, and thereby gaining an appreciation of how it feels to successfully execute the movement. This point is equally relevant to the coach. Essentially we need to become proficient with the skill to have the necessary appreciation of what the action feels like in order to coach it successfully. It is this sensory experience that we are striving to provide for the performer in the first instance; we then strengthen and fine-tune this internalised template via repetition during practice.

PAINTING MENTAL PICTURES...

As we noted previously, a crucial task when coaching is to enable the individual to conceptualise the task so that they have a clear representation or picture in their mind of what they are trying to do. The same tools that provide understanding of the task can also help the performer to conceive the movement solutions, leading them to execute the action or technical refinement in the intended manner.

Analogies offer a great tool in allowing us to depict complex skills as an imaginary task that is evocative and easily understood [147]. An illustrative example is coaching the basketball free-throw shot using the cue 'imagine reaching into a jar on a shelf to grab a cookie' [148]. Use of metaphors similarly allow us to create projections in the mind of the performer. In this way we can impose imaginary constraints during practice that help steer performers towards the movement behaviour we are seeking [149]. Well-chosen depictions also serve to steer attention, guide intention, and direct the performer's efforts when they execute the task.

In order to take full advantage of these tools, once again we need to find what resonates for each given individual. By extension, we need to be prepared to come up with novel ways of depicting the task or solution. The coaching process requires us to be creative and adaptable so that we can describe and prompt in a myriad of different ways, and come up with a host of different cues to ultimately achieve the 'light bulb moment' for that individual.

Finally, we need to be prepared for the fact that a cue or analogy that works for a given individual at one moment in time may not necessarily have same effect at a later date. Returning to the wisdom shared by Dan Pfaff, we must be ready to discard it if it no longer fits and try something else.

BRINGING AWARENESS...

Earlier in the chapter we introduced the '5A model' of technique refinement [133]. As a reminder to the reader the first step was analysis. The second 'A' is *awareness*. This points to the fact that in order to change the learner's existing strategy and adopt an alternative way of working, they need to first become aware of what they are doing currently.

In the realm of athletics and the performing arts, some individuals are highly 'body aware' in that they are finely attuned to the nuances of their bodily movements and therefore highly able to differentiate subtle deviations. Others have far less of an appreciation. In this case, it will be an ongoing process to develop their *kinaesthetic awareness*, or in other words their 'feel' for what is going on. What we are aiming for is a high degree of *specificity* and *sensitivity*. Essentially we want the performer to be able to identify exactly what just happened, and to detect small changes with a high degree of acuity.

To illustrate this idea, when making a technical refinement to a particular movement pattern the performer needs to gain an appreciation of what the new version feels like, and recognise how it differs to what they are doing currently. Gaining a 'feel' for the respective variations allows them to detect which version they are closer to, and differentiate between the respective movement patterns during successive attempts [133].

Part of our role as coach during this process is to shine a torch and direct the performer's awareness and attention to particular features. We can support this process by providing periodic feedback to assist with the ongoing calibration, or recalibration in the case that we are instituting a change. As they become more attuned and their conscious awareness of the performance grows, the individual will also naturally become better able to detect subtle differences and to identify errors for themselves [150]. This is an important precursor to developing their ability to troubleshoot and correct errors between attempts independently of external feedback.

CONSISTENCY AND VARIETY...

When seeking to effect change in behaviour there is a need to satisfy the diverging needs for both consistency and variability. The effect of and need for variability during practice is somewhat related to the nominal or functional difficulty of the task for the learner. For instance, if the degree of variation employed in practice overwhelms the learner's capacities, they are not able to engage in any learning or make sense of the information available within the constantly shifting learning environment.

It follows that during the early stages particularly there will be a need to keep things relatively consistent to ensure that the individual is able to come to grips with the new task. We need some opportunity to explore the task under stable conditions to gain a real appreciation of what the task entails and get a firm grasp on what we are trying to do before we can begin to problem solve.

The necessity for frequent exposure to consistent practice also has a neurophysiological basis. Critical elements include the new neuronal connections made during the initial acquisition of cognitive and motor skills. There are experience-dependent *neuroplastic* changes, which grow and strengthen the neuronal networks that correspond to the new skill [151]. These processes that underpin learning and the subsequent consolidation and retention of motor patterns, require frequent and sustained exposure [152]. Repetition under relatively stable conditions is therefore beneficial and necessary.

Furthermore, it is still possible to explore different solutions when repeatedly tackling the same task under stable conditions. This simply requires that we do not restrict the performer from exploring different solutions in the way we present the task and provide instruction. Equally, there is merit to providing sufficient variability in task constraints imposed in practice, so that athletes are afforded the opportunity to solve the task under a range of conditions. The learner should therefore be progressively exposed to tackling the task under different scenarios to come up with variations on the solution.

APPROPRIATE VARIATION...

In the context of sport, imposing different constraints during practice offers one way to prompt performers to come up with different ways to solve the task. We can manipulate the learning environment in a way that favours developing flexibility in problem-solving and adaptability, as the individual is challenged to perform under different conditions and constraints.

By changing the constraints of the task or how we stipulate the task should be executed we can manipulate the challenge placed on the athlete. This allows us to direct the stimulus in terms of movement execution and also steer the problem-solving process. Practically, variation can be introduced at either the level of the task (i.e. changing task parameters) or how the task is executed (the rules of the game).

In relation to task execution, we should seek to expose performers to the 'manifold' of combinations and permutations of movement variables that produce a successful outcome [139]. To illustrate this, let us use the example of shooting a basketball into the hoop. Without changing the location of the player in relation to the hoop, the ball can end up in the hoop via a variety of trajectories or flight paths, so there are a range of different permutations of release angles and velocities that can achieve a successful outcome. The athlete can also employ different release heights with a jump shot, which opens up further manifolds of angles and velocities to get the ball in the hoop.

It is also important that we recognise 'adaptive movement variability' does not solely come from manipulating task constraints or practice conditions. When we closely observe even a closed skill, successive repetitions are not in fact identical. Variability is an inherent feature of movement skill practice even for a closed skill under stable conditions. During the learning process the variation we see between trials is part of the purposeful 'motor exploration' of potential task solutions that learners engage in [153].

Bernstein used the phrase 'repetition without repetition' to describe this phenomenon [135]. Bernstein's study of blacksmiths at work noted that the movement was subtly different each time they swung the hammer, yet the hammer still struck the metal at the precise point with a high degree of accuracy and consistency. Regrettably, in recent times the 'repetition without repetition' concept has been misrepresented and misunderstood by some in sport who have taken it to mean that we should change the drill or the task constraints employed in practice with every repetition.

CONCEIVING THE SOLUTIONS...

For each individual the potential solutions that are available to them will be shaped by the confluence of three aspects. The first is how they perceive the constraints of the task. The second is the constraints of the environment in which the task is being undertaken (which may vary in each instance). The final factor concerns the constraints of the individual performer (physical attributes, capacities, and capabilities).

There are two key things to note here. The first is that each individual brings a unique set of options or playbook for potential solutions or ways of performing the task. The less obvious but equally salient point is that the solutions we conceive are not only unique to our physical attributes and capabilities, but also how we see the world and how we conceive the possibilities of the task.

What determines the possibilities is therefore not just the capabilities of the individual but also their perception of those capabilities and their ingenuity in how they conceive of tackling the task. By extension, it would be doing a great disservice to restrict an outstanding performer to a very limited range of possibilities for how to 'correctly' perform a given task, simply based on our narrow frame of reference for what is possible based on normal mortals.

STEERING EXPLORATION...

As noted earlier, trial and error is an important feature of how we learn and acquire skills. When engaging in this exploratory learning process we directly perceive the task and its possibilities. We also perceive the environment in which we are performing the task in order to explore the opportunities it offers. In turn the possibilities we perceive, with respect to both the task and performance environment, are shaped by what we perceive to be within our capabilities.

To illustrate the point, our perception of objects and features within our environment is scaled to our height and reach. We thus directly perceive these features and objects according to our subjective sense of our own bodily dimensions and capabilities [154]. The various features and objects in our environment can also invite particular actions [155]. For instance, when we see a ball, we are naturally drawn to kick it, or to pick it up, perhaps to bounce it, or to throw it.

"Affordance points both ways, both to the environment and the observer"

— J.J. Gibson [156]

Aside from permitting the performer some opportunity to freely explore to task and 'perceptual workspace', there are various ways in which the coach can help steer exploration during learning. For instance, we can manipulate how we design the practice environment or simply present the task to the performer in a particular way. Either by practice design, or via the instruction provided, we can impose different constraints on how the task is performed. The latter may range from obstacles to negotiate to altering the rules of the game when performing the task. Similarly, we can employ practice activities that demand, encourage and reward creative problem solving. Finally, use of well-directed questions can help shine a torch onto salient features of the task or environment, or to hint at potential solutions.

FACILITATING PROBLEM-SOLVING…

Having figured things out to the extent that the performer has acquired the rudiments of how to perform the task or new technical refinement, we then progress onto the next stage of the 5 A model process, which is *Adjustment* [133].

When navigating this process, we should recognise that in effect there are always two coaches (i.e. the coach, and the 'inner coach' within the performer's own mind). In fact, we might argue that there are actually three coaches, on the basis that the task environment also serves as a teacher.

By extension, there are three sources of feedback (performer, coach, and environment), so it follows we should allow the performer to make use of all three. Accordingly, there is a need to give consideration to the timing and extent of our feedback. We should also consider allowing the individual some opportunity to choose when and even how feedback is provided. Our input should essentially serve to guide the trial and error process as they figure out the task and experiment with different solutions. We can likewise help direct the process of refining solutions, providing a nudge when there is a need for a course correction, and being a resource to help the individual to fix things when the wheels come off.

As we have noted, engaging in practice is in large part about developing the performer's own awareness and their ability to detect errors or deviations for themselves. Our role here is to help facilitate the reflection process and fill in the gaps as necessary, whilst giving them a chance to fix it themselves before we jump in.

Ultimately our aim is that the performer becomes able to self-regulate independently without the need for external input. This applies to modulation of output in real-time and the fine-tuning that occurs over time. As they successfully complete the task or execute an approximation of the skilled movement, the performer develops an increasingly detailed sensory template and in turn this serves to guide ongoing refinement. The performer thus becomes better able to troubleshoot and self-correct [150]. In the sporting domain, developing the athlete's faculties for detecting, troubleshooting, and correcting errors during practice will serve them well when they come to perform in competition. Acquiring the ability to think on their feet is equally beneficial to performers in all domains.

Whilst we can assist the athlete in developing these tools, it is also critical that we acknowledge that we are also the biggest potential impediment to this development.

MINIMISING OBSTRUCTION...

As coaches we need to recognise that over-provision of input and feedback is maladaptive and unhelpful to the performer's learning, retention, and execution under pressure. Excessive intervention and explicit correction during the process of acquiring and refining skills is a problem particularly when it restricts freedom to explore alternative solutions. We need to be mindful that wherever possible we must afford the performer sufficient opportunity to work through the problem and figure it out for themselves.

It has been suggested that excessive provision of information and instruction during learning and practice might encourage an overtly conscious 'online control' of skilled performance. The tendency to 'reinvest' conscious control over well-practiced motor skills has the potential to negatively impact performance, particularly when there is something at stake [157]. In the context of sport and the performing arts this is strongly related to the phenomenon of 'choking' under pressure. Whilst the evidence for this phenomenon is somewhat equivocal [158], it would seem pragmatic to avoid it nevertheless.

When coaching a new skill we should perhaps think of first prize as being that we demonstrate the task and the learner immediately picks up the salient features and successfully performs the skill without us having to say anything. Second prize, we provider verbal instruction, but convey the information in a way that is indirect or abstract, such as an analogy or a mental image, allowing the performer to grasp the essence and put it into practice. Third prize is that we convey the necessary information directly but concisely (i.e. in as few words as possible).

The scenario with a technical refinement is somewhat different, as there is a need to convey more detailed and specific information [81], so inevitably there is a greater need for direct and explicit instruction. Whatever the scenario, when providing direct instruction and feedback our aim is nevertheless to be as sparing and concise as possible. Similarly, when providing guidance and input as the learner practices we should limit ourselves to one or two key themes or cues at a time. Our task is to deliver the information in bite-sized chunks using language and imagery that resonates with the individual.

In the case of learning motor skills, wherever possible we should also try to speak directly to the body. In other words, we want to encourage the performer to *feel* the movement. After each repetition, rather than providing input immediately, I first ask 'what did you feel'. We can similarly prompt the athlete to replay the execution of the prior repetition in their mind and then reflect on it in a systematic way, in order to mobilise their 'inner coach'.

Our role as coach is to lend the performer our eyes and provide an external viewpoint to verify and cross-reference their own perception. This can also be augmented with visual feedback in the form of video replay as appropriate, but once again coaches need to be wary of utilising video too extensively, as athletes can easily become over-reliant on this form of external feedback. Video replay can also divert the athlete away from tuning into the intrinsic feedback provided by their own body and the task environment.

Prompting the learner to engage in 'somatic reflection' between repetitions should therefore form an integral part of our coaching practice [150]. This discipline provides the opportunity for the performer to refine their existing solution and to conceive new solutions. Similarly, we should encourage the performer to take time to consciously rehearse the particular refinement or novel solution in preparation for the next attempt.

Conversely, thinking too much during execution paradoxically serves to impede or throttle the execution of skilled movements. This is particularly the case when we are dealing with ballistic actions, which rely more on feed-forward control. Likewise this applies to complex movements, especially those executed at high velocity, whereby a lot of cognitive noise disrupts the smooth coordination and flow of the movement.

Whilst the discussion has largely been focussed on learning and refining motor skills, these themes equally apply to skilled execution of any complex task that require professionals to be attuned to changing dynamics. In each case, the actor needs to allow themselves to rely on their skills so that the can reserve their attention for the shifting terrain they are navigating and responding to what is being signalled by others, rather than getting stuck in their own head and second guessing themselves. In essence, there is a time to think, such as when reflecting on prior attempts and planning the next one, and then there is a time to act.

GET THEM OUT OF THEIR HEAD...

Some individuals are more prone to adopting an internal attentional focus and locus of control when performing, and it is demonstrated that individuals with these traits show a greater propensity for 'choking' under performance pressure [84]. A similar propensity for conscious control and heightened awareness is likewise observed among athletes following injury [124]. In both of these instances, there is a specific need to get the performer out of their own head when performing.

Having attained a level of mastery of the skill, executing well-practised 'chunks' of component movement skills does not require or benefit from conscious control. Clearly, we must address this in how we prepare the performer; by the time they reach the competition environment it is too late to manage the crisis.

On this theme, the penultimate stage in the 5A model is *(re-)automation* [133]. Having acquired a new skill, or made an adjustment or refinement to an existing movement pattern, it is necessary to embed and automate the new movement pattern. Practically, this means logging repetitions of the new solution or movement pattern in practice without making any further changes or tweaks.

Of course this does not mean that the performer should not exercise conscious awareness as they perform. Indeed this will be important in order to permit the performer to reflect on the quality of their execution afterwards [150]. Returning to the theme of autonomy not automatons, the important distinction is that what we are seeking is the performer to be attentive to the sensory experience as they execute the movement, as opposed to trying to consciously control the execution of the skilled movement in real-time.

That said, when the athlete arrives in the competition environment this is a time for acting rather than deliberating. In the performance arena skill execution should be largely spontaneous. There should not be the same necessity to think about the appropriate response in the heat of battle, or attempt to consciously control how movement is generated. When performing on this stage, the performer must be able divert their mental resources to attend to what is in front of them, particularly in a dynamic and unpredictable environment.

The final stage in the 5A model is therefore *Assurance* [133]. In sport, all athletes aspire to a 'flow state' when performing, which is associated with the sensation of 'letting it happen' [159]. As a precursor for attaining flow, it follows that performers must first become very familiar with the new or remodelled movement patterns and develop a high degree of comfort in executing them independently. From a coaching perspective, the important thing to note is that this can only be acquired in the absence of excessive coaching and without continual intervention.

TO WRAP UP...

So there we have it: coaching intervention is an act in three parts. A central theme is that irrespective of our professional discipline we find ourselves coaching others, so it is important that we are clear on what roles we should fulfil, what the scope of our involvement should be, and what specifically our objectives are.

The first step is to enlist the performer in the process and take the time to make the case for change, in order that they can be part of the decision to proceed (or not) with the intervention. When devising our intervention we must make sure that whatever we advocate respects the essential nature of the task and adheres to the fundamental physics that govern the task and desired outcome, so that we align all relevant aims and objectives. Finally, as we deliver coaching and facilitate learning our overarching aim must be to promote the role of the individual and foster their contribution, so that they are ultimately able to self-regulate and self-correct without our input. In essence, our end goal as coaches is to make ourselves redundant.

REFLECTING AND CONNECTING THE DOTS...

To what extent do you think this exploration of coaching is relevant to the world in which you operate?

Where do you observe the elements of coaching described within the context of your day to day professional duties?

To what are the respective stages of initiating and implementing a coaching intervention evident within your environment?

Where are the major gaps that you observe?

Are the staff concerned typically briefed on the 'why' behind proposed changes and granted the opportunity to indicate their support (or express reservations) prior to the decision to proceed with the intervention?

Are there opportunities to adopt and integrate the practices to improve engagement and ultimately enhance the success of interventions?

To what degree are staff enlisted and engaged in the process when changes in operating practices are initiated and implemented on an individual and collective level?

Are proposed changes judged and evaluated in relation to the fundamental 'physics' or market forces that govern your particular field or industry, or do other factors such as trends and conventions influence thinking and practices?

What is your opinion on the extent to which the present processes for implementing change creates dependency on top-down management, versus facilitating the capability of staff to operate independently?

In other words, how would you judge present practices in terms of encouraging autonomy versus creating automatons?

Would you say coaching is a feature of your life beyond work? How might these principles and processes apply in your interactions with humans outside of a professional context?

'Tempering' to Future-Proof Performers

Tempering is a process used to impart strength and toughness, and essentially serves to bring out the intrinsic properties of the material under stress. Performers who are forged in the crucible of severely testing conditions may be similarly rendered highly resilient to future challenges and stressors. Those who successfully come through such trial by fire paradoxically often prove stronger from the experience. The notion that stressors can not only make systems more resilient but in fact stronger and better as a consequence speaks to the concept of antifragility, a phenomenon observed in nature and highlighted by Nassim Taleb [103] who famously coined the term. With this chapter we will bring an antifragility lens, along with a general reticence to accept that sports injuries 'just happen', to reframe how we think about the quest to 'future proof' performers to risks and scenarios that we cannot fully anticipate. In place of the conventional approach of seeking to safeguard and protect, we will make the argument for tempering performers to harness and develop their intrinsic reserves and coping abilities. Adopting this perspective and general strategy for managing injury risk, we will outline some tactics to help guide us in our approach.

I began my career in sport working in the contact sport of professional rugby union. Sports injuries are not entirely avoidable in the chaos of game play when violent bodily contact is a feature of the sport. When I subsequently moved onto working with other (non-contact) sports, I was not willing to accept that injury was a fact of life in the same way. Whilst contact injuries are not entirely avoidable, I viewed the non-contact and overuse injuries typically seen in these other sports as a different matter.

To my colleagues in the field the position I adopted might have appeared naïve. Happily I was not swayed by such opinions and the general refusal to accept the inevitability of sports injuries has stayed with me. My reasoning was (and remains) that if we have a thorough understanding of what the sport demands and we can anticipate the types and magnitude of stresses involved, then it is up to us to ensure the athlete is prepared to cope with these rigours. In essence, we should deploy any and all tools at our disposal in our quest to make the performer unbreakable.

I share this personal viewpoint to set the tone for the discussion to follow, as it differs in fundamental and important ways from the norm among practitioners and the viewpoint adopted in much of the sports injury prevention literature. The contention that I and notable others share is that despite the best intentions we have become too conservative and over-protective in our approach, with unanticipated and paradoxical consequences. As I hope to make the case, we can better serve performers and ultimately shift the odds in their favour by being bolder and more progressive.

"If something is future-proof, it will continue to be useful or successful in future if the situation changes"

— Collins Online English Dictionary

A REVELATION: WE ARE NOT MACHINES...

There is a temptation in sports science and medicine to model the human body as a machine. Such a machine approach assumes that failure limits and structural capacities are predetermined and unchanging, so by extension it is assumed that musculoskeletal structures will degrade over time. Here is an example of how we apply this machine model to relate workload and injury: the story goes that when cumulative loads exceed predetermined failure limits, the inevitable result is injury to the structures involved.

Contrary to this 'human body as machine' model, biological systems have not evolved this way, which invalidates many of the assumptions that underpin related approaches. Unlike machines, our capacities, stress tolerance, capabilities, and coping resources are fluid and adaptable. Failure limits are flexible and dynamic, and the boundaries are constantly shifting as our system continuously responds to whatever conditions and stressors (or lack thereof) it is exposed to. Paradoxically we observe that injury may result from either too much or too little exposure to mechanical stress [160].

Aside from the notion of a fixed ceiling, another assumption of the machine model is that there is an unchanging equilibrium that our system will default to (like a thermostat with a fixed setting). Based on this premise it is advocated that we should keep training loads within a narrow bandwidth around some predetermined fixed point to operate effectively and avoid pushing into our failure limits. The *acute-to-chronic workload* concept as currently applied is an exemplar of this approach, whereby arbitrary restrictions are imposed to minimise deviations between successive training days.

Once again, the notion of a predetermined equilibrium is flawed when we attempt to relate it to biological systems and with humans. As John Kiely notably pointed out, we are dealing with *allostasis* rather than simply homeostasis [75]. What this means is that any default 'set point' and associated parameters are not fixed, but are dynamic and responsive to whatever conditions are encountered. Rather than operating within a narrow and predictable range, our systems require and respond well to perturbation, such as random fluctuations or mini shocks. Acute (short term) exposure to a variety of stressors of varying magnitudes ultimately serves to stretch the bandwidth of what we are able to readily tolerate.

Tolerance to training stress at any time varies widely between individuals, depending on their individual make up, previous exposure, and present status [161]. Individual thresholds and the theoretical ceiling of what a given performer can tolerate are not fully knowable. After all, the limits of human endeavour are constantly being redrawn. Whatever our individual limits may be, we can also expect them to fluctuate over time in a manner that is also not entirely predictable.

To further confuse matters, biological organisms such as humans also have inbuilt redundancy and reserve capacity. As complex adaptive systems, we comprise a host of constituent parts and subsystems that are interconnected and have redundancies (or back up subsystems) inbuilt. Any stimulus or stressor has ripple effects and adaptations throughout the constituent parts of the system, which cannot be fully anticipated. Due the complexity of the systems involved, the relationship between input and output is not linear or predictable. This presents a problem for injury prevention strategies that involve monitoring workload, as they rely upon the assumption that there is a direct relationship between cause (workload) and effect (injury).

Clearly the models we use to think about training stress and injury are in need of revision. The assumptions that underpin many of the approaches in current use are not only flawed, but have made us ultra-conservative in our practices. Ultimately, our urge to protect may paradoxically be serving to compromise the ability of athletes to cope with the stress of training and competition.

Conversely, stress testing serves to strengthen biological systems, assuming we remain within tolerable bounds. Fundamentally, we must be exposed to stressors in order to confer protection. This is quite opposite to 'protecting' from exposure to stressors. When viewed in the this way, the common approaches of protecting, constraining what stressors we are exposed to, and eliminating unpredictability can be expected to create fragility and ironically render performers more vulnerable to injury.

STRESS IS NECESSARY...

By our nature, we are complex adaptive systems. Fundamentally, exposure to stressors is the trigger that elicits the adaptation that fortifies structures, increases stress tolerance, and improves our reserves to create a buffer against future stressors. In essence, the only route to altering our tolerance to stress is via exposure to stressors.

"The goal is certainly not to avoid stress; stress is a part of life. But in order to express yourself fully you must find your optimum stress level and then use your adaptation energy at a rate and in a direction adjusted to the innate structure of your mind and body"

– Hans Selye [162]

Epigenetics describes the interaction between our genes and our environment (or nature and nurture). Epigenetics is essentially the process by which we express our potential and 'switch on genes' (whilst 'switching off' others) to mobilise coping resources following exposure to stressors, shocks, and survival pressures. Genetics (or genotype) might help to determine our potential capacities and theoretical individual limits; however, the degree to which this potential is realised, in terms of what qualities are expressed and what tolerance we exhibit (i.e. phenotype), depends on our training history and what stimuli and conditions we have been exposed to.

The term 'eustress' is used to differentiate beneficial stress from 'harmful' (distress). But the situation is not binary when it comes to stress. An illustration of how even potentially harmful stress drives adaptation is *hormesis*.

Hormesis describes the adaptive response of biological organisms to exposure to an agent that is toxic and even lethal in larger doses. Biological systems not only tolerate but paradoxically benefit from periodic short term exposure to low doses of potentially toxic or harmful agents [163]. This is the case as long as the dose or exposure does not overwhelm our present coping resources, otherwise it can prove fatal. It turns out there is some truth to the old adage; what doesn't kill us makes us stronger.

As demonstrated with hormesis, when it comes to any type of stressor it is not a simple case of good/bad or beneficial/harmful, but rather depends on dose and context. The duration of exposure is also crucial. In general we cope well and can even benefit from acute (short term) exposure to 'negative' stress, whereas chronic or persisting exposure is typically harmful and causes maladaptation. With this caveat in mind, intermittent and controlled exposure to a variety of hormetic stressors, such as periodic food restriction or intermittent mild heat shock, can improve health and longevity by up-regulating favourable *epigenetic* signalling and gene expression [164].

Conversely, as we noted earlier in the chapter, if we deprive the performer of a stimulus or stressor this also creates unforeseen ripple effects through the system. When we eliminate or excessively restrict our exposure to stressors we deem to be 'harmful', paradoxically this can make us more fragile. In the absence of the necessary stimulus, the signalling pathways are down-regulated and so our coping resources diminish.

Stress adaptation equally applies to psychological and emotional coping resources, as we will explore in the chapter that follows. Interventions such as cognitive behavioural therapy adopt a stress inoculation approach. Rather than avoiding or eliminating the stressor or trigger, the strategy is to systematically expose the individual to a controlled dose of the stressor, whilst providing the support and assistance to guide their coping strategy and ultimately bolster their coping resources.

Supercompensation that follows exposure to a tolerable stressor is an extension of biological systems' drive for adaptability that favours redundancy and reserve capacity. By definition, supercompensation is an overshoot phenomenon, which serves to ready us for future exposure at a level exceeding what has been encountered to date. Essentially, our natural adaptive response is to *over-prepare* us for the unprecedented.

Clearly this approach is somewhat counter-intuitive; we naturally have the urge to protect those in our care and our instinct is to keep them out of harm's way. The default strategy is thus to avoid, in order to protect the individual from any and all exposure to potential harm. With our urge to protect and with the best of intentions we unwittingly risk making those in our care more susceptible when they inevitably encounter stressful events.

COMPLEX ADAPTIVE SYSTEMS WITH A MIND ATTACHED...

It bears repeating that we have no concept of what the individual limits might be for a given performer. What is clear is that we will never allow performers to express their full tolerance and coping resources unless we permit the necessary exposure to stressors. We should also not be afraid to engage in some trial and error to explore the boundaries. A key tenet of *antifragility* is that the harm from errors is more than compensated by the benefits derived, in terms of information and discovery. The only caveat is that mistakes need to be of a magnitude that the system can survive them.

Conventional wisdom presently holds that we should avoid spikes in load or shocks when preparing athletes. Variability and volatility in conditions are not negative as long as the system is sufficiently adaptable. Conversely, requiring things to be highly predictable with little tolerance for deviation is the very definition of a fragile system. By artificially controlling fluctuations and striving to eliminate unpredictability we can unwittingly create fragility. Depriving the system of variability and volatility renders it less adaptable and makes performers less able to cope with future unforeseen events. Clearly this is the opposite of what we are aiming for in our quest to future-proof.

The role of the mind in all this is evident in the realisation that our appraisal and subjective experience is part of what mediates the response to a given stressor. To use the example of physical preparation in sport, there are a host of non-training factors relating to how athletes anticipate, perceive, experience, and reflect upon the workout that can alter how they respond to a training stimulus.

"The magnitude of the stress response is not directly dependent on the magnitude of the stressor... our personal emotional interpretation of the applied challenge amplifies or dampens the subsequent cascade of bio-chemical events constituting the stress response"

– John Kiely [75]

A fundamental truth that we need to recognise in our capacity as coaches is that a major source of performers' anxieties stem from doubts and concerns about their ability to cope. By exposing the individual or group to stressors in a deliberate way we provide the opportunity for them to face this under practice conditions. Working through these trials promotes a sense of self-efficacy and these experiences can thus serve to reduce anxiety. If the process is managed well, the subsequent knowledge that you have survived stressful situations naturally makes you less daunted by the prospect of facing such trials in the future when there is likely to be more at stake.

Teams, working groups, and essentially any system or process involving humans can be conceptualised as a complex adaptive system. We can describe humans as complex systems with a mind attached; if what we are dealing with involves multiple individuals, there are of course several minds attached. The perceptions of each individual and the collective hive mind as a whole thus come into play. Whilst this adds a further layer of complexity, we can nevertheless implement a broadly similar tempering approach as we seek to develop the resilience of the collective and improve the ability of the group to cope with stressors and unforeseen events. In doing so, we will need to manage perception.

AN ALTERNATIVE APPROACH TO MANAGING INJURY RISK ...

What we have been building towards is that we can be bold and take more of an aggressive 'stress adaptation' approach as we seek to mitigate injury risk. We can effectively switch mode and seek to prepare and equip, rather than getting locked in the default defensive or protective mode. Such an approach to managing injury risk differs to conventional *injury prevention* initiatives in important ways, some of which may not be obvious at first glance.

Firstly, adopting a more progressive tempering approach acknowledges the reality that it is not feasible to devise preventive countermeasures for something that we cannot entirely predict. Returning to 'future-proofing', we have a forecasting problem in that we cannot anticipate future events with any degree of accuracy. Equally, this does not give us an out; we cannot simply accept that injuries will happen and there's nothing we can hope to do about it. Rather, we should seek to prepare and equip athletes for the uncertainty and unpredictability of what awaits them.

Going on the offensive is an important departure in strategy. The major failing of injury prevention initiatives is that they are typically too conservative and narrow in scope. Aside from offering only limited solutions, the more glaring issue is that standard interventions do not provide sufficient challenge. For instance, most initiatives in sport generally feature repurposed rehabilitation exercises, which by definition are designed for use with injured athletes so it is little wonder that healthy athletes find them tedious. The lack of challenge and the fact that these initiatives are often delivered by the medical support staff rather than as part of the athlete's normal training goes some way to explaining the poor compliance that plagues these interventions [165].

If we want to adopt a 'stress adaptation' approach then a prerequisite for any intervention is that it must be sufficiently challenging to mobilise the performer's coping resources, otherwise it will not prove effective. Whatever measures we employ must create reserve capacity, improve capability, or result in the performer moving in a more mechanically efficient way when they reach the performance arena.

Adding reserve capacity is the most obvious avenue to future-proof the performer by extending their failure limits. The inclusion of strength training is accordingly what commonly differentiates the injury prevention interventions in sport that prove to be effective [166]. In essence we can create a buffer by building spare work capacity, reserve load tolerance, and extra capacity to store, return, and dissipate energy within muscle and tendon. Rather than simply preparing athletes for the expected demands, we should take a lead from nature and seek to 'over prepare' the athlete for what they might face practice and competition. Our objective should therefore be to ensure the performer is equipped to handle the aberrant and the unprecedented.

As we embark on the task of developing the requisite capacities with a performer, clearly we need to first meet them where they are. It is often a trial and error process to determine each individual's presence tolerance, in terms of what volume and density of work they can handle at the outset. Frequency is important from a dose-response viewpoint [167-169]; however, *density* of exposures with respect to time is also a key factor. The limits of tolerance with respect to intensity or magnitude of loading are likewise dynamic, so once again it takes some ongoing trial and error to push the envelope whilst working with the moving target of the performer's present capacities.

From a capability viewpoint, we can leverage mechanical effectiveness to mitigate risk and also find efficiencies. As we noted in the previous chapter, physics applies universally, so we can employ these principles to guide interventions. Enhancing mechanical effectiveness of athletic movements directs and distributes forces to greater effect, and so benefits both performance and load tolerance [146]. Improving mechanical efficiency similarly allows us to effectively reduce and redirect the stresses placed on respective parts of the kinetic chain.

Capability thus involves expressing qualities more effectively during athletic movement. One aspect is removing restrictions and improving function (or addressing dysfunction) to facilitate movement efficiency. Another critical element that relates back to capacity, targeted strength development is often necessary to provide the means to open up different options and facilitate the sought after changes. We can illustrate this with the scenario that is common with female athletes: if you wish to shift a female performer from their characteristic knee extensor dominant strategy it is first necessary to ensure that they have the requisite hip extensor strength to make alternative options available to them [170].

Capability also relates to the host of aptitudes we describe as athleticism. Instead of providing a single solution, we should seek to provide a playbook of solutions that the athlete can bring to whatever scenario or movement problem they encounter. Practically this means encouraging the performer to explore a range of solutions; whatever variations and permutations they come up with just need to respect the physics of the task. Returning to trial and error, the attempts where they get it wrong are also a necessary part of the process. Assuming these errors cause no lasting damage the experience often proves beneficial (hormesis again). Adaptability and the ability to improvise will also help the performer get out of trouble in live scenarios. To serve the wider aim of making the individual able to deal with the unanticipated, we can incorporate progressive and systematic exposure to unpredictability and uncertainty, which likewise develops the ability to react, adjust, and adapt in real-time.

Finally, from a context viewpoint, our efforts in the physical and athletic preparation realm should seek to support technical refinement in the sport. As we covered in the previous chapter, rather than restricting and attempting to make the movement 'safe', we need to continue to support performance outcomes. To that end, our objective here is to enhance the performer's ability to express the skill in a way that is most mechanically effective and efficient. We can support this by developing the individual's *somatosensory awareness* and feel for the movement as they experience relevant postures and shapes as they move. These efforts are generally directly towards specific links in the chain that are likely to be failure points.

Whilst this discussion has focussed on the specific example of mitigating sports injury risk, we can extend this approach to the task of rendering individuals, teams, systems, and processes more resilient and lessen the odds of things 'breaking down' in a wider human performance sense. The same elements (capacity, capability, context) can help to direct our efforts in various realms. We can seek to create reserve capacity at the level of the system, team, and individual. We can endeavour to improve capability in ways that favours adaptability, problem solving, and ability to improvise solutions. Finally, we can undertake context-relevant initiatives to refine processes and practices and make them more effective and efficient, and introduce specific countermeasures to address potential failure points and apparent rate-limiting steps.

PRE-EXISTING CONDITIONS...

The majority of athletes at higher levels of competition bring with them some history of injury (in many cases recent) and even 'healthy' athletes are generally managing some sort of niggle or complaint. The presence of pre-existing or current injury clearly affects a performer's present tolerance and capabilities. On the other hand, given that previous injury is the number one risk factor for future injury, this makes it more important to develop reserve capacity and mobilise additional coping resources, not less.

If anything the existence of prior injury should prompt us to take a more progressive approach, given the need to mitigate the higher risk that the athlete will otherwise be exposed to. This notion contrasts sharply with how injuries are managed and most *return to competition* protocols in present use. Most often we adopt a defensive approach and seek to protect the athlete by restricting and constraining their exposure; as the reader might have guessed by now, this tends to make athletes more vulnerable.

It bears repeating that we need to meet the performer where they are and cater to their present tolerance. Exercising caution in our initial approach, some trial and error will allow us to determine what magnitude of stress they can presently handle, and what density and volume of work they can presently tolerate. Equally, thereafter our objective should be to push the envelope to extend their limits and periodically provide perturbations to expand what they can tolerate, in terms of fluctuations and variability in stressors.

The human body has abundant resources, reserves, and redundancies that are at our disposal. When handled appropriately performers can leverage these intrinsic qualities and continue to perform at the highest level, even in the presence of pathology. These inherent properties equally apply at a collective level, and so it follows we should adopt a similar approach to developing team resilience through progressive exposure to conditions that exploit and mobilise the intrinsic strengths and coping resources of the group [171].

LEARNING COURAGE...

There are strong psychological and emotional elements at play when dealing with injury and coping with similar adverse events. The initial injury and ongoing symptoms naturally take an emotional toll on the performer. Indeed, the mere prospect of injury can provoke a lot of fear and anxiety, particularly in the case of reinjury.

Following a significant injury we see characteristic *neuroplastic* changes that result from both disrupted input from the injured structures and central changes stemming from the motor cortex. To compound these issues the athlete's motor control strategy is also often altered in other ways, as they turn their attention inwards and attempt to revert to conscious controlling every moment [124]. An extreme manifestation of how injury can alter motor behaviour is *learned helplessness*, which presents a major barrier to restoring function [127]. This phenomenon is described as an 'altered neurocognitive state', given that whilst it might seem to have psychological origins it is also manifested as inhibited motor drive during activity.

Another common behavioural aspect of the debilitating effects of severe and chronic injuries is *kinesiophobia* – i.e. the athlete comes to fear and avoid movements and scenarios that might elicit pain. Clearly these responses are maladaptive, rendering the athlete more fragile and reducing their odds of successfully returning to performance and avoiding further injury.

Persuading the athlete to confront fearful movements and situations, and to get out of their head and 'let go' when performing skilled movement, demands considerable faith and courage. With their permission, we must nevertheless expose the performer to stressors (both physical and mental) in a staged manner in order to master these emotional and psychological demons. This approach of systematic exposure, or 'stress inoculation', is akin to the premise of cognitive behavioural therapy. Stress inoculation should be an integral part of how we rehabilitate injuries and confer protection against future injury.

Sadly, the fear and anxiety that underpin the aversive behavioural responses to injury are contagious – and sadly it is often those providing care who are the unwitting source of this *stress contagion*. The need to rehabilitate the performer from a mental and emotional standpoint in itself should make us reconsider how we typically manage injuries and the return to performance process that follows injury. As practitioners we also need to learn courage, otherwise our anxiety will inevitably communicate itself to the athlete; this is not only unhelpful but also likely to prove detrimental to their successful return.

The treating practitioner who works with the performer during the acute phase similarly needs to recognise that they may be in a vulnerable place and can easily form an emotional attachment, particularly following significant injury. Retaining excessive involvement in their ongoing recovery thus carries the risk of fostering dependency throughout the rehabilitation phase and the return to competition process that follows. Practitioners must be aware of this important point and remain conscious of the potential unintended consequences of their continued involvement.

Consequently, it is important to take steps to allow the individual a longer leash and foster autonomy as early in the rehabilitation process as possible. There is a need to create the necessary distance and separation by stepping back at the appropriate point. To that end, individual benefit from a phased process, whereby non-treatment elements of rehabilitation progressively transition to a suitably qualified and informed coach. Such a staged approach best serves the physical, emotional, and psychological needs of the performer. In recognition of the benefits of a different face and voice during the rehabilitation and the subsequent return to competition process, we created the role of 'Performance Rehabilitation Coach' at my former workplace for precisely this purpose.

Once again, whilst we have focused on the highly specific example of recovering from sports injury, many of these themes apply to leading and managing individuals and teams in other realms. There is similarly a need to be brave and to resist the urge to intervene and micromanage, especially when the stakes are high. As in the examples cited, we need to be prepared to let go of the reins and delegate responsibility to others, accepting that things will go wrong on occasion. In doing so we signal that we have faith in the team and individuals we manage. To that end, it is important to communicate in words and actions that whilst they will inevitably make errors on occasion, we are confident in the ability of the team and individuals concerned to fix mistakes, take the lessons (so they don't make the same mistake twice), and come up with solutions for future scenarios.

From this viewpoint, when seeking to right the ship after adverse events or a dip in performance, there is merit in resisting the urge to take back sole charge and rather use the opportunity to engage other team members in the task of putting things right. By definition, developing team resilience means affording the group the opportunity to bounce back after setbacks [171]. Our role as leaders and managers is to support the group and guide each individual in this endeavour. Our objective is to provide the conditions and guidance to grow individually and collectively, and in doing so develop the tools and capabilities to be better able to cope with future problems and unforeseen events.

IN CLOSING...

In part this chapter represents a call to overcome our natural aversion to risk, and reconsider the default response of protecting from exposure to potential harm when attempting to manage risk of injury. With our overzealous attempts to regulate and restrict participation to make it more 'safe' we may be paradoxically rendering performers more vulnerable to injury or to breaking down under load. We need to consider these potential adverse effects (and iatrogenic risks) of our well-intentioned interventions.

To that end, we need to rethink conventional 'preventive' approaches in current use, such as artificially imposing arbitrary restrictions on workload imposed and excessively controlling exposure to stressors. For some practitioners this may mean challenging the underlying and unspoken assumption that the particular activity or participation in sport and life in general is inherently injurious.

Conversely, the stance of the 'just make them strong' camp is also somewhat myopic. The more progressive approach of tempering athletes via systematic exposure to relevant stress conditions should not be confused for the suggestion that we should just lock athletes in the weights room. We need to be clear what capacities we are seeking to build, and under what conditions they need to be expressed. For instance, structural integrity and force generating capacity must be expressed in extreme ranges and positions in many sports. Clearly developing these specific qualities necessitates more than just the conventional view of what strong is.

In the context of sport, advanced or specialised training modes can prove highly potent tools for developing capacities, improving tolerance, and extending failure limits. A range of modalities similarly have application for developing the capabilities that athletes require to adapt and improvise. Finally, a deep knowledge and thorough understanding of technical aspects and the performance model for the sport and performer is critical in helping to refine specific skills. Whatever tools we employ we need to test our imagination when it comes to preparing for worst case scenarios, and rather aim to equip performers for the unprecedented. Each of these considerations can similarly be applied in guiding our efforts in other domains and contexts.

Ultimately our task is to embrace the challenge and continually explore the boundaries of the performer's present tolerance and capabilities to ensure that they are equipped to not only survive but to excel in the uncertainty and unpredictable context of the performance arena. Returning to the familiar themes of ego and humility, rather than wrestling over spheres of influence, or which part falls within our domain or respective areas of expertise, the only consideration in terms of delivery should be what best serves the physical, emotional, and psychological needs of the performer. Finally, whilst stress adaptation and tempering requires that we allow performers to be exposed to stressors, equally we need to be watchful for adverse effects and remain ready to provide breaks and modify exposure, as appropriate to the individual and the circumstances.

REFLECTING AND CONNECTING THE DOTS…

What are your initial thoughts? Does conceptualising resilience as a process and something that emerges following exposure to the right conditions resonate with your experience?

How might the principle that systems adapt and become robust under stress be applied in the context of the domain you operate in?

To what extent is stress testing, or stress inoculation standard operating procedure within your profession?

Are there opportunities to introduce and integrate future-proofing initiatives with systems, working groups, and staff members?

To what extent is developing team resilience a defined management objective? Is there merit in adopting this approach?

What are your thoughts on how we might leverage the benefits of exposure to trying conditions given our typical preference for conditions of comfort?

Developing Psychological Resilience

In the previous chapter we observed how exposure to stress is a prerequisite for imparting resilience and bringing out the intrinsic toughness of biological structures. Principles such as tempering similarly apply when we are speaking about psychological resilience or *mental toughness*. Performers need to be exposed to stressors that elicit a psychological and emotional response in order to develop the necessary tolerance. Practices to help develop performers' psychological resilience have notably been explored in competitive sports and military settings. Some authors have termed such interventions 'mental fortitude training' [172]. In this chapter we delve into the different ways we can assist in developing the ability to perform under pressure and acquiring the *psychological hardiness* to better tolerate stressors both within the performance arena and beyond.

ADVERSITY AS OPPORTUNITY...

For most of us, terms such as 'adversity' and 'stress' typically have negative connotations. The phase 'I am stressed' is generally not viewed as positive. Yet the coping strategies that serve us in the most trying times cannot be developed in the absence of stress. A concept that we introduced in the previous chapter is the notion that resilience is not simply an inherent quality, but rather a capability that emerges over time through a process of tempering and exposure to trials. We might have a predisposition towards hardiness, but this potential will only be realised under the appropriate conditions. This applies both on an individual and collective level (i.e. team resilience) [171]. There might be something to the superhero movie storyline whereby exposure to extreme stress reveals our super powers.

It is only during times of hardship that we are prompted to assemble our toolbox of coping resources and afforded the opportunity to hone these tools. This perspective leads us to the revelation that adversity is not only necessary but is in fact desirable for performers in training. We might thus switch modes from regarding adversity as something to be endured to instead think about what opportunity it presents. In this sense, trials and periods of difficulty become something we can exploit to serve our purposes.

How we deal with adversity and what we take from the experience is in a large part a matter of what perspective we adopt. Perspective and appraisal are crucial elements in a more general sense in shaping *affect*. How we perceive stressors and what sensations we are feeling goes a long way to determine what emotions we experience. These factors profoundly impact how we anticipate situations and serve to shape our entire experience, in terms of our psychological and emotional state.

"Adversity does not build character, it reveals it"

– James Lane

Times of adversity also provide illumination. These are the times we not only find out about ourselves but also those around us. What all of this illustrates is the multiple meanings of the term *integrity*. Much like character, our true commitment to our stated values and the strength of our convictions are only revealed when tested. Stress testing reveals what our core values really are. How individuals respond under testing conditions is highly revealing. Until those in our circle have been with us during trying circumstances we cannot fully anticipate how they will respond or have real certainty that they will stand with us. Rather than being unduly troubled, we should perhaps be intrigued about what the situation might reveal. Adopting this mindset allows us to focus on the clarity these experiences.

Until our mettle has been tested we cannot have any real certainty that we can endure. The lived experience of coming through times of adversity thus provides assurance of our ability to cope moving forwards. Accordingly, exploration of athlete development and the path from junior competition to elite level reveals that the bumps on the 'rocky road to success' are an integral part of the journey for developing high performers [173]. Times of adversity and setbacks are thus not simply a feature of the journey for any high performer; these experiences serve a critical function in the process. The trials that are encountered on the way represent invaluable opportunities for learning, developing, and providing clarity that serve the performer moving forwards, as long as they are managed appropriately.

MENTAL TOUGHNESS…

The terms mental toughness, mental resilience, and psychological hardiness are variously employed in the literature in a way that suggests they are somewhat interchangeable. We can come up with a working definition that draws on the respective terms, in order to identify what specific factors we should be seeking to develop. Resilience is a featured of adaptive biological systems, and has its origins in genetics, neurobiology, and physiology. Psychological hardiness essentially describes the extent to which we remain robust under conditions of stress, and whether the observed immune and neuroendocrine stress response is healthy versus maladaptive [174]. Mental toughness is generally employed in relation to performance, which adds additional layers and a focus on specific capabilities.

Rather than relying on academics to come up with a theoretical framework, it is instructive to go to the source and enlist elite athletes to share what constitutes mental toughness in the context of preparing and performing in the sport. The athletes who participated in one such investigation described mental toughness as being both an innate quality and something that is developed over time [175].

Notably the latter part is good news for leaders and coaches who seek to develop mental toughness in the performers they serve.

Based on the surveyed responses of elite athletes there are some distinct themes and attributes. The highest ranked trait that separates mentally tough performers is an unshakeable belief in their ability to ultimately succeed. A second hallmark of mental toughness is how the individual responds to setbacks and how well they are able to regain their equilibrium after adverse events. Two other prevalent themes identified were insatiable desire and determination, plus the ability to retain focus amidst distractions. The ability to tolerate and endure physical and emotion pain was also highlighted. A final theme was that mentally tough performers are not unduly affected by what competitors are doing.

Another element that is commonly identified in relation to mental toughness is *self-concept* [176]. Self-concept has a major influence on how performers appraise and experience challenges and obstacles. Those who are secure in their sense of self are better able to entertain challenge. To perceive obstacles and adversity as a challenge rather than a direct threat, the individual's sense of self needs to not be contingent upon their status as a performer and it must extend beyond the particular domain. The performer needs to exist in their own minds as an individual and part of the wider community, beyond their 'athlete' status within the particular sport.

PERFORMING UNDER PRESSURE...

The capability to perform under the pressure of competition is a defining characteristic of mentally tough performers. An investigation of triathletes and Ironman athletes revealed that ratings of mental toughness showed a positive association with dispositional factors relating to their ability to achieve *flow* when performing [177]. Mentally tough performers are generally more secure in themselves when competing and hence less troubled by distracting thoughts, allowing them to more readily 'let it happen'.

Beyond achieving flow state, what is described as *clutch* performance more specifically relates to performing at crunch time. What constitutes a clutch performance is when a performer raises their level under pressure situations to excel at the critical moment when there is something riding on the outcome [178]. In contrast to 'flow', which is described in terms of 'letting it happen', clutch is characterised as 'making it happen' when it matters.

The ability to demonstrate clutch performance under pressure conditions is association with individuals' ratings of perceived control [178]. It follows that as coaches we need to develop a feeling control as the performer appraises whatever challenge they face. Essentially we want to instil the sense that 'I've got this' when the performer steps up to perform at the critical moment.

Psychological resilience involves not only our cognitions, but also how we regulate our thoughts and emotions as we anticipate event and step up to perform. Athletes recalling their experience of clutch performance describe an effortful attempt to mobilise their full attention resources and summoning hyper focus as they strove to rise to the challenge [179].

If these meta-abilities are crucial to performing under pressure, it follows that we need to devise ways to help develop them. One such strategy to facilitate performers to acquire these skills during practice is *affective* learning design. Affective learning design essentially involves replicating conditions of pressure and physiological arousal during practice. Exposing the performer to pressure conditions in a systematic manner during the course of their preparation would seem to be a sensible way of allowing them to devise coping strategies and develop tolerance. This is analogous to the tempering process described in the previous chapter with respect to physical qualities.

LESSONS FROM ATHLETE BURNOUT...

Burnout is the ultimate expression of a maladaptive stress response. Burnout is the eventual outcome when coping resources are overwhelmed. The cumulative adverse effects of stressors can wear the performer down to such an extent that they are not able to bounce back. Studying this phenomenon can allow us to identify the critical factors and in turn protect performers by informing interventions that can prevent the situation escalating to such a degree.

Returning to our earlier definition of psychological hardiness, it is important that we elucidate what makes the difference between eliciting a healthy stress response versus one that is maladaptive.

Studies have sought to identify factors that are protective and assist with coping on the one hand, and negative factors that contribute to stress experienced in a negative way and ultimately increase the likelihood of burnout on the other. Relationship and social factors are associated with burnout among athletes. Clearly the coach-performer relationship is a critical relationship, given the propensity to affect the individual's state in both positive and negative ways, and this seems to be the case particularly with younger athletes [180]. As leaders and coaches what we can take from these findings is the need to establish that our aims are aligned and communicate that our methods are complementing the individual's efforts to achieve success.

Another important factor in relation to burnout is what social bonds exist within the collective, such as the team or organisation. The impact of prosocial versus antisocial behaviour of team mates has recently been given some attention in this regard [181]. Somewhat naturally, prosocial behaviour of team-mates during practice and competition is associated with positive affect among individuals, whereas antisocial conduct prompts negative affect. There are also demonstrated knock on effects for task cohesion, which becomes increased with prosocial behaviour, whereas it is reduced with antisocial behaviour. Perhaps unsurprisingly, antisocial behaviour is also an antecedent of burnout in the athletes studied [181].

It is open to question the extent to which leaders and coaches can directly influence social bonding or create cohesion within the group with our intervention. That said, we can have an indirect positive effect by maintaining standards of conduct, including mutual respect and consideration towards others. Accordingly, we should be ready to take action to demonstrate our commitment and to communicate its importance, particularly when there are transgressions.

There are other relationships in the individual's personal life that have the potential to add to the stress or conversely provide some protection. Perceived social support can be either mediate or moderate burnout risk [182]. Higher ratings of perceived social support are protective and buffer the effects of stress. Conversely, lower ratings are associated with heightened risk of burnout. Parents play a significant role in this regard, particularly in the case of younger performers. Once again, parental influence may serve to add or to relieve stress on the performer, depending on the nature of the relationship and the circumstances.

It follows that coaches should seek to enlist the parents and significant others in the process and strive for alignment on mission and message. Whilst there is clearly a limit to what influence coaches and leaders can exert here, it remains important to leverage positive influences and mitigate negative effects as far as possible. For instance, ring-fencing family and social stressors is an important consideration when preparing performers to compete at major events.

Ultimately psychological resilience is the biggest protector against burnout [183], albeit this can be something of a circular relationship. Those who interpret conditions of stress and adversity in a more positive way are more likely to have a healthy stress response and in turn to exhibit greater resilience over time. In contrast, the same conditions and events interpreted in a different way can create negative stress and lead to maladaptive stress responses, which over time might lead to burnout, especially in the presence of the other co-factors described above.

Once again, interpretation and perception appear to be at the heart of what makes the difference between those who succumb under the strain and those who persist and ultimately flourish. The question becomes how we might steer performers towards a more positive interpretation of challenging events and alter their perception so that the experience proves to be positive and beneficial.

EMPHASISING AGENCY AND PURPOSE...

In an earlier chapter we introduced the concept of agency, and once again it has a central role in how we prepare individuals to cope with pressure. Restoring a sense of agency when the performer is feeling nervous and perhaps a little overwhelmed can be very powerful. A starting point is to remind the performer of their purpose and return to what originally motivated them to pursue the path that led to them being here. It is likewise helpful to simply bring to the performer's attention that they have a choice in all of this. Once the athlete recalls they choose to be here and do this, in itself that can serve to dispel feelings of dread and any sense that they are not in control of the situation.

Of course for this to be effective it does help when from the outset the performer is clear that they are in fact doing it for themselves and not for anybody else's benefit. On occasion the process can get hijacked during the course of the youth sports journey, particularly as athletes advance towards the professional ranks. Nevertheless, we can bring the performer back to what originally made them choose to participate and return them to an earlier time when they were performing for their own sake. In this way we can seek to restore intrinsic motivation and a sense of purpose that they can draw on under stress.

TAKING THE POWER BACK...

As we have noted, interpretation is key. Perception goes a long way in shaping our experience and in turn the nature of our response to stressors. The emotions we experience are fluid and highly malleable. The same is true of the cognitions that surround our emotions and contribute to our mood state. Once we have figured out that the emotions we feel are largely projections constructed by our own minds, it becomes much easier to stop being a slave to them.

With coaching we can arm the performer with the knowledge to be able to interrogate their own emotional state and determine the origins of what they are feeling. The term *affect* describes the sensations we feel arising from our own body that are in part a reflection of our internal state and also partly elicited by external conditions and the situations we encounter. Being able to parse how our physiological state is contributing to the sensations underpinning the affect we feel, versus a reflection of external circumstances, can help us to divine the cause of what we are feeling. For instance, when we are in a sleep deprived state our cognitive and physiological state is impacted, so this will inevitably have an impact on our affect. We therefore should not rush to judgement in labelling the emotion and ascribing the cause to external situations or actors. Things may feel very different after a good night's sleep.

With guidance it is possible for the performer to take back the power to manage their perceptions and to shift their own perspective. With the right awareness and tools we can enable individuals to redefine their cognitions and what emotions they experience in a way that empowers them to change their own emotional and psychological state.

"You have power over your mind — not outside events. Realise this, and you will find strength"

– Marcus Aurelius

There is a critical distinction to make between what is under our control and that which is outside of our control. As coaches we can counsel performers to direct their attention and energy towards managing their own perception and perspective, which are under their control, rather than wastefully dwelling on and railing against what they cannot change. To that end, we can illuminate what is within the individual's power. For instance, it is up to us whom we grant access into our circle.

CHANNELLING THE STOICS...

"Stoicism is about the domestication of emotions, not their elimination"

– Nassim Nicholas Taleb

Stoicism is widely misunderstood, both among the majority who are only peripherally aware of Stoic philosophy and by those who proclaim themselves to be proponents or aspiring Stoics themselves. A common but incorrect assumption is that stoicism advocates that we should act without emotion and effectively means suppressing our emotions. In fact, the wisdom shared by the Stoics can help us to better understand and work more effectively with our emotions, rather that excluding them. The enlightenment that Stoic wisdom offers can also help performers to deal with externalities and the habits of thinking which can otherwise hijack their emotional state.

"Any person capable of angering you becomes your master; he can anger you only when you permit yourself to be disturbed by him"

– Epictetus

As a general rule, performers should be highly selective in who they grant the power to affect their state. From a purely rational perspective, very few have the privileged access required to formulate any legitimate judgement of another individual. If we are objective and critically evaluate the source, they typically lack the requisite insight and relevant information to have any sound basis for whatever opinion they might express about us.

By this rationale, no person is really entitled to an opinion (good or bad) in relation to another individual, unless they happen to have intimate knowledge of them. The fact that hordes of people may express their ill-founded opinions and illegitimate judgements irrespective of this irrefutable fact is not something that performers should be unduly troubled by. If an individual has the power to permit others' opinions to affect them, it follows that it is also within our power to refuse to grant this permission.

"When someone is properly grounded in life, they shouldn't have to look outside themselves for approval"

– Epictetus

By extension performers need to learn that they do not need to look outside of themselves for affirmation and approval. The only person who has all the facts and insider knowledge that would provide a legitimate basis for making these judgements is ourselves. Nobody else can or should have this power. Those who seek others' approval and external affirmation will find their feelings and behaviour enslaved by others.

Social evaluation and the judgement of others are arguably the biggest stressors for performers. Professional athletes especially are always in the public eye. In the digital era, this also means constantly being subject to evaluation via social media. Any judgements expressed on these platforms are a reflection of the source's projections based on the athlete's public persona, which is itself a fiction. The person expressing the opinion has likely never met the athlete in person or spent any time with them. We can help performers to recognise that others' criticisms are typically based on misrepresentations and misunderstandings of what is anyway a fictional character. Making this distinction allows us to differentiate ill-informed opinions of a fictional persona, as opposed to legitimate criticism of the person in reality.

One effective coping strategy is to tune out. To that end, we should encourage performers to limit their exposure to social stressors and sources of negative affect. Social media certainly falls into this category, not least given that it purposely amplifies the most emotive content. However, this also extends to other sources, including mainstream news media, which increasingly operates on salacious headlines and sensationalist reporting. Sensationalist media of any type is by definition intentionally editorialised and specifically engineered to provoke a strong affective response. It follows that we should consider limiting our exposure, given it is purposely designed to affect our state.

"Keep company only with people who uplift you, whose presence calls forth your best"

– Epictetus

It is important for performers to realise that they possess the power to grant others access. All of us have a choice in who we associate with. Those we spend time inevitably influence our thoughts and our emotional state. It follows that we should reinforce this point, with the suggestion that performers remain mindful and carefully curate who they permit in their inner circle. This should not be misconstrued to mean we should only engage with sycophants and 'yes men'. Rather the selection criteria should favour those who have our genuine interests at heart, and as such are candid with feedback and challenge us to be better.

"What you're supposed to do when you don't like a thing is change it. If you can't change it, change the way you think about it. Don't complain"

– Maya Angelou

Indulging in complaints and self-pity is a luxury we can ill afford, particularly at times of adversity. As coaches we should therefore intervene and highlight this point to performers when they are complaining and railing against things that are beyond their control. Aside from being a self-defeating indulgence, complaints and raging against what is not in our power to change expends emotional energy. It is important that we bring this to the individual's awareness and prompt them to invest the time and energy more productively to find workaround solutions, or else redouble their efforts to overcome the obstacle via means that are under their control.

MANAGING PERCEPTION...

We will explore the topic of working with our emotions during times of stress at length in a later chapter, but a key theme is that awareness is a prerequisite for regulating our emotional state. Interpretation and perception are thus central in determining how we respond to stressors. The labels we assign to what sensations we are feeling exert a profound influence over our emotional experience, our surrounding thoughts, and how we respond to external events and actors.

Cognition and emotion therefore work in both directions. Our cognitions assign labels to external events and our internal feelings. We interpret events and we feel emotions based on the labels and the representations we construct in our own minds. Conversely, the emotions we are experiencing at any given time serve to influence our surrounding thoughts and colour our representation of events. How we reason is often based on the emotions we are feeling (hence the term *emotional reasoning*).

As coaches we should certainly impart this revelatory knowledge to the performers we serve. After all, if we reinterpret our affective state (what sensations we feel) to give it a different label we can effectively hack the process to alter what emotions we experience and in turn reshape what thoughts our emotions give rise to. Investigations of *reappraisal* thus focus on how we interpret the somatic feelings that accompany physiological arousal [96].

One thing that is critical for performers to understand is that arousal is not only integral to performing but also serves a purpose. This knowledge alone can take much of the stigma away when athletes are feeling nervous. Often a major cause of much of the surrounding anxiety among performers is the mistaken perception that what they are feeling is not entirely normal, and that elite performers are somehow meant to be immune from feeling nerves prior to performing.

Nerves prior to the big event should be accepted rather than denied, and certainly it should not be taboo for performers to speak about feeling nervous. Rather than being a sign of weakness, sensations of nervousness should be reframed as part of the natural process of readying the body and nervous system to perform. Physical sensations of physiological arousal such as butterflies in the stomach should be readily acknowledged and embraced as functional by coaches and performers alike. A nice line that was shared by a coach is 'get your butterflies flying in formation'.

SYSTEMATIC REFLECTION...

How we reflect on events is similarly key in determining our response, and in turn shaping how we entertain future challenges. When we are seeking to develop resilience, it is not a question of artificially creating conditions of adversity or manufacturing challenge, as there will generally be ample opportunities that will present themselves without our intervention. There is however a need to be systematic in our approach in order to derive the full benefit of these trials as they arise and fully leverage the opportunity for learning. Leaders, managers, and coaches clearly need to understand this, but it is equally helpful to impress this point on the performer. Beyond general awareness, as coaches in the process we can also implement processes and practices to facilitate the endeavour.

Military leaders are noted for scrupulously keeping detailed records, allowing them to reflect on events and decisions after the fact. Reflective practice is similarly identified as a key process and an important discipline for coaches and practitioners to engage in. It should be recognised that the practice of keeping a daily record equally has merit for performers in different realms. Coaches involved with individual pursuits such as track and field athletics will often encourage the athlete to keep a log to capture not only detailed records of the workouts they perform, but also their reflections on the session and other day to day events. Whilst this practice is less prevalent in team sports, there is nevertheless merit in individual performers in these sports adopting this approach.

Each individual involved in the endeavour should therefore be encouraged to maintain a log or diary to capture key occurrences and notable moments, and to record any associated thoughts and feelings. These records thereafter provide a means for independent reflection. Similarly, this practice also forms the basis for conducting regular debriefs, either individually or as a support staff, including periodic in-depth reviews.

TEAM RESILIENCE...

From a team or organisation perspective, social support is an element that contributes to the individual and collective ability to cope. Key relationships include coaches, other support staff, colleagues and team-mates, and those in the individual's personal life. These respective relationships can be a vital source of assurance, or indeed a source of stress, depending on the dynamics involved.

Just as individuals experience periods of hardship, so too do teams, working groups, and organisations. Much like with an individual, times of adversity prompt the group to mobilise their collective coping resources. When operating as a group, coming through hardship and bouncing back from setbacks is naturally a shared endeavour. Team members are inter-dependent and successful team functioning relies upon cooperation and collaboration. It follows that team resilience is a collective effort [184].

Team resilience is an emergent property of a dynamic system and hence emerges over time with exposure to testing conditions [171]. When considering team resilience, we can generalise the resilience factors that we have described for individual performers, albeit we can expect social elements and interpersonal dynamics to play a particularly prominent role.

Elite sport provides a fertile environment for developing team resilience – after all the mettle of the team is tested every time they compete and poor results inevitably prompt a great deal of scrutiny from both within and outside the organisation. There is inevitably pressure and expectation from various sources and competitors are of course seeking to exploit any weakness, not least when facing them in the performance arena. In this context, sports teams will inevitably experience setbacks, which provides ample opportunity to see how they respond to these experiences [185]. Champion teams embody the traits that underpin team resilience, and are often used in case studies of team resilience and cohesion [186].

During stressful times and challenging conditions the interactions between individuals within the group become all the more crucial. The leadership provided both from above and from within the peer group according helps to determine whether the group draws together or pulls apart under pressure. The quality of communication within the team and social dynamics between team members in particular are critical for team cohesion and staying on task [187]. A sense of shared accountability is also central to this endeavour [184].

If navigated well, the shared experience of coming through periods of adversity together greatly strengthens the bonds between team members. These times are when these relationships are tested, but also proven. As such, champion teams exhibit very strong social identity among members of the group [186].

Sadly, coaches and leaders in sport and other domains have at times been misguided in their efforts to build 'grit' and team resilience. Bootcamp style punishing workouts and 'Hell week' inspired gruelling excursions have frequently been adopted for these purposes. Aside from lacking any relevance from the perspective of preparing individuals and teams to perform in their specific context, it is also very difficult to make the case that these methods will have any efficacy in achieving the outcome of developing resilience factors. If anything, putting performers through these largely pointless ordeals will harm our relationship with them and diminish our credibility as leaders in their eyes, particularly if there are independent thinkers within the group.

GET A LIFE...

Single-minded commitment, including what might be characterised as obsessive drive and total investment in the pursuit, are often part of what makes for a successful ascent to the highest level. However, performers need a life beyond their chosen sport, performing art, or profession to sustain them if their career at the top is to have any longevity.

By extension, each individual needs to create some separation between their performer or athlete persona and their wider existence as a human beyond the performance arena. If the performer's self-concept is inextricably linked to their athlete or performer status, then every challenge in effect becomes an existential threat. Cleary this makes for a precarious existence and is ultimately not sustainable.

It is a relatively common scenario that the performer has subjugated other aspects of their life in the pursuit of their goals as they made their ascent. Accordingly, there may be a need to invest time a d effort cultivating a life beyond the performance (and practice) arena. This will necessarily include developing human relationships that are not directly linked or contingent upon their status as a performer and independent from whatever domain they are involved in. These relationships are part safety valve, part safe haven. We all need a sanctuary, and for performers this means spending time in environments and engaging with people that are entirely separate from life as a performer.

These principles equally apply to leaders, coaches, managers, and practitioners in all domains. As professionals we also need to have a life and a viable existence as a human that is separate from our profession. To that end, our family and friendships that pre-date or are entirely independent from our status in the profession or the professional environment are paramount. Work-life balance is often looked on with scorn by high performers, but we need to alter our perspective, not least because it will aid our ability to continue to perform at the highest level.

As leaders we must model these behaviours, in order to foster a sustainable performance environment for all members of the team. Setting the example should be part of a wider effort to impress upon those we serve the importance of maintaining the necessary balance and separation to exercise sound judgement, conduct ourselves appropriately, and help avoid burning ourselves out.

IN CLOSING...

Acquiring the tools to deal with setbacks and the ability to respond to times of adversity in a way that ultimately makes the individual stronger for the experience is central to sustainable high performance. An integral part of long-term athlete development in youth sport is developing the necessary life skills, and this necessarily includes the emotional aptitudes to function and to thrive amidst the stressors of participating in sport over the long-term. The life of an athlete has arguably never been more turbulent, given the challenges and distractions posed by social media in this era of hyper-connectivity. Unfortunately, young performers across all domains are increasingly proving to be ill-equipped to cope with the attendant stress and emotional struggles.

A central theme in this chapter is that the same stressors and conditions have the potential to make or break us. Another recurring theme is that the element of coaching can be decisive in determining which of these scenarios prevails. As coaches and practitioners we can help guide those we serve to develop the aptitudes and coping abilities underpinning the psychological resilience to come through the trials that performers will inevitably encounter on the journey. Beyond sport, this equally applies to leaders, managers, and humans in all domains.

Part of our duty of care is to help the individuals we are responsible for to acquire the necessary understanding and tools to handle the trials and tribulations that are part of the life of an aspiring high performer (and being a human in general). What this ultimately amounts to is coaching; once again, regardless of what sphere we operate in, we are ultimately coaches of humans.

I can anticipate that some may protest that dealing with such matters as psychological skills and tools for developing resilience is outside our expertise or scope of practice, and should be left to psychologists or mental skills consultants. I would counter that our defining purpose is to prepare the performer to perform at their best on a consistent basis and in a manner that is sustainable over the long term. As such, given how mental aspects profoundly influences human performance it would be a glaring omission were we not to account for such a fundamental part of the performance equation.

REFLECTING AND CONNECTING THE DOTS...

In general, how much attention do you feel we give to the role of psychological resilience in a professional setting?

Would you say the ability to endure and bounce back from setbacks is generally viewed as an innate quality, or something that we can and should seek to develop?

What are your reflections on the idea that times of adversity are revealing? Have you had the experiences of discovering something about yourself and others during the course of enduring challenging periods?

To what extent is this concept of adversity as opportunity prevalent in your current setting? Do you see merit in bringing this perspective?

Based on what your own experience what do you feel makes difference in determining whether our stress response is healthy and positive versus maladaptive? Do you see a role for coaching to help others to better cope with challenge and stressors?

Do you feel that leaders and managers are sufficiently aware of the coaching aspect of guiding individuals and teams through difficulty? In general how equipped are those in leadership roles to provide this input?

What is your view on the relative importance of individual versus team resilience in coping with stressors and challenges in your particular occupational setting?

What strategies, if any, are employed to leverage opportunities that might arise to foster cohesion and develop resilience as a team or within working groups?

Based on the information presented, what measures might you consider implementing to support efforts to develop resilience for individuals and team resilience for the collective?

Part Four: Managing Self

"Physician, heal thyself!"

Luke 4:23

The human element of coaching and leading necessarily means turning the focus upon ourselves; in essence, we need to understand ourselves, and what influences our behaviour and our interactions.

As with athletes and those we serve, operating in the modern climate of hyper connectivity presents a host of challenges and necessitates that we arm ourselves with the requisite knowledge to develop appropriate countermeasures, both for our athletes and ourselves.

Our physical and mental wellbeing is integral to our ability to fulfil the requirements of our role in service of athletes; we have an obligation to fulfil these responsibilities.

It is contradictory and harms our credibility when we counsel others on 'self-care', and then fail to adopt this behaviour ourselves; if we seek to influence others we bear the responsibility to model these behaviours.

Meta-Abilities for Human Performance

Meta means above or beyond. We can thus define meta-abilities as 'higher order' skills, and relate them in terms of our 'executive functions'. As they are above or beyond, meta-abilities effectively determine how well we are able to make use of our capabilities, and ultimately how successfully we are able to function in each respective area. With this short offering to open up this final part of the book we explore the meta-abilities in relation to human performance. In doing so, we will unpack the superpowers that we can harness to enhance our practice in a variety of realms as coaches, practitioners, and athletes, and help educate ourselves and those around us to make use of these tools.

EXECUTIVE FUNCTIONS...

Executive functions can be defined the faculties that allow us apply some top-down control to regulate and modulate our responses, decisions, and actions. Executive function and self-regulation are thus related concepts. This type of 'top-down' control is effortful and involves a deeper level of processing than the more immediate first glance assessment and default response. Daniel Kahneman famously characterised the two scenarios as thinking slow and fast [35].

In essence, executive functions allow us to make a more considered and reasoned response, adapt our actions to the specific circumstances we face, and play a long game rather than simply being reactive. Three core executive functions have been identified, which are inhibition, working memory, and cognitive flexibility [188]. From these core functions we derive the higher order executive functions of planning, reasoning, and problem solving. It is worth noting that there is considerable overlap between the respective meta-abilities, as the reader will discover.

META-LEARNING...

The first meta-ability on the list is *meta-learning*. Meta learning describes our awareness and understanding of how we learn. This meta-skill also encompasses the ability to deploy and apply our learning skills in different realms. For instance, meta-learning relates to how we approach acquiring skills in general, irrespective of the type of skill. Being clear on the process allows us to learn more effectively and we can apply this knowledge to both cognitive tasks and motor learning.

Having the awareness to self-regulate is clearly a crucial starting point, but there must also be the willingness to do so. To give an example of meta-learning from the realm of sport, the self-directed *deliberate practice* behaviours that performers engage in are revealing. Deliberate practice in itself is a manifestation of meta-learning, as it is both effortful and directed towards a particular outcome [189]. Moreover, part of what separates performers who compete at a higher level is that they choose to practice the skills that they are weakest at, whereas sub-elite performers opt to engage in practising the skills that they are already adept at performing. The observation that performers at different levels exhibit such marked differences in their practice strategy provides a great illustration of meta-learning in action and also provides some insights into the differing results the respective approaches may yield over time [107].

META-COGNITION...

Meta-cognition describes the extent of our awareness of our own mind. More specifically, meta-cognition concerns the degree to which we have insight into the mental processes surrounding our thoughts and actions, and in turn our ability to regulate them [190]. Understanding and being able to monitor our own cognitive process is an important first step to being able to be selective in not only what we engage in, but also how and when. By extension, this meta-ability encompasses how we process and filter different inputs and forms of information from various sources. In this way, meta-cognition relates to our capacity for critical thinking, which many would contend is the critical higher order skill for the Information Age.

"Elite athletes are not just experts in movement execution but conceivably they are also experts in planning, metacognition, and reflection"

– MacIntyre and colleagues [190]

Meta-cognition is central to expertise, as it guides our decision-making and governs what informs our actions in different realms, and this of course includes sport performance. In particular, exercising control over how we allocate cognitive resources (notably attention) is a crucial part of operating within a dynamic environment. Being attuned to what is going on within our own minds is an inherent part of meta-cognition, but equally we need to able to selectively focus on what is relevant to the task at hand.

The executive function of *inhibition control* also comes into play here. Inhibition control is integral to harnessing attentional resources and maintaining concentration, allowing us to tune out or at least turn down the volume of inputs that might otherwise interfere or detract from our endeavour. Beyond enabling us to handle distraction, these abilities allow us to stay on task and resist the impulse to engage in something less taxing [188].

A meta-cognitive function that supports our capacity to learn over time concerns our ability to evaluate ourselves and objectively rate our present capabilities. Readers familiar with the *Dunning-Kruger* phenomenon will be aware of the scenario whereby those with lesser knowledge or low skill paradoxically tend to hold an over inflated view of their own competence [191]. Such an inability to recognise the limits of our own competence (or the extent of our incompetence) represents a failure of meta-cognition. Some authors have also suggested that this might also reflect a choice on some level to protect our self-concept [192]. What is clear is that until we are ready to face the current reality we are likely to not only continue to get things wrong but also fail to register our role in failures, and naturally this will greatly impede our efforts to become better.

As our cognitions and emotions are inextricably linked, meta-cognition also converges on the realm of *emotion regulation* [193]. Likewise, given that meta-cognition relates to how we engage with factors that are external to ourselves, which naturally includes our interactions with others, this brings *social cognition* comes into play [190]. These elements of intra- and inter-personal intelligence bring us neatly onto the theme of emotional intelligence.

EMOTIONAL INTELLIGENCE...

In earlier chapters we considered the role of emotional intelligence from leadership and coaching perspectives. Various aspects of emotional intelligence are equally pertinent to the performer themselves. The role of emotional intelligence within the context of competitive sport is thus becoming increasingly well-established [55].

It is clearly crucial that the performer is able to regulate their own emotions within the highly charged environment of the performance and practice arenas and under conditions of fatigue and stress. Emotion regulation goes a long way to determining whether there is a neutral, positive, or negative impact on performance and the general wellbeing of the individual. The ability to harness and regulate emotion clearly has implications for performance in the moment, but will also impact how the performer fares over time.

Given the importance of social support, the role of emotional intelligence in supporting the performer's ability to interact successfully with other humans and foster healthy relationships within and particularly beyond the performance arena is also highly relevant. This is evident for those who engage in individual pursuits, but it becomes all the more crucial for performers who are part of a collective, notably team sports athletes.

Emotional intelligence is arguably the ultimate meta-ability as it encompasses a host of elements, which could each be considered meta-skills in their own right. Broadly we can classify these elements under the banner of intra-personal intelligence and inter-personal intelligence, respectively.

INTRA-PERSONAL INTELLIGENCE...

Intra-personal intelligence describes our inward looking sense and our capacity for introspection. Intra-personal intelligence therefore comprises a significant element of self-awareness. Beyond this, performers also require a higher level understanding of how their emotional responses and mood state have the potential to impact various facets of performance in different scenarios.

Our knowledge and understanding of own feelings necessarily relies upon self-reflection and online monitoring 'in the moment'. Other related aspects include our awareness and understanding of our own emotional state and our emotional responses to external events. In other words, emotional awareness is the extent to which we can not only decipher what we are feeling, but also be aware of what might be beneath it.

Beyond the ability to tune into our emotions, intra-personal intelligence as it relates to emotion regulation further encompasses our capacity to harness our emotions and regulate our emotional state. Once we have determined our emotional state, we need to be able to reflect on our own emotional responses and make some sort of rational judgement on them. A critical factor from a performance viewpoint is our ability to be conscious of emotional responses that do not serve us, particularly in the moment. By extension, we require the ability to modulate our emotional state accordingly to limit the negative impact.

Effective emotion regulation to support our ability to perform thus encompasses a few overlapping meta-abilities, as there are a number of different elements and accordingly various strategies we can employ [194]. We will explore these themes at length in a later chapter.

INTER-PERSONAL INTELLIGENCE...

Inter-personal intelligence is the keystone of our social intelligence. This meta-ability governs how well we are able to recognise, understand, and navigate social situations and interactions with others. Critical factors include our knowledge of social structure and conventions, such as power relationships and social dynamics between members of the group.

Successful human-to-human interaction means being able to read other people and social cues, which includes perspective taking and empathic sense. This is what us to respond accordingly and tailor our verbal and nonverbal communication in ways that serves us. As we explored in an earlier chapter, interpersonal intelligence encompasses not only the ability to consider the other person's viewpoint, but also attend to and intuit what might lie behind their position and what they are expressing in ways that allow for a deeper level of understanding.

IN CLOSING...

A common theme among elite performers in various realms is that they are highly self-directed and doggedly persistent in the pursuit of better. The meta-abilities and executive functions concerned with self-regulation and goal-directed behaviour are therefore highly relevant to all those who aspire to excel in their particular domain. A number of meta-abilities or higher order skills are similarly central to the processes of how we acquire and apply our expertise in different contexts.

Given their utility for performers, it follows that we should seek to explore ways to develop these meta-abilities. Psychological skills training and mental performance coaching are well established in sport and are becoming prevalent in different realms. The practice of *mindfulness* is likewise ubiquitous in all spheres and professions at the present time. Whilst this is a positive step, these practices nevertheless remain vague and ill-defined, and by extension there is a general lack of clarity when it comes to how best to apply these methods to develop specific meta-abilities.

Such issues aside, an important route to developing the meta-abilities we have described is simply through greater awareness. For instance, a necessary first step is for us to be aware (or *mindful*, if you like) of the relevant higher order processes taking place in the moment. Introducing these concepts to performers in itself helps to encourage each individual to contemplate what this means for them, and consider how they might alter their approach to account for these aspects. Engaging in reflection after the event on a regular or at least periodic basis is likewise an integral and essential part of the endeavour.

Beyond the question of trainability, what is important is how we might best deploy these meta-abilities to navigate the miscellaneous challenges we face both within the performance arena and in our daily lives. These are the questions that we will explore in the chapters that follow.

Reclaiming Mental Faculties in the Information Age

The information age has given rise to this present era of hyper-connectivity. With the ubiquitous presence of smartphones and other devices we now have an almost endless source of distraction at our fingertips at all times. The smartphone quickly assumed such a prominent role in our lives and these devices proliferated so rapidly that it largely escaped our attention that we might have a problem on our hands. When we are in public spaces everybody else around us is also immersed in their device, so we have come to accept this constant immersion and distraction as standard behaviour. This situation might have snuck up on us, but of late a number of authors and voices have begun to sound the alarm. With this chapter we delve into the smartphone and social media phenomenon, and explore the extent to which they present a problem in our professional and personal lives. We will also consider some countermeasures in an attempt to plot a path back to using these tools in ways that serve us rather than being a slave to the technology.

'PROBLEMATIC' SMARTPHONE USE...

With the proliferation of mobile smart devices and the pervasive role of online technology in modern society, our use of these tools has come to shape the actions we take in our everyday lives. As more elements of our everyday lives move online, increasingly smartphones and other mobile technology have emerged as the primary means that many of us employ to engage in these daily online activities [195]. The capability provided by these tools to readily access online media and various applications when we are on the go certainly provides unparalleled functionality. Equally, having such ready online access so close to hand at all times carries an imminent risk of encroaching on our daily lives, especially when it comes to our in-person interactions with other humans.

Against this backdrop, the notion of 'problematic smartphone use' is becoming more widely recognised and studied [196]. The data that are emerging reveal the level of dependence we have developed and it all makes for troubling reading. Based on reports, around half of smartphone owners surveyed stated they could not live without their smartphone [197]. The fear of being without one's smartphone has even been given a name (*nomophobia*) [198]. At present it is typical for us to reach for our smartphone as soon as we wake up in the morning, and thereafter interact with our phone with dizzying regularity (an average frequency of 85 times each day) throughout our waking hours [199]. A staggering three quarters of those surveyed admitted they continue to use their device whilst walking, and what is all the more alarming is that two thirds of respondents state that they check their smartphone during the night [196].

The dysfunctional aspects of our present smartphone use are manifested in multiple ways [196]. As in the previous examples, compulsive use of these devices is clearly evident. The second category is behaviour that we would consider antisocial, as we will explore in the sections that follow. Finally, smartphone use is implicated in dangerous behaviour. One prominent example of the latter is distracted driving due to the prevalent use of smartphones whilst in charge of a motor vehicle, which is presently a major contributor to road traffic accidents (despite the acknowledged risks and contravening the laws introduced in many countries to prevent it). The increasing number of deaths occurring whilst taking 'selfies' would also seem to fall into the 'dangerous behaviour' category, albeit arguably this is an example of Darwinian natural selection at work. As an aside, the fact that the term 'selfie' has been adopted into everyday language in itself demonstrates the pervasive role of the smartphone in shaping thoughts, words, and actions in the present digital era.

Amidst such findings, many authors have raised the spectre of *smartphone addiction*. Whilst it would be prudent to be careful with the use of terms such as addiction (given there are clinical criteria involved), smartphone *dependence* is certainly increasingly prevalent to varying degrees. There is something of a generational effect whereby younger people are particularly prone [195], albeit the grown-ups (including parents of young people) are certainly not immune to the lure of these devices, as we will explore. Despite the behaviour having become somewhat normalised, many commentators are expressing their concern about the obsessive use of these devices that we can recognise in ourselves and observe among those around us on a day to day basis. Indeed in 2015 the World Health Organisation acknowledged that problematic smartphone use might present a public health issue.

Part of the dysfunctional effect associated with smartphone use relates to our cognitive habits and related behaviours. For instance, the fact that distraction and entertainment is available at our finger tips is not conducive to impulse control [200]. In this way, the technology is at odds with the executive functions we described in the previous chapter. Increasingly, whenever we get a spare moment we automatically reach for our mobile device. Having these devices to hand at all times provides the constant temptation and the means to 'bail out' mentally whenever the task or situation in front of us becomes onerous, and it is all too easy to succumb to this temptation.

Engaging with our mobile device to relieve boredom readily morphs over time into constantly seeking distraction for its own sake. This brings a new dimension to the phrase 'when left to our own devices'. It bears repeating that the smart technology works in constant opposition to the higher order functions we met in the preceding chapter that are involved with self-regulation and goal-directed behaviour [201]. In effect, the constant distraction and immediate gratification available at our fingertips provides the option of not having to engage in deeper thoughts or troubling ourselves with matters of real life. It means we do not have to reflect on events that might have occurred and what we might be feeling. Clearly none of this is conducive to exercising the meta-abilities that allow us to demonstrate emotional intelligence.

ABSENT PRESENT...

It is apparent that our increasing online interaction via our smart devices may be to the detriment of 'offline' or in-person social interaction [202]. The growing time spent online naturally reduces the time available to interact with others in real life, or *IRL* – the fact this now merits its own acronym speaks to the extent of the issue. Even when we are present in body, our mind is often elsewhere as our attention is captured by our smart device. It is increasingly common for us to neglect the person in front of us in order to attend to our phone [196].

The irony of seeking social connection via social networking applications on our smartphone when real and in-person social connection is immediately available should not be lost on us. Once again, this behaviour has become so prevalent that a term ('phubbing') has been invented to describe the scenario of snubbing the person in front of us in favour of our smartphone [203]. Another description offered for this scenario is being 'absent present'.

Preliminary evidence also suggests that using digital devices during real life experiences affects our recollection of the experience [204]. Our memory of the lived experience is stronger and more vivid when experienced in the absence of technology. In other words, using technology appears to paradoxically diminish our memory of the experience that we are trying to preserve by capturing it with technology.

All of this raises the spectre of humans in modern society acting like zombies spellbound by their electronic device. The allure of the technology places us in some danger of sleep-walking through our days, failing to fully register real life experiences and inattentive to those around us.

BEING A PEFORMER IN THE DIGITAL ERA...

Performers in the realm of sport are far from exempt from the influence of digital technology. Athletes are as prone to the compulsive use of these devices and digital media as the rest of us. This was illustrated by media reports of a coach of a professional team who felt compelled to provide breaks during practices for players to check their smartphones.

The online realm and social media in particular has added a capricious new dimension to the social context of participating in sport, particularly as the athlete's profile grows. The majority of athletes, now have a social media profile (and this is also increasingly true of coaches and practitioners in sport). High profile cases in the news of high profile athletes being sanctioned or falling foul of public outcry following ill-considered social media posts underline the perils that high profile performers face in the digital era. Such incidents have prompted national sporting organisations, professional teams, and even college teams to provide social media training for athletes [205].

"Are you here to tweet, or are you here to compete?"

— Peter Haberl, Senior Sport Psychologist at the United States Olympic Committee

There are a number of incentives (including financial) to maintain a social media profile and cultivate an online following for athletes and other performers, and this is becoming a focus for performers at a younger and younger age. For performers in the digital era the challenge of managing social media output and balancing the potential benefits of their online activity against the downsides has become a key priority. Competitions present athletes with opportunities to promote themselves, but equally this can be a major distraction [206] to the extent that it interferes with their ability to perform at their best when it matters. Online activities and social media use can also prove detrimental to performers in other ways, as we will explore in the next chapter.

Social media can be problematic even when things are going well. Female athletes in particular report concerns about the type of images they are expected to post on social media channels and dealing with unsolicited comments and messages from followers is another source of stress [207]. Conversely, when things are going badly social media can become a hugely malevolent influence. As we will explore in a later section, social media platforms can be a forum for toxic and negative comments. Performers can be drawn into exchanges on these platforms in response to critical comments and abuse, which tends to exacerbate the issue [208]. The toxic elements of social media are naturally especially problematic for young performers; after all it would take herculean self-assurance to shrug off this sort of unsolicited abuse even for mature adults.

Digital technology also presents a problem from a talent development viewpoint given it has become a major source of external recognition and validation. The affirmation and feelings of popularity young athletes derive from their social media accounts adds a further element that fuels their compulsive use. In this way, social media can infringe on performers' participation in the sport, becoming a distraction during practices and even competition. We even see the bizarre scenario where an athlete can start to derive validation from the social media attention and associated rewards in such a way that displaces the need to achieve competitive success in the sport itself. Any intrinsic motivation to engage in the sport for its own sake has been long since extinguished by this point.

COGNITIVE PERFORMANCE COSTS OF DIGITAL TECHNOLOGY...

It is increasingly acknowledged that hyper-connectivity and the prevalence of smart devices likely comes at a cognitive cost and has the potential to be detrimental to 'off screen' performance [199]. Just as it is at odds with our executive functions, there is a strong argument that technology-related distraction is the natural enemy of cognitively demanding work. Cal Newport proposed the term *deep work* [209] to distinguish complex tasks and creative projects that demand immersion and extended periods of focussed attention, as opposed to the superficial 'busy work' that takes up much of our time but demands far less investment of mental resources. When attempting to engage in deep work that requires our full attention it serves us to recognise that our mind has a tendency to rebel and seek out less cognitively taxing tasks. In mobile technology our rebellious minds have found a potent ally.

We have become accustomed to working with the continual interruption of notifications from mobile electronic devices (not only smartphones but also now smart watches) and pop-up alerts on laptop and desktop computers demanding our immediate attention. Investigators have begun to explore how these interruptive notifications are impacting our professional and personal lives. The effect on our work performance is unsurprisingly not positive, particularly when it comes to our creative output and capacity for other deep work.

What is most apparent is that the stream of interruptions lead to the primary work task taking longer to complete and with a higher likelihood of errors [210]. The distraction provided by another device such as our smartphone is not the only issue: interruptive notifications on the same device we are using to work (laptop or desktop computer) can also significantly extend the time taken to complete the primary task [211]. Even if we resist the urge to attend to whatever the notification is calling us towards, there is still a cost in terms of attentional resources and task performance solely as a consequence of the notification itself (i.e. simply the alert tone or vibration) [212]. Whilst the constant nagging interruption and demands for our attention have become a fact of modern life, on some level we do seem to register the negative impact. These frustrations are increasingly evident in elevated subjective ratings of anxiety, annoyance, and reduced work satisfaction [213].

Even if we disregard the incessant notifications, our tendency to have our smartphone (or smart watch) close to hand at all times is in itself a barrier to undivided attention. Our use of these devices between tasks or mid-task when taking a break from cognitive work is not conducive to doing quality work, partly due to the cognitive costs involved with switching between inputs. It has been demonstrated that the mental refreshment we experience from taking a break is diminished when this time is spent with our smartphone [214]. As a result, our cognitive performance is impaired following the break: time taken to complete the task, efficiency, and quality of output (number of errors) are all negatively impacted.

What these studies reveal is the myth of multitasking. Attempting to attend to multiple inputs at the same time or in rapid succession forces us to switch our information processing faculties as we go back and forth. Switching between tasks and inputs is costly from an attention viewpoint. There is a residual effect, whereby our mind does not immediately disengage from whatever we switched over to, however briefly [215]. This causes a lag, during which we are not able to mobilise our full attention and cognitive capacity for the primary task at hand. As a result of these lingering effects our limited working memory capacity can also quickly become overwhelmed as we switch back and forth.

The mere presence of smartphones and other devices in our working environment shows adverse effects on our attention, concentration, and working memory resources. Even when we are able to resist engaging with our smartphone when working on a task, simply having our device close at hand serves to reduce our working memory capacity and what cognitive resources we are able to invest [199]. Unsurprisingly the drain on our mental resources not only negative impacts our ability to process what is in front of us, but also reduces our capacity to retain any new information [216].

Rather than using these tools to support how we work, the technology is providing a constant source of temptation for wandering minds seeking distraction from tasks requiring mental effort. Smart devices and mobile applications have become the perfect accomplice that enables endless prevarication. Clearly this is not supportive of our ability to engage in cognitively demanding 'knowledge work' requiring sustained periods of concentration. In his book *Deep Work* [209] Cal Newport therefore proposes that the increasingly rare ability to mobilise our full cognitive resources and resist these distractions now represents a major competitive advantage in the knowledge-based economy.

There are parallels here to the game-changing capability of top athletes for *clutch performance*, which is similarly underpinned by the ability to harness their full concentration and mental resources through effort and by their own volition to raise their game and execute when it matters. Interestingly, smartphone use has equally been suggested to negatively impact our ability to achieve *flow* [217], i.e. the state of intense but effortless concentration and total absorption in the task, which is the other mental performance state that high performing athletes aspire to.

DEVELOPMENTAL ISSUES...

Hyper-connectivity and constant presence of digital technology has a clear tendency to foster unfocussed and hyperactive behaviours, such as compulsively checking smartphone applications for updates. There is a growing argument that the habits we form with the constant use of this technology is impairing the executive functions we outlined as underpinning mental performance. It increasingly appears that the meta-abilities required to mobilise our full cognitive resources of our own volition and selectively direct our attention to support focussed action are becoming degraded due to these trends.

The welfare and wellbeing of children and adolescents has been a major focus of investigations of smartphone use and the use of social networking applications in particular. Childhood and adolescence are fertile periods when behaviours and habits are acquired. Many authors accordingly raise the concern that young people are highly susceptible to the influences of the mobile technology that is now ubiquitous in many parts of the world [218].

The internet, and the devices we use to connect with it, represent a newly introduced and prominent feature of the environment in which children are raised. The *i-Generation* born in the internet era and after the advent of smart phones are described as 'digital natives', having grown up with this technology. Mobile digital technology represents a potent environmental factor during childhood and adolescence, and as such these devices have considerable scope to influence and potentially interfere with cognitive and psychosocial development. There is some early evidence to support these concerns. Notably, studies from the realm of neuroscience indicate a measurable effect on the development of structures within the brain [219]. In one investigation quantifiable differences in white matter were found from brain imaging scans. Structural alterations were further evident in parts of the brain among those participants who were categorised as 'smartphone dependent' based on their habitual use of mobile technology [220].

Of all of our cognitive faculties, executive functions are likely most susceptible to the influences of mobile technology. Online activities and the behavioural effects of digital technology has considerable scope to hinder off-line development of the higher order skills involved with meta-learning and meta-cognitive abilities that allow us to regulate and direct mental resources and foster associated behaviours. These influences are clearly particularly problematic during stages of development when we are still acquiring these executive functions. Adolescents who habitually media multi task accordingly show poorer executive function [221]. Notably self-regulation and impulse control are highly prone to the influence of digital technology [198].

Part of maturing is developing the ability to exercise the executive function of inhibition and learning to modulate how we respond to the impulses we feel to act. Regulating impulsive behaviour involves managing how rewards shape our behaviour. For instance, a characteristic of maturing is the ability to delay immediate gratification in order to pursue longer term objectives. The advent of mobile technology has introduced a constant source of temptation and immediate gratification that has a high degree of potential to retard the development of the relevant executive functions and meta-abilities that underpin goal-directed behaviour [211].

We should note that the social networking applications developed for use with mobile technology are specifically engineered to elicit reward-seeking behaviour and leverage our urge for instant gratification. The influence of the digital technology is so pervasive and the associated bad habits are now so prevalent that this behaviour has sadly become normalised, largely removing the social cues and external feedback that might otherwise help foster these self-regulation abilities. The consequences of these trends are starting to become apparent. Levels of media multi-tasking among adolescents show a negative relationship to scores on executive function. What is all the more striking are the reported negative effects on real-world academic performance [221].

ACADEMIC PERFORMANCE...

Aside from impairing the development of meta-abilities and executive functions, the presence of mobile technology has considerable scope to directly interfere with learning. In the digital era the use of smart devices in the classroom has become integral from an early age. The use of mobile technology can of course be applied to support the learning experience. However, whilst digital media has a host of advantages, crucially it is not as effective as print media when it comes to our ability to process the information presented on the page [222, 223].

Aside from the apparent limitations of digital media in supporting learning, it is equally commonplace for smartphones to be used during class to engage with mobile communications, social networking applications, and online media that bears no relation to what is being taught. Extraneous smartphone use during class is highly prevalent among students both at high school level and in higher education [224]. Distracting use of technology in the learning environment has the power to affect not only the individual but also fellow students who are within sight line of the screen of the device.

It is also evident that these devices can interfere with independent study beyond the classroom environment. Measures of smartphone use and hours spent on social networking applications has repeatedly demonstrated a negative relationship with academic performance, based on a host of studies [211]. This is the case whether the engagement with mobile technology and online activity occurs during class or when completing homework. The distraction of mobile technology robs the learner of precious mental resources and working memory capacity in a way that has measurable negative effects on retention [216]. Clearly this is also not conducive to learning to understand.

DEVELOPMENT OF SOCIAL INTELLIGENCE...

The internet era and the advent of smart devices has certainly added an extra dimension that young people must learn to navigate. In essence, today's youth now face the challenge of developing their own identity and figuring out the rules of social interaction in both real life and virtual society. Moreover, there is typically little guidance to support their efforts to navigate the virtual world and to reconcile their online and offline lives; after all this is not something that their parents had to face when growing up, and the kids are undoubtedly more familiar and adept with the technology.

Just as digital technology may conceivably impact the development of other executive functions, potential issues have been highlighted in relation to psychosocial development. As we explored in the previous chapter the meta-ability of emotional intelligence is built upon both intra-personal (i.e. inward looking) and interpersonal or social intelligence. The elements of empathy and perspective taking are integral to exercising interpersonal emotional intelligence. Unfortunately, trends in the data indicate that empathy in young people may be on the decline in the digital era. A study examining measures of empathy in college students indicated this seems to be a relatively recent trend that began to emerge after the year 2000 [225].

As with other meta-abilities, the qualities that underpin social intelligence are primarily developed during childhood and the adolescent years. Social awareness and ability to read and respond to social cues are acquired through by interacting with others, and through these social interactions we become more aware of the thoughts and feelings of others. In particular, empathy is a major determinant of prosocial behaviours observed among adolescents [226]. The development of empathy during the adolescent years further shows a strong association with the social intelligence that individuals exhibit in adulthood [227]. Once again, the digital life of children and adolescents is implicated in each of these aspects. As we noted earlier in the chapter, the allure of our smartphone may be making us less attentive to those around us. By extension, it is conceivable that growing up in the digital era may lead to becoming more absorbed in ourselves and our online lives, and hence less thoughtful to the needs of those around us. Whilst this is speculative, what is clear is that any such effects will leave a legacy that extends into later life [228].

Both social acceptance and social standing are primary concerns for young people, as they learn to navigate complex social structures and find their place in the world. As such, adolescents in particular are highly sensitive to the opinions of others, and to their status among their peers. These factors have a highly potent (and measureable) neurophysiological effect that is also manifested in the psychological and emotional wellbeing of the individual [219]. From this perspective, the virtual world and social networking platforms have a prominent role in the day to day life and overall development of modern youth. These forays into the online world can be to the detriment of the young person's real world existence. When we are troubled we tend to become withdrawn. We now have the virtual world inside our smart devices to withdraw into, which can sadly exacerbate the issue.

Aside from these growing pains, there is also a darker side to the online world. The social networking applications on our smartphones can become weaponised and provide a medium for vindictive antisocial behaviour. Cyber bullying has become prevalent and should be recognised as a cause of serious potential harm [229]. The one-to-many format of social media sadly makes these applications a highly effective tool for publicly shaming or ridiculing another individual in front of an online audience of their peers. The asymmetrical format makes it very difficult for the subject of these attacks to defend or protect themselves, particularly given the mob mentality that social networking platforms encourage. In this way mobile technology and social media can represent a highly toxic influence during a vulnerable time in young people's development when they are most sensitive to the scrutiny and evaluation of their peers.

Against this backdrop, it is perhaps unsurprising that issues of mental health and general wellbeing among children and adolescents have begun to surface over the recent period.

IMPACT ON WELLBEING...

As the body of data continues to grow, a statistical relationship is emerging between smartphone use and measures of anxiety. Screen time and psychological wellbeing has been studied in children and adolescents in particular, and negative associations with psychological wellbeing is a common finding [230]. Excessive and compulsive use of mobile digital technology ('smartphone dependence') has demonstrated links to symptoms of depression and psychological distress [197]. Whilst there have been calls for moderation given some of the alarmist reporting to date [231] there is nevertheless consensus that excessive use of digital technology does represent an apparent source of harm, even if the degree of the negative impact is debated [232]. What is also evident is that adolescents appear to be the group who are most susceptible to these influences.

Studies have attempted to parse out the effects of specific types of online activity on subjective wellbeing. Beyond screen time in general, the use of social networking applications on these devices has been highlighted as a specific issue, based on the apparent negative impact on indices of psychological and emotional wellbeing. Given the vulnerability of children and adolescents to peer influence, the impact of social media engagement on wellbeing in young people would seem to merit research attention.

One such study investigating social media use and subjective wellbeing throughout the day reported that the greater the use of social media in the preceding hours, the worse participants reported feeling [233]. Oddly this led them to use social media even more during the subsequent time interval, causing a further decline in self-reported wellbeing. Such maladaptive social media use has been reported by a number of studies. What researchers term 'problematic use' of social networking applications has been identified as contributing to symptoms of social anxiety, depression, and most alarmingly reported suicide ideation [234].

Once again, adolescents are identified as the group most affected and early adolescence appears to be an especially sensitive phase. There is also some suggestion of a gender effect, whereby adolescent females are particularly susceptible to the potential negative effects associated with social media engagement. Accordingly, there is data indicating that use of social media applications during early adolescence among young females especially has adverse implications, with negative trends in wellbeing reported in the years that follow [235].

As noted in the previous section, adolescents are highly sensitive to their standing among their peers. Certainly the advent of social networking applications has done nothing to lessen the social anxiety. If anything, offline or 'real world' social interaction has become a more daunting prospect, due to the need to simultaneously keep up appearances online. This is also not helped by the distorted view of the lives of others and interactions among peers that are portrayed on social media.

Whilst young people might be most susceptible, there is also evidence of ill effects among older generations. The nature of our engagement with social networking sites appears to be a determining factor. Passive use of social media, that is browsing other users' profiles and entries without contributing, seems to undermine our subjective wellbeing to a greater extent than engaging more actively by posting content and communicating with others on these platforms [236].

Persistent use is further associated with more negative effects, including paradoxically higher ratings of loneliness [237]. Frequency and duration of use among social media users has similarly reported negative relationships with subjectively rated measures of life satisfaction [238]. The evidence thus suggests that the more time we spend engaged on these platforms, the less satisfied we tend to be with our lives.

The warped perception offered by social media lens and the distorted version of reality that individuals choose to present to the world via these platforms by their nature tend to provoke anxiety and elicit feelings of inadequacy. The ongoing pressure to present a highly embellished version of our lives to the world and continually add to the highlights reel on these platforms becomes a strain for many people. Whilst these issues have been emphasised in relation to young people, the grown-ups are certainly not immune to these effects.

Evidence is emerging that our online social media engagement may render us less resilient to the social stressors experienced in our real life social interactions [239]. This is yet another feature of the tension that exists between our online activities and our ability to conduct our social lives and negotiate in-person interactions offline. These investigations highlight the interaction between our social media activity and how we respond to real life events, which was reflected in physiological measures of stress and recovery recorded from participants [239].

HUMAN RELATIONSHIPS...

As noted previously, the lure of our smartphone and social networking applications can frequently lead us to neglect in-person social interaction, even when we are in the company of others. The fact we are unable to drag our attention away from our smartphone is clearly not conducive to building rapport. This behaviour also signals our apparent disregard for the other individual, albeit this effect is moderated somewhat by the fact that increasingly they too are immersed in their smartphone.

The potential for what in any other era would be considered disrespectful behaviour to harm relationships is evident. There is some suggestion that we do have some level of awareness of these perils. Investigations report that more intensive use of online social networking applications shows a negative relationship to participants' satisfaction with their offline relationships, which in turn elicits feelings of social anxiety and thereby further impacts psychological wellbeing [240]. It should be noted that social networking applications can equally facilitate our social lives offline. However, once again how (and when) we choose to engage with the digital technology serves to determine whether it is a net positive or negative effect.

More specifically, the use of mobile technology during the time we spend in the company of others appears particularly detrimental, and once again this is reflected in the subjective ratings of satisfaction derived from these social interactions [241]. Adolescents are often particularly guilty of this behaviour, with recent reports indicating that nearly half of teenagers surveyed admitting to using their smart phone 'constantly'. Aside from what this behaviour signals to the other person, being less attentive to those we are with also makes us less vigilant to social cues. In this way, the intrusive and distracting presence of our smartphone makes us less adept in social situations, simply as a result of the growing tendency to attend to our device rather than the person in front of us [202].

The most important relationships in our lives are equally susceptible, and it is here that our compulsive use of mobile technology can do the most harm. As an illustration, this is even manifested in the interaction between parent and infant. In public spaces you can often observe kids striving to get the attention of their parents who are immersed in their smartphone. Ironically the solution that many parents opt for to placate their children is giving them a device of their own, essentially to keep the child occupied and allow them to continue phubbing their offspring in peace.

As a social species, interaction with other humans is integral to our physical and mental health. Where we seek emotional support has a bearing on our psychological state and wellbeing. In person interaction remains critical from this point of view. Whereas face to face emotional support received is protective against depression symptoms, seeking emotional support via online sources paradoxically worsens the situation [242]. The data indicate that offline social interaction remains the most important (positive) determinant of our wellbeing and self-reported health status, as opposed to online social networking engagement [243]. It follows we should prioritise our in-person relationships and social interactions above all else. From physical and mental health perspectives, the choices we are increasingly making to favour online interaction via our smartphone over in person interaction are thus all the more self-defeating.

INTERVENTIONS AND COUNTERMEASURES...

The information presented in the preceding sections would appear to demand countermeasures to help protect ourselves and minimise the potential impact of digital technology on our personal lives. Beyond that, from a human performance perspective devising effective strategies to better navigate the technology would seem a smart move. Developing the faculties that will allow us to continue to produce at a high level in the digital era are thus equally crucial to confer a competitive advantage in our professional lives.

A host of interventions have been proposed to reduce smartphone dependence, ranging from the mild to the more extreme. On the mild side, some authors advocate switching the smart device to a monochrome display to make it less visually stimulating. Towards the other end of the spectrum, an intervention advocated by prominent authors is to undergo a full digital detox, whereby individuals go 'cold turkey' and completely abstain from smartphone use for an extended period of time [244]. A pragmatic strategy that is somewhere in the middle is to batch online tasks, such as scheduling discrete periods of time for electronic communications. As a general strategy batching tasks tends to be more efficient as it avoids the cognitive costs and lag effects associated with repeatedly switching between tasks.

Having our smartphone in the immediate vicinity (even in silent mode) provides more cognitive interference, including a greater urge to compulsively check the device, particularly for those who are predisposed [198]. Conversely, liberating ourselves from our devices, even for short periods of time, improves our ability to resist distraction and prevent our mind wandering to extraneous matters [245]. A strategy that extends this approach is to schedule enforced offline periods that are prioritised for cognitively demanding work. To give an example, when writing this book I took to staying offline during the morning on writing days, with devices in flight mode and kept in another room.

When taking breaks it will serve us well to resist the urge to engage with our smartphone given the apparent cognitive costs involved. Engaging in some other activity with low cognitive load, for instance simply getting up to stretch our legs and move around, is much more conducive to maintaining cognitive performance. Resisting being drawn into the virtual world on our smartphone guards against our attention and mental resources becoming captured by extraneous matters, avoiding the cognitive residue of switching between tasks and the toll on our cognitive resources following the break. Moreover, preserving our reserve mental capacity also allows our minds to continue processing the cognitive work we are engaged in during these offline periods. Resisting the urge to go online during breaks can thus facilitate creativity and offline problem-solving.

Clearly our professional and personal lives require that we respond to electronic communications, but we must equally avoid the scenario that is presently commonplace whereby we are constantly at the mercy of intrusive alerts. On a fundamental level we need to overcome the imperative we feel to drop everything and respond immediately when messages arrive, and incur all of the cognitive costs of switching between tasks that this involves.

To that end, we can adopt the tactic of batching the task of responding to email or smartphone notifications. However, the key is not simply to batch the task of responding to alerts; equally important is that we confine these interruptions to discrete periods of time [246]. If we have scheduled discrete time slots to respond the electronic communication, it follows that we should switch off alerts and messaging applications during the hours in between, or perhaps just remain offline entirely. In doing so we create extended blocks of time that are free of interruptive notifications. Such practices permit us to harness our full cognitive resources and immerse ourselves in our work without the threat of interruption, at least from electronic communication and smartphone alerts (avoiding interruption from other humans is another challenge entirely).

When it comes to communal activities in our work and learning environment a necessary step is to eliminate smart devices from meeting rooms and the classroom as far as possible. The effectiveness of this intervention has been demonstrated in a university setting, where instituting a smartphone ban in the classroom led to measureable improvements in academic performance and scores on important examinations [247]. If laptop computers or tablet devices are to be used for taking notes during meetings or lectures, it should be mandated that they are switched to offline mode for the duration.

There is also an apparent need for strategies that enable us to be more intentional in how we use mobile digital technology within our home environment. A simple but powerful practice that is an important step in this direction involves resisting the urge to engage with our smart device immediately upon waking up in the morning so that we spend some time immersed in the real world before we go online. Just as with our working environment, devices should be offline and kept away from where we are and whatever we are attending to. If this strategy has merit for our work, it follows we should similarly adopt the approach of creating protected time spent offline in our personal lives. For instance, during evenings and weekends we might take steps to restrict access or at least switch devices to flight mode for extended periods to safeguard the quality of time spent with friends and family.

Another important measure to enhance both our in-person interactions and our general wellbeing is to regulate our use of social networking sites. If we choose to engage with social media, then it is best we do so in a more intentional and active manner, in the interests of our mental health and wellbeing. There are benefits to social media use for many professions, can be a great tool to support and facilitate offline social activities in our personal lives. Equally, using these platforms with greater purpose will allow us to enjoy the benefits whilst avoiding the downsides of mindlessly scrolling and subjecting ourselves to the distorted view of reality and fabricated versions of the lives of others that tend to be displayed on these platforms.

Finally, despite the versatility of digital media, print media still have a role to play for both learning and leisure. When seeking to read for comprehension or to process the information more deeply, there remains advantages in reading hard copy. This applies both to how we consume nonfiction materials and our reading for pleasure. Despite the convenience of e-books, paperback books are here to stay. So feel free to enjoy this book in both print and electronic format!

TO SUM UP...

Smart devices and mobile technology are without doubt incredible tools that provide us with unprecedented processing capacity and access to resources and information. Given the continuing rapid advances in both the functionality and availability of this technology it seems natural that there would be a lag period as we figure out how best to engage with it. Nevertheless, in the interim the tendency has been for our behaviour to be led by the technology rather than the other way around.

There is however a growing realisation that the wealth of online resources that we now have available at our fingertips inevitably comes at a cost. The evidence is accumulating to suggest that over time these effects might be causing deficits in our own capacities and capabilities when it comes to navigating the real world and our offline interactions with other humans. The capability this technology provides us clearly supplements and augments our human capabilities. Equally, over-reliance on these tools may conceivably displace and diminish our cognitive faculties, not least the meta-abilities that are so critical to human performance. By extension the availability and pervasive use of these tools throughout childhood and adolescence is conceivably disrupting development, and once again it is the development of executive functions that seems most affected.

Our smart devices provide a ready means to indulge the urge to relieve any momentary boredom and seek refuge online. With such access it has become easy to lose ourselves in the virtual world. We can also speculate that this might be to the detriment of creativity: why daydream when we can go online? When we fill our spare time passively browsing social media it is also evident this has the potential to negatively affect our feelings of wellbeing.

Equally there is a need to avoid being alarmist and some of the reporting on this topic has verged on hysteria. The data on the effects of mobile technology are still emerging and so we should exercise some caution in drawing premature conclusions. That said, the preliminary evidence is certainly not positive and there is already sufficient data to give us pause. There is a legitimate need to tackle these issues and develop strategies to mitigate the potential negative impact of our growing over-reliance and misuse of the technology.

With prudent and intentional use these devices and technology remain a phenomenal resource that can enhance our professional and personal lives. However, there is a need for a reset in how we presently use these tools. Being mindful will allow us to exercise greater restraint, but more practically we need to impose some constraints on how we engage with our devices so that we can interact with online media in ways that serve us. In other words, let us press reset and adopt strategies to avoid the prospect of living our offline lives at the mercy of the technology.

REFLECTING AND CONNECTING THE DOTS...

What is your opinion? Do you feel the concerns raised about problematic smartphone use and social media are warranted?

Commentators have noted that attention spans seem to be shrinking, and the ability to apply our undivided attention to a given task is becoming more rare – is this your experience or do you think the narrative is over done?

Relating the information presented in this chapter with the meta-abilities and executive functions introduced in the preceding chapter, to what extent do you feel mobile technology is a barrier to fostering the capabilities and behaviours that underpin high performance?

How would you characterise your present use of your smartphone? Who would you say is master versus slave in your relationship with mobile technology?

Do you feel there is a tension between our online and offline lives in the present digital era?

What is the present extent of your engagement with social media? How do you feel this affects your work satisfaction and general sense of wellbeing?

Does the message about the potential for smartphones and social media use to negatively impact in-person human interactions offline resonate with you?

What are your views on the generational effect? What are your observations in relation to younger generations who are growing up as digital natives in the smartphone era?

Which of the interventions and countermeasures outlined do you feel are most likely to prove effective? What strategies do you employ to regulate your use of digital technology?

A Wake Up Call on Sleep

Sleep is essential to sustaining life. Yet the majority of us are casually dismissive when it comes to sleep. We routinely deny ourselves this most critical sustenance of our own volition. The attitudes towards sleep among high performing individuals in different realms and society in general are quite baffling. We also largely fail to make the connection between the reckless lack of care and attention we give to our sleep and the dizzying array of consequences that inevitably follow. Objectively this behaviour is bizarre and our present failure to prioritise sleep defies logic, particularly as we continue to discover how crucial sleep is to every facet of our ability to function. With this chapter we explore the myriad ways you lose when you don't snooze sufficiently.

Like other animals humans have a biological drive to sleep. Yet unlike other animals we are increasingly choosing not to heed the call. Among high powered types it has been a badge of honour to work long hours and sleep sparingly. Cool kids stay up late, just as rock and roll types rejoice that they will sleep when they're dead. Such attitudes have influenced societal norms when it comes to sleep habits. Those of us who operate in the realm of sport are far from immune from this lemming-like behaviour.

Perhaps due to our sleep-deprived state, we have been slow to connect these trends with the burgeoning public health issues that have coincided. The apparent chronic sleep shortage in modern society is a problem of our own making. Whilst this is a relatively recent phenomenon, given how lifestyles are evolving in the digital era, the declining sleep that seems to be becoming epidemic in countries like the United States may become a pandemic across the developed world given how technology is fuelling this trend.

A DAWNING REALISATION...

For athletes, coaches, and practitioners in the sporting realm sleep is not only critical to success, but is also essential to athlete health (and of course those two things are inextricably linked). The recent period has seen a growing level of recognition and a number of publications in the sports science and medicine literature on the topic of sleep. It is increasingly widely acknowledged that sleep is crucial for athletic performance, particularly in sports that rely on perception, cognition, and decision making [248]. In the wider realm of human performance increasing attention is being given to the role of sleep for tactical athletes, such as in a military setting [249]. Sleep is also finally becoming acknowledged in business and commerce, which would seem to make some sense as we move towards a knowledge based economy [250].

The consequences of failing to pay attention to sleep of course goes beyond inhibiting performance [251]. Chronic lack of sleep is implicated in the prevalence of 'human error' accidents. Increased incidence of injury is similarly associated with sleep shortage. Higher rates of illness is another price that we can expect to pay for chronic lack of sleep.

Yet amidst this greater recognition of the importance of sleep for athlete health and performance in the literature sleep remains widely neglected among performers. This is the case even at elite level [252, 253], but it is especially prevalent at youth and collegiate level [254]. Moreover, coaches and practitioners themselves seemingly fail to realise that they are not exempt [255]. The failure to prioritise sleep equally applies to those who operate in other domains beyond sport. It turns out we are all human; it follows we can expect to suffer the consequences of failing to prioritise sleep from a human performance perspective. This has a host of implications for our professional lives, relationships, and health.

I consider myself quite 'woke' when it comes to the critical importance of sleep. I had the realisation early in my undergraduate studies that if I wanted to avoid succumbing to whatever cold or flu virus was circulating the student body I needed to double down on my sleep. At the time the notion that sleep could have such a profound impact on my health and immune function was something of a life-changing revelation, so the lesson has stayed with me. Like many others I have also suffered from insomnia at various times in my adult life, which very much teaches you to appreciate sleep and the degree of impact that lack of sleep can have.

"There does not seem to be one major organ within the body, or process in the brain, that isn't optimally enhanced by sleep (and detrimentally impaired when we don't get enough)."

— Matthew Walker [256]

In the face of the ever-growing body of data in the scientific literature, supported by the pioneering efforts of Professor Matthew Walker [256] and others to bring this information into the wider consciousness, we are only now beginning to fully appreciate the extent to which sleep is essential to every part of how we function. The reader should prepare themselves for the barrage to follow.

STAYING IN THE GAME...

Studies have established that a major factor in whether athletes achieve their sporting goals is the extent to which they manage to avoid enforced absences from practice and competition due to illness or injury [257]. The links between insufficient sleep and the incidence of accidents and injuries are firmly established. For instance, a notable finding for youth athletes from the investigation by Milewski and colleagues [258] was that the adolescent athletes studied who averaged less than 8 hours' sleep reported disproportionately higher incidence of injury.

"Sleep is the universal healthcare provider"

— Matthew Walker

Sleep is part of our adaptive response to stressors. As I can personally attest to, sleep is central to immune function and our immune response to pathogens [259]. Our immune response is dampened by acute sleep loss, to the extent that getting a flu shot when short on sleep reduces the protective effect considerably [260]. Another indication of how sleep is integral to our adaptive immune response is that when we do fall ill we have a biological drive to sleep more [261]. During these times sleep serves to support the immune system in fighting the illness and restoring us to health, so naturally we crave more of it.

Just as with injury, habitual sleep patterns are directly implicated in the incidence (how many times you get sick) and severity of illness (i.e. how long you're out of action) among athletes, as with other humans [262]. An illustration of this is that if we expose participants to an active cold virus those who slept less are significantly more likely to succumb to the cold virus during the follow up period, compared to those who slept for more than 7 hours [263].

In the context of sport, sleep is central to maintaining immune function and health in athletes, both during regular training and when competing [264]. For instance, sleep is an integral part of the restoration of immune function during the recovery period following exercise [265]. A prolonged bout of demanding physical exercise leads to a transient suppression of immune system function, creating a time window in which the athlete is more susceptible to opportunistic infections [264]. Other stressors involved with competing at elite level can similarly serve to suppress immune function, which can compound the issue [266]. Against this backdrop, sleep represents the most potent weapon in the athlete's armoury to combat the effects of training and non-training stressors to support immune function and remain resistant to illness.

In other words, given that success in sport is directly linked to avoiding enforced absences due to illness and injury, and incidence of illness and injury are in turn directly linked to how much sleep athletes report, then sleep represents a major performance factor that determines an athlete's ability to be successful.

SLEEP AND HUMAN PERFORMANCE...

Physiological capacities are acutely impaired by lack of sleep. Endurance and time trial performance appear especially susceptible to these deleterious effects [251]. The acute physiological response to exercise is altered when in a sleep-deprived state, with changes in both metabolic function and autonomic nervous system responses occurring during and following a bout of training or competition [267]. Perceived exertion also tends to increase, so that the same relative intensity feels harder.

Performance capabilities over time are also compromised by chronic sleep shortage. As performers experience less of the restorative effects of sleep, including repair of tissues, the regeneration between practices and competitions is impeded [268]. The adaptive response to training is also severely impacted, negating much of the benefit that would otherwise be derived.

It is also evident that lack of sleep can adversely affect fine motor skills. Clearly this has implications for the execution of sports skills requiring a high degree of coordination and accuracy. For instance, acute sleep loss has been shown to harm serving accuracy in tennis players, so that after a poor night's sleep serving percentages were significantly poorer in the players studied [269].

Negative physiological and performance effects of acute sleep restriction are thus evident from many studies. However, the more consistent findings of negative effects are reported with chronic sleep shortage accrued over time, such as average nightly sleep duration.

"Sports requiring speed, tactical strategy, and technical skill are most sensitive to sleep duration manipulations. Furthermore, longer-term sleep manipulations are more likely than acute sleep manipulations (whether deprivation or extension) to affect athletic performance"

— Kirschen and colleagues [270]

Another way to illustrate the adverse effects of lack of sleep on performance is the significantly improved performance observed following interventions redressing the sleep debt. Implementing extended sleep over a period of days can significantly improve physical and skill performance metrics for athletes in different sports. For instance, significant improvements in field goal and free throw shooting percentages in college basketball players [271] and serving accuracy in tennis players [272] have been reported following sleep extension interventions. Even an acute intervention on the day (simply having a nap) can confer significant short-term performance benefits [273].

Various aspects of neurocognitive function are also significantly impacted by lack of sleep. Reduced function may be observed even with very mild sleep deficit of as little as an hour, particularly with susceptible individuals [274]. The degree of impairment with moderate sleep restriction is akin to being legally drunk [275]. Cognitive lapses accordingly become more frequent when sleep-deprived [276]. Psychomotor vigilance is particularly affected, even with normal variation in sleeping patterns in athletes, so that reaction times become sluggish [277] and the coupling between stimulus and response goes awry. As a result both speed and accuracy may be impaired, affecting both what response we select and how we execute the chosen action.

Higher cognitive functions are especially prone to the effects of sleep deprivation. Cognitive tasks that require more conscious attention and directed mental effort are thus highly affected [278]. With acute or chronic sleep shortage we tend to revert to autopilot, becoming less vigilant and more prone to lapses in attention. Various aspects of executive function is compromised by lack of sleep, which means that the working memory and attentional resources at our disposal are reduced. To compound the situation our ability to manage, direct, and switch attention is also impaired. All of this is particularly pertinent to student athletes, as both athletic [279] and academic performance [280] are liable to be affected.

A notable finding for those involved in human performance in all spheres is that decision making may be impaired when sleep deprived. When short of sleep we are not only less able to attend to and process relevant information, but we are also less capable of strategic thinking. Our capacity for rational thinking is also impaired in this state, owing to a combination of impaired executive function and the mood disturbance that is common when sleep deprived [276].

Each of these factors individually and collectively harms performance [270]. Case studies in elite sport suggest this is likely to be reflected in team selection, and the minutes that players get on field or on the court [256]. Professional athletes' activity on social media offers a very public indication of when they are awake late into the night (and might be better served sleeping). What should be a very real concern for athletes is the finding that professional basketball players' late night tweeting habits were associated with impaired next day game performance, observed from their game metrics on the following day [281]. With a nod to the previous chapter, this also demonstrate the role of smart devices and social media applications in driving sleep restriction and disrupted sleep patterns.

DEVELOPMENT IN CHILDREN AND TEENS...

Sleep plays a fundamental role in our development during the early years and throughout the pivotal periods of childhood and adolescence. Sleep remains integral to neuroplasticity throughout life but the function of sleep is especially crucial to brain development during infancy, childhood, and adolescence [282].

There are three main discrete categories of sleep: light NREM, deep NREM, and REM. One of the defining characteristics of REM sleep is rapid eye movement, hence this quality has been used to separate the three types, but there are other characteristics that differentiate them, including the nature of the brain waves observed [256]. We cycle through these respective stages but the relative proportion of deep NREM sleep is greater early in the night's sleep, whereas REM sleep and light NREM sleep predominates later in the sleep bout.

Young infants have a higher proportion of REM sleep than at any other time in life. During this time the ratio between NREM and REM sleep is 50:50. The distribution between NREM and REM sleep only arrives at the 80:20 split sleep seen in adulthood once we reach late adolescence. NREM and REM sleep works in combination to create, remodel, and update our neural circuitry. REM sleep is involved in building the architecture of neural circuits; NREM sleep in turn prunes the mass of circuitry laid down and organise the neural connections made.

Deep sleep (encompassing both REM and deep NREM sleep) is the driver for brain development and maturation, as well as being central to the formation of neural circuitry underpinning cognitive and motor skills. Sleep in young infants is involved in the construction and development of the cerebral cortex [282]. Development of the frontal lobe, which is instrumental to reasoning, rational thought, and critical thinking, is the final part of brain development that occurs during the latter stages of adolescence. Once again, prefrontal cortex development in adolescents is highly sensitive to both quantity and quality of sleep [282].

For student athletes the central role of sleep in how our brains develop is highly pertinent. During adolescence, when frontal lobe development takes place, there is a critical need for the deep sleep and the requisite blend of sleep components. Sleep supports the neural development that young adolescents need to navigate the increasing complexities of the world around them, including social structures and interactions with others. Both duration and quality of sleep is therefore paramount for youth athletes.

Given the integral role of sleep in brain development and neurocognitive function, the consequences of chronic sleep shortages in young people clearly extend beyond sport. Aside from sporting performance, sleep in children and adolescents also shows a direct statistical relationship with tests of IQ and scholastic performance [283]. Shorter sleep duration is associated with lower scores on general IQ and verbal IQ [284]. In another study adolescents who recorded less sleep on weekdays and weekends exhibited smaller volumes of grey matter in specific regions of the brain, and these individuals also had lower grade point averages [285].

The association between sleep and the grade point average has also been demonstrated among student athletes at collegiate level [280]. Clearly these findings are a major concern for all parties involved. What is all the more troubling is that sleep disturbances are further linked to the mental health issues that are becoming increasingly prevalent among student athletes.

INFORMATION PROCESSING AND MEMORY...

Our capacity to process and retain information is directly linked to our sleep status. As we have identified, sleep is integral to making new connections in the brain, termed *synaptogenesis*. Acquiring new information and task based knowledge is accordingly supported by sleep during adulthood as it is in childhood [286].

Acquiring new knowledge and consolidating information into memory are sleep dependent processes [287]. Sleeps supports the 'offline' learning that occurs between lessons or practices [288]. For instance, if you take a nap after a bout of learning, or sleep between consecutive practice sessions, the new memory is stronger and you have superior retention than if you had stayed awake in between [289]. Of interest to both performers and coaches is that the benefits of sleep for consolidating learning also applies to the acquisition and retention of motor memory as we will explore in the next section [290]. This consolidation of newly acquired information into memory occurs during non REM sleep [291]. Next day retention and recall is therefore correlated with the relative quantity of NREM sleep the previous night.

Another critical function that is specific to stage 2 light NREM sleep is serving to free up working memory capacity for new information [287]. The role of sleep in managing our working memory capacity means that the duration and quality of our previous night's sleep has a direct bearing on our ability to take on board new information and to acquire knowledge the following day [292].

In keeping with its role in pruning neural circuitry, NREM sleep is also central to the process of selectively retaining pertinent information and discarding what is less relevant from the masses of inputs and bytes of information we are exposed to each day. In the Information Age, this function of sleep has never been more crucial.

ACQUIRING SKILLS...

As we have noted, beyond acquiring facts and new explicit knowledge, sleep has a central role in motor skill learning [293]. This includes the implicit learning that is a major part of how we acquire language and motor skills. For instance, the quality of the sleep we receive is demonstrated to impact how able we are to acquire motor skills on successive days [294].

The acquisition, consolidation, and refinement of motor skills is thus supported by sleep. Participants demonstrate enhanced speed and accuracy measures for the motor skill being learned when practice bouts are separated by a night's sleep [290]. This effect is not observed when the same practices and assessment are undertaken without sleep between practices. It therefore appears that, rather than practice alone, it is actually practice accompanied by sleep that leads to mastery of movement skills [293].

When we allow sufficient sleep, we are effectively able to continue to work on and refine our motor skills offline. In particular it is the stage 2 NREM sleep that occurs later in the night which is implicated with this offline learning effect. Equally, REM sleep is also involved in building associations within our mental representation of the skill. REM sleep essentially allows us to divine the higher order structure that links and governs elements of complex tasks, which helps with figuring out how best to employ our skills and execute in the performance arena.

INSPIRATION AND CREATIVE SOLUTIONS...

It has long been known that sleeping on a problem serves us well. In the dream domain of REM sleep we are freed from conventions and constraints on our thinking as we mull over the problem. During sleep the mind has free rein to conceive improbable scenarios and consider the task or situation in unconventional and abstract ways.

Our executive functions and meta-abilities are particularly reliant on sleep [278]. Consistent adequate sleep on a regular basis thus brings enormous value to how we are able to think and solve problems. Sleep can directly assist the process by bringing novel insights and alternative perspectives on the problem. Sleep further supports our ability to be imaginative, providing the space for unconstrained and divergent thinking that allows us to conjure up prospective solutions.

Sleep grants us the capacity for free thinking that lends itself to creativity and the genesis of new ideas [295]. Sleep is thus a source of inspiration, which is important as in many instances the best solution is not necessarily intuitive, forcing us to look beyond the more immediately obvious alternatives.

If sleep is so integral to coming up with inspired solutions and our ability to be creative, it follows that failing to get the required amount of sleep on a consistent basis robs us of these gifts. Without sufficient sleep we can become automatons. Whilst functioning on autopilot might suffice for less cognitively demanding tasks, it is clearly not conducive to creativity and free thinking. From a human performance perspective this has implications for all those who wish to be successful, given the necessity to continually evolve and innovate in order to gain and retain a competitive edge whatever our chosen field.

BODY COMPOSITION AND DIETARY INTAKE...

When we are getting insufficient sleep we tend to alter our dietary habits and over time the effects of periodic or chronic sleep shortage can lead to adverse changes in body composition. Clearly this presents a potential performance issue for athletes and is not particularly conducive for coaches or practitioners in sport. Equally, on a much larger scale this represents a health issue for all of us.

Sleep affects both our appetite and food choices. This is mediated via the effects of lack of sleep on the hormones that direct our feeding behaviours [296, 297]. We get hungry when we are tired and sleep deprived, so we tend to eat more and in bigger portions [298]. We also crave particular types of food, driving us to disproportionately increase intake of high energy snack items and this compounds the issue.

Just as the metabolic and physiological response to exercise is altered when in a sleep-deprived state our biochemical response to feeding is also altered. In particular, our insulin response and how we regulate blood sugar quickly become impaired [299]. Following less than a week of insufficient sleep we can exhibit effects that would classify us as 'pre-diabetic'.

Sleep is thus crucial for those seeking to make positive changes in their body composition [300]. What is under recognised is the central role of sleep in regulating body mass changes, including what bodily stores this comes from. In most instances, athletes are seeking to reduce fat mass and conserve or increase lean mass. With habitual sleep shortage the opposite occurs: fat mass is conserved, so any weight that is lost is at the cost of precious lean mass [300].

MOOD AND EMOTION REGULATION...

Sleep is integral to *affective brain homeostasis*. In other words, adequate sleep provides the reset to restore both our emotional state and our capacity to handle whatever the next day might throw at us [301]. Conversely, lack of sleep adversely affects our mood and psychological state. Disrupted sleep is thus associated with mood disturbance among athletes at all levels [302, 279]. One example is that athletes' sleep duration and quality prior to competition is demonstrated to affect their mood state entering the competition [303]. The likelihood of negative affect (self-reported negative emotions such as anxiety, fear, and anger) is increased when in a sleep-deprived state, whereas positive affect (positive emotional states) is reduced [304].

Aside from mood state, our ability to control our emotional equilibrium and regulate our emotional response to external events is also impacted by sleep. The most apparent demonstration of our compromised emotional regulation when we have not had sufficient sleep is an increase in 'emotional reactivity' [305]. For instance, we are quicker to anger and other negative emotions are also triggered more easily. The knock on effects of this elevated emotional reactivity can create a vicious cycle. The greater likelihood of over-reacting increases the odds of emotional disturbance following any outburst, affecting our sleep afterwards, which in turn impacts us the following day, and so on [306].

Aside from not being much fun to be around when we are tired and irritable, the effects of lack of sleep are also likely to affect how we conduct ourselves and our effectiveness as professionals, given that cognitive function and our propensity to interact with others tends to be compromised [307]. Performers are further likely to become frustrated more easily. In a sporting context, clearly this is not conducive to learning or performing, whether in the practice environment or during competition [279]. The adverse effect of sleep on mood and emotion regulation adds to the miscellaneous stressors and renders athletes less able to handle the challenging situations that are ubiquitous in performance sport.

Happily when extended sleep opportunity is permitted (or imposed) for a week, mood scores quickly rebound and show a significant increase, as demonstrated by an investigation of female college track athletes [308]. A similar improvement in motivation as well as physical and cognitive performance was observed following an extended sleep intervention in military officer training corps recruits, when compared to their habitual sleep patterns [249]. Whilst these findings underline that our mood and mental state are dragged down under the weight of insufficient sleep, the positive news is that this can be lifted when we make the decision to prioritise our sleep and make the necessary changes to our schedule and behaviour.

SOCIAL AND EMOTIONAL INTELLIGENCE...

As sleep is integral to our emotional fitness, it follows that sleep is central to our ability to not only develop but also to demonstrate social and emotional intelligence. Our emotional faculties and the ability to read and respond to social cues contribute to our ability to navigate social interactions, and each of these aspects is linked to sleep status [307].

Lack of sleep conversely impacts how we view the world and perceive the actions of those around us. As an example, sleep status affects our acuity in detecting non-verbal cues, such as body language and facial expression. We are considerably less accurate in how we interpret and differentiate between different expressions and gestures when short on sleep [307]. Not only are we more likely to misinterpret these social cues, but also more inclined to perceive them as hostile.

There is some evidence that those who report habitually sleeping longer also have higher frontal cortex grey matter volume; and they also rate higher on emotional intelligence, with lower self-reported mental health issues [309]. A related finding is that sleep habits among adolescents appear correlated with measures of brain development, with reduced grey matter volumes observed in different regions of the brain among those who reported less habitual sleep on weekdays and weekends [285]. The specific regions affected are those we have highlighted as being integral to emotional intelligence and functioning in social environments.

Both in our professional and personal lives, sleep can impact our ability to successfully navigate interpersonal relationships. For professions that rely on human interaction it follows that the role of sleep can be decisive. This is especially the case for leadership positions and those engaged in people management roles at all levels. For instance, it is demonstrated that leaders and managers who report shorter duration and poor sleep quality score lower on ratings of interpersonal effectiveness, as rated by those staff who directly report to them [310]. This may in part be due to the impact of lack of sleep for us to express ourselves effectively, both verbally and nonverbally [307].

In a sport performance context, whether we are an athlete, coach, or practitioner, the impact of sleep on our social capabilities has a host of implications. Successful performers know it takes a village to sustain performing at the highest level. Even in individual sports, athletes still rely on the integrated support provided by dedicated service providers and practitioners across various disciplines. The ability of an athlete to foster and maintain good relationships with those who support them on the journey is accordingly paramount. Clearly in a team sports context the social dynamics between the players and with the respective members of the coaching and support staff are absolutely critical to team success. The effect of sleep status on personal relationships beyond the practice and competition environment similarly have a major bearing on the global stress and wellbeing of the performer, impacting performance in the short term and ultimately their odds of burnout in the long term.

MENTAL HEALTH AND WELLBEING...

In view of the integral role of sleep in brain development in general and the brain regions associated with emotion and social functioning in particular, it follows that both chronic and acute sleep patterns have a huge bearing on the emotional disturbance we experience [301]. Sleep exerts a major influence on our mental health and wellbeing, through its impact upon our emotional state, our interpersonal relationships, and the associated stresses we experience [307]. Stress and sleep exhibit a bi-directional relationship: daily stress tends to affect the subsequent night's sleep and lack of sleep serves to elevate the stress we experience day-to-day [311].

Aside from being a source of stress, lack of sleep further impacts our coping resources to deal with that stress. Sleep plays a direct role in how we process emotions [301] to the extent that some authors have characterised sleep as 'overnight therapy' [312]. Both sleep duration and quality are thus integral to emotional resiliency and our faculties for coping. Sufficient sleep, and REM sleep in particular, is crucial to providing the nightly emotional reset to cope with daily events [301]. Dealing with events that have befallen us in the dream domain effectively helps take the emotional sting out of what has happened and readies us for future challenges [313].

Once again, this relationship between sleep and coping is bi-directional. Those who possess greater resiliency and coping faculties find their sleep is less impacted by emotional disturbances prompted by external events and outside actors. Conversely, shorter habitual sleep durations are negatively related to measures of 'resilient coping' in response to adversity [314].

As described in relation to mood, sleep status affects our feelings of wellbeing. Chronic sleep shortage tends to instil a general sense of malaise. The world appears a less appealing place when we are short on sleep. Positive events may not bring the same joy as we labour under the effects of sleep deprivation; this is termed *anhedonia* and is symptomatic of depression. To compound this, we are more likely to perceive the actions of others as hostile or provocative.

It is not hyperbole to assert that REM sleep is crucial for our sanity. Impaired duration and quality of sleep over time has 'pathopsychological' implications with respect to our mental health and incidence of mental illness. In severe cases chronic sleep disturbance can lead to psychosis. Whilst this might seem extreme, what this underlines is the seriousness of the impact that sleep can have on our mental health. It is crucial we recognise that sleep is a likely factor in the rising incidence of mental illness. A nationwide study identified that self-reported insomnia was a consistent predictor of suicide ideation [315]. Similar findings are reported in student athletes (and non-athletes); both insufficient sleep duration and symptoms of insomnia were found to be independent predictors of reported suicide ideation in the college students studied [316].

CHRONIC DISEASE AND LONGEVITY...

Sleep is essential to sustaining life and as such sleep behaviours are directly linked to all-cause mortality [317]. In plain terms, depriving ourselves of sufficient sleep will shorten our life expectancy and negatively impact the quality of life we do have. Total lack of sleep for a sustained and prolonged period will in fact kill you as surely as a lack of food, and in roughly the same amount of time.

Earlier in the chapter we noted that disrupted sleep makes us more susceptible to opportunistic minor infections. Habitual sleep is further linked to the incidence of major illness and conditions that shorten our life span and impact our quality of life. Sleep is integral to supporting our innate immune function. As demonstrated by immunisation studies, sleep is also essential to our acquired immunity and the adaptive immune response that follows exposure to pathogens [317].

Lack of sleep shows an association with inflammation, and being central to how we regulate and direct our immune response sleep is thus implicated in the risk of inflammatory conditions. Chronic lack of sleep is linked to both compromised immune responses on the one hand and autoimmune conditions, whereby the immune response attacks healthy host cells, on the other [317].

Sleep represents a major, albeit modifiable, lifestyle risk factor for a host of chronic diseases. Not least due to the effect of sleep on insulin resistance and biochemical response to feeding, sleep shortage is linked with the 'Metabolic Syndrome' that includes diabetes, obesity, and heart disease [318]. Ongoing deficits in duration and quality of sleep likewise tends to elicit a chronic state of low grade inflammation, and so sleep is implicated in chronic diseases with an inflammatory component [259]. Sleep is further linked with the risk of developing different forms of cancer, as well as the survival rates of cancer patients [317].

Finally, sleep seems to play a major role in brain health and cognitive decline with age. Both quantify and quality of sleep are identified as mediating factors for the onset and progression of neurodegenerative conditions, such as Alzheimer's. Sleep disturbance is implicated as a co-factor contributing to the incidence of all-cause dementia and is specifically linked to the amyloid formation and aggregation within the brain that occurs with Alzheimer's disease [319].

LOGISTICAL CHALLENGES AND PRACTICAL COUNTERMEASURES...

Clearly there are logistical challenges and practical obstacles to getting the sleep we need on a consistent basis. Equally, we now also have a greater appreciation of what is at stake. By first identifying likely obstacles we can devise appropriate strategies and countermeasures. Furthermore, we can take pre-emptive steps to come up with contingency plans for when things go awry.

In professional sports, many athletes (and support staff) have to contend with demanding and highly variable competition schedules involving extensive travel, in some instances across time zones. The scheduling of training and practice sessions is similarly a constraint on daily sleep patterns in many sports [320]. This is a prevalent issue in sports such as swimming that favour early morning practices [321] partly as a result of the conventions in the sport, but also due to logistics of facility access.

Scheduling and related logistics are likewise a common issue at sub-elite and youth level, given the need to fit training and practices around work and school schedules. A notable example is the practice and academic schedules imposed on high school student athletes particularly. In many cases, high school athletes are required to attend early morning practices and then train again in the evening; naturally this leads young athletes to stay up late simply to get their homework done. The logistics of the situation thus present major obstacles to getting the duration and quality of sleep that is so crucial for student athletes during adolescence particularly.

Work schedules and the demands of travel are clearly not limited to the realm of sport; performers in all domains will face these obstacles from time to time. Despite the logistical challenges and notwithstanding unavoidable periodic interruptions, it remains critical to maintain a consistent sleep schedule as far as possible. Maintaining a routine serves to support the regularity of the circadian rhythms that drive both the onset of sleep and sleep quality. Consistent daily wake-sleep cycles are similarly important to support the biological processes that accompany our normal circadian rhythms. Aside from maintaining regular patterns, adopting an effective sleep schedule clearly also means allowing adequate time to receive the hours of sleep we require. For many of us, this means adjusting to the reality of an earlier bedtime.

Whilst we should strive to adhere to a consistent sleep schedule as far as possible, inevitably there will be periodic disruptions to our normal schedule due to travel, work, and life commitments. During these times it is important to remain mindful of minimising the disruption to our circadian rhythms. However, beyond circadian factors, we also need to account for the fact that we have a homeostatic drive to sleep. Essentially this means we should aim to address any sleep debt incurred in a timely fashion. Whilst we may not be able to ensure the recommended number of hours' sleep every night, we can nevertheless adapt what we do to ensure that the cumulative total sleep time we receive over the period of a week averages out to the required nightly amount.

Opportunities for sleep extension (i.e. more than our usual sleep allocation) over a period of days and napping are two practical ways to correct the sleep deficit for performers [322]. Clearly we do need to do this in a way that avoids compromising our normal sleep to ensure have a net gain in the sleep we receive. Whilst it can provide a short term improvement in our cognitive, physiological and motor performance when we are sleep deprived [273], napping can be problematic from this viewpoint as it may impact the subsequent night's sleep.

In the sporting realm, it is consistently reported that athletes' sleep is often disrupted the night after competing [253]. This is particularly the case following evening competitions, in part due to having to come down from the psychological and physiological arousal elicited when competing. For similar reasons, it has been suggested that training in the evening should be avoided. Interestingly the data do not seem to support this, with the exception of 'highly vigorous exercise very close to bedtime' [323].

One lifestyle and diet factor that athletes and non-athletes alike should pay attention to is the use of stimulants and caffeine intake, particularly later in the day. Caffeine directly blocks adenosine which regulates our drive to sleep. Caffeine also has an extended *half-life* (the time it takes to reduce by half), so significant concentrations can remain in our system some hours after consuming a caffeine-containing food or beverage. Recognising that caffeine directly interferes with sleep, a fairly straightforward step to address the issue for athletes and the rest of us would be to restrict our intake of caffeine (and other stimulants) later in the day.

This recommendation is clearly at odds with the increasingly popular convention of taking 'pre-workout' supplements containing stimulants such as caffeine prior to training, particularly when training later in the day and evening practices. Many athletes use caffeine as an ergogenic aid when competing; however, any benefit needs to be weighed against the reported contribution of caffeine use prior to evening competitions to the difficulty falling asleep and impaired sleep quality among athletes [324].

The commonly reported finding of disrupted sleep prior to competition [303] illustrates that our ruminations and anxious thoughts have the potential to impact both duration and quality of sleep, and this similarly applies to non-sport related stressors. Just as the anticipation of an important match and completion can affect an athlete's sleep, we might experience something similar during the days leading up to work and life events we deem to be important. Clearly our thoughts, ruminations, and anxieties are something that we need to manage in order avoid sleepless (or sleep-disturbed) nights. This is the case with athletes and those who work in sport, but applies more generally to performers in all realms.

Sleep hygiene is integral to our efforts when seeking to enhance sleep duration and quality. It is important to respect the sanctity of the space we use to rest and sleep. To that end we should aim for a dark and quiet environment without distractions (and banishing electronic devices to another room during the hours of sleep). Temperature is another factor we need to account for. Our core temperature drops during sleep, so it follows we should seek to ensure the ambient temperature in the bedroom is not too warm and take steps to help reduce our core temperature prior to going to bed.

Technology has become a major factor from a sleep hygiene perspective. As we have explored, mobile digital technology represents a highly potent source of distraction and prevarication and so use of these devices often delays going to bed. Screen time, particularly later in the evening, is linked to increased sleep latency (that is, it takes longer to fall asleep) and decreased sleep quality among athletes [325]. And as we have noted, late night social media use impacts performance for athletes even at the highest levels. For the many who admit to continuing to use their smartphone after the lights have gone out, clearly such behaviour is also not conducive to falling asleep. All of this helps to explain how performers frequently fail to get sufficient sleep even when their schedule permits adequate opportunity to do so.

Beyond the stimulation, part of the reason that digital technology disrupts our sleep is simply due to blue light exposure from these devices. This extends to our light exposure in general during the evening. From an evolutionary perspective, daylight and darkness are naturally major drivers that govern our wake-sleep cycles. Modern devices and ambient light exposure can disrupt this, purely by exposing us to excessive light. Once again, ensuring our sleep environment is fully dark is one important factor, but we should also attempt to minimise our light exposure and blue light exposure in particular, during the hours prior to bedtime.

Bringing all this together, we can institute a pre-bedtime routine that avoids exposure to stress and other stimuli as far as possible later in the evening. In part this involves being strict in regulating our use of electronic devices. Other measures to wind down and support relaxation can also help quieten our thoughts and reduce any feelings of anxiety, particularly during the interval prior to bedtime. We can further account for thermal aspects, notably the ambient temperature of the room(s) where we are spending time prior to bed and we might consider other measures to help lower our core temperature in preparation for bedtime. Cold water immersion following training and competition is one intervention that has been employed with athletes, but the findings with respect to sleep duration and quality are equivocal [326]. A shower before bedtime is arguably a more practical measure that can shorten the time it takes to drop off to sleep, as has been demonstrated with youth team sports players [327].

IN CLOSING…

Sleep is essential for all humans but particularly those who seek to push the boundaries of human endeavour. As we have explored, failing to prioritise this most vital source of sustenance for our mind and bodies impacts our ability to function in every part of our daily life. As noted throughout the chapter, this has numerous implications for athletes (and coaches) in performance sport. However, these considerations equally apply to leaders in business, knowledge workers, professionals engaged in human performance across all domains.

Humility is likely to be required for the reader as you evaluate your present situation and consider what action might be necessary. This is particularly the case for those of us (including myself) who are more susceptible to the effects of sleep disturbance. There is some degree of individual variation in the amount of sleep we require and also the degree to which we are affected by acute (short term) lack of sleep. However, despite the claims of many to the contrary, the section of the population who can remain effective (and healthy) on less than five hours sleep is minuscule.

For the vast majority of us the recommended 7-8 hours for adults applies universally. And once again, for athletes and others who engage in regular intensive training, the minimum to support health and performance is higher than this, with estimates of 9-10 hours for competitive athletes not uncommon [322]. This disparity emphasises the degree of the correction required for those athletes who report failing to get 7 hours on a consistent basis [253].

The current picture is particularly troubling for young people. It is evident that vast numbers of children and adolescents people are presently falling far short of the recommended minima to support their development and what is required to support their physical and mental health. In a large part the shortfall is simply due to lifestyle factors. Unless we are able to address these issues and successfully modify behaviours, there is the distinct possibility of severe public health issues and other adverse consequences that will plague an entire generation.

Hopefully the information presented in this chapter serves as a 'wake-up' call (pun intended) and helps to provide the impetus to take action and make lasting changes.

REFLECTING AND CONNECTING THE DOTS...

How would you rate your sleep? Based on the information presented and your own experience do you think you generally get enough?

Would you say you are particularly susceptible to the effects of sleep?

How does lack of sleep typically affect your ability to perform at work or life in general?

Have you experienced insomnia at any point in your life? How did this impact your ability to function?

To what extent have you previously considered the role of sleep in relation to human performance?

When you recall a personal experience of training or preparing for an event, to what extent did you consider sleep in supporting the endeavour?

Have you experienced periods where you were particularly prone to illness that you can retrospectively link to sleep and related lifestyle factors?

Have you observed (or been party to) accidents or injuries at work or at home that you can trace back to being sleep deprived?

Can you relate to the information in the chapter on sleep and neurocognitive function? Would you say your short term memory, capacity for thinking, or ability to concentrate are impacted by sleep?

Were you aware of the role of sleep in memory, learning, and skill acquisition? What implications might this have, and how might you alter your approach in view of this information?

Are you a parent or do you have young family members? Are you concerned at all about sleep and related lifestyle factors, based on the information presented on how inadequate sleep may affect development during childhood and adolescence?

Do you find sleep affects your mood and ability to regulate your emotional response? Does this impact your relations with others?

Are you better at remaining patient with others after a good night's sleep? Do you find that you are more irritable or less rational after a poor night's sleep?

What obstacles and challenges do you face in attempting to keep a consistent sleep schedule from a work and life point of view?

What practical countermeasures could you employ to mitigate these barriers?

Do you make use of contingency measures after disrupted sleep, such as sleep extension or napping?

How would you rate your 'sleep hygiene', based on the information presented?

Are there changes you would consider making from a sleep hygiene perspective, such as restricting screen time or alterations to the bedroom environment?

Do you currently employ any practices in your pre-bedtime routine to unwind or help you fall asleep when you go to bed? Would you consider implementing any changes or adopting a new routine?

What lifestyle and dietary changes (such as restricting caffeine intake) would you consider, based on the information presented?

What were the major insights or key messages from this chapter that you would share with colleagues, friends and family?

Marshalling the Mind Under Stress

High stakes and heightened emotions are characteristic of competition; and both the stakes and the accompanying emotions are correspondingly higher at the top level. For those who operate in elite and professional sport the presence of stress seems ubiquitous. Coaches and athletes alike regularly face high pressure scenarios where there is a great deal of expectation and much riding on the outcome. Anticipation of an important event such as a big game, major competition, or selection trials naturally inspire a host of feelings, thoughts, and emotions ranging from excitement to anxiety and even dread, sometimes simultaneously! These elements are likewise a feature of human performance environments beyond the realm of sport. In this chapter we explore how we can equip ourselves to meet the psychological and emotional challenges that high performers inevitably face on the journey.

REVELATION: HIGH PERFORMERS ARE NOT IMMUNE TO STRESS AND ANXIETY...

There is a longstanding myth that elite athletes (and coaches) are somehow a different breed of human that is immune to stress and not troubled by doubt and anxiety as other mortals are. Over the recent period high profile athletes have shared their personal battles with mental health issues, which has gone some way to dispelling these myths and reducing the stigma. Athletes are certainly more open about sharing their experiences and happily mental health is no longer the taboo topic it once was.

Despite such positive developments unhelpful attitudes still persist among performers, coaches, and leaders in sport and other realms. Somehow we have retained the impression that as a high performer we should be above such petty anxieties and doubts. The imaginary archetype of a high performing athlete or coach that many still hold in their heads is not prone to such human failings. Once again, these issues are not restricted to sport and many individuals in different realms of human performance face similar battles with such misconceptions.

Due in part to these enduring attitudes and stereotypes we often assume that others do not grapple with the same negative thoughts or feel the anxiety that we do. Often these perceptions are reinforced by the show that performers put on for their peers' benefit. Such misapprehensions compound the nerves that we all feel periodically. Our thoughts and judgements that we are somehow not meant to be affected in this way ironically represent a significant source of anxiety.

On an individual level, it is true that different athletes and coaches are affected to varying degrees. Those of us who have a dispositional tendency towards introspection may also have a stronger response to outside events. *Perceived stress reactivity* is increasingly considered as a disposition-related variable with regards to individual performance and coping with competition-related stressors [328]. Personality traits have also been studied in relation to individual susceptibility to the debilitating effects of performance anxiety [329] and conversely how resilient performers are to competition related stress. The terms 'trait-' and 'state-anxiety' describe how certain personality types may be more prone to anxiety.

Elite sport or any competitive endeavour at the highest level constitutes a high stress environment. In such circumstances seems eminently natural and entirely understandable that we will feel nervous or anxious from time to time. Objectively it is somewhat baffling that athletes and coaches respond to such feelings with adverse thoughts and judgements. Perception is hugely powerful, a theme which will recur often in this chapter. This certainly applies to our expectations of the degree to which we should be affected by stress, what thoughts we are supposed to have, and how we are meant to feel in particular scenarios.

STRESS AND PERFORMANCE...

Leaving personality traits aside, how we respond to stress remains highly individual. Beyond our state at a given time, our response to a stressor likewise remains highly changeable, as it depends not only on the circumstances but also how we frame whatever scenario that we are facing [330]. The statement 'affected by nerves' is generally construed as negatively impacting how an athlete performs on the occasion. In reality the impact of conditions of stress on performance may be negative, neutral, or positive [331]. In the same way, how we respond to anxiety can serve us in a positive way, have a neutral effect (i.e. no impact), or negatively affect how we perform.

Aside from the physiological response and how it impacts our performance in the moment, there are also structural and behavioural adaptations that follow episodes of stress. A stressor is after all simply a stimulus that shapes how we interact with our environment and respond to external events. The nature of these changes, and whether the net effect is adaptive or maladaptive, does however depend on factors such as the duration of the stressor. Whilst this might be outside of our control there are other factors that are within our power to influence, such as our perception and how we interpret whatever events or circumstances we encounter.

For the purposes of the discussion we should also differentiate between *acute stress* that occurs in response to the situation at hand and is transient or short-lasting, versus *chronic stress*, which is sustained over an extended period. The short-term stress response provides the mechanism by which we can elevate our performance capabilities and our preparedness for future stressors [332]. In contrast, chronic stress is typically associated with maladaptation and compromised performance, manifested both directly and through adverse effects health, motivation, and altered behaviour.

Coming through the trials of youth level competition to some degree prompts young performers to figure out ways to manage acute stress and anxiety as they attempt to mitigate the negative impact on their performance. Once they reach higher tiers of competition performers have generally cobbled together some countermeasures and coping strategies. For the most part, this is a problem-solving process that relies upon trial and error, and it is largely an independent endeavour.

The present Darwinian process of natural selection is far from perfect and it is clearly a daunting task for young people who are finding their way in the world (not least given their brains are not yet fully formed). Failing to independently figure out the puzzle of dealing with stress and performing under pressure is a reason that so many young performers fail to fulfil their potential. This is even identified as a reason that many young athletes drop out from participating in their chosen sport prematurely [328].

It is typically only when athletes arrive at elite level as a senior athlete that they encounter sport psychologists or mental skills coaches and even at this stage access to specialist support is far from assured. Whilst things are becoming more evolved, there is still relatively little consideration for how we might help athletes (or coaches) to cope with chronic stress and anxiety from a performance and health viewpoint. Whilst this question is arguably not adequately addressed in sport, in other realms of human performance there is often no provision whatsoever. The majority of individuals who aspire to operate the highest level in their chosen domain presently have to figure this out on their own.

Stress is an integral and necessary part of life. Equally, how we appraise and respond to stressors has a major bearing both on performance in the short term and how we cope with conditions of stress to sustain performing over time. This has important implications: if we can arm ourselves with the necessary understanding it should be possible to modify how we respond and adapt to stressors. For performers in all domains there is a great deal of opportunity to take greater command of the process. We can learn to engage with stressors in a way that is more conducive to performing over the long term, and in doing so guard against the potential negative health and performance consequences of chronic stress [333].

‘FLOW’, ‘CLUTCH’, AND ‘CHOKING’...

Flow state is characterised as spontaneous and fleeting, albeit authors have started to investigate how we might go about ‘hacking’ flow or triggering these states [334]. In contrast, what is termed *clutch performance* is more purposeful, as it pertains to elevating performance at a very specific crunch time. Whereas flow is characterised as effortless and 'letting it happen', clutch performance is described in terms of 'making it happen' [335].

Clutch performance is arguably more relevant to performing under pressure, as it specifically relates to elevating performance when it matters, with all the attendant pressure on the outcome and weight of expectation this entails. In the context of sport clutch performance is described as an act of effortful focus, whereby the athlete enlists their full mental resources in order to perform at the crucial moment [179]. At present we typically do little to help performers acquire the capability for clutch performance, beyond exposing them to pressure conditions and hoping they will figure it out.

For performers who would like to acquire the superpower of clutch performance, there are however a few helpful leads. For instance, managing inner dialogue would appear hugely important to this endeavour, given the scope for negative thoughts and judgements to distract and take up precious mental resources. Perceiving that we have some degree of control over the situation is also cited as a facilitator of clutch performance [179]. This presents something of a circular challenge. To some degree we need to experience successfully executing clutch performances in order to gain confidence and a feeling of control when we step up to perform under pressure, yet having confidence appears somewhat necessary in order to exhibit clutch performance in the first instance.

Returning to perception, there is also a need to address the stigma attached to occasions where we might demonstrate such human frailties as being negatively affected by the pressure. *Choking* is the term commonly used to describe the scenario where performance is impaired under pressure, so that conditions of stress negatively impact execution [336]. The term is used widely both in the scientific literature and among commentators and sports fans. The label of choking represents a huge problem given the negative connotations and naturally this presents an added source of anxiety for performers. Being saddled with this label and having to deal with the attendant psychological baggage is clearly not conducive to approaching future scenarios involving performance pressure with a feeling of control or confidence.

THE ROLE OF COGNITION...

The thoughts that occupy our minds profoundly influence how we feel, and in a circular fashion how we feel influences how we think. In a human performance context, what goes on within our own mind affects other processes within our body. Our thoughts or 'cognitions' influence our emotional state and this is manifested physically in our body, which in turn has a cascade of effects that affect our brain chemistry, physiology, autonomic nervous system activity, and even immune function.

The impact of cognition and emotion on our physiological has a host of implications for athletes, not only in the context of performing in competition but also in relation to regular training. For instance, the physiological and stress hormone response to both performance stress and training is affected by the individual's mindset going into a training session [58]. Measures of life stress similarly affect how individuals recover following a workout, both in the hours [337] and days that follow [338]. What is going on in the mind of the athlete thus impacts how they are able to tolerate training and how they engage with practices. What psychosocial stressors athletes are exposed to and how they are handled by the individual further affects their risk of illness and injury [339].

Cognition encompasses our internal representations of the outside world and how we appraise other individuals and interpret whatever situations we encounter. Cognition is also central to our sense of self; this includes how we think about ourselves in general and in relation to others. We bring this perception of ourselves to the different scenarios and external events we encounter.

Cognition further concerns our conscious thoughts and the tacit knowledge that we acquire through learning and experience. As prior experiences shape our cognitions, the downstream effects of preceding events thus influence how we engage with whatever stressors we subsequently encounter and how we behave in response.

Why all of this is important is that our cognitions represent the key to our perceived coping abilities. It bears repeating that our cognitions go a long way to determining how we appraise and process the myriad stressors and different situations we face [330]. If we have some degree of confidence in our ability to cope, we tend to engage with the same stressors in a very different way [340].

Athletes (and coaches) will periodically find themselves in a negative head space, particularly when the circumstances are trying. For instance, periods of poor physical health can negatively impact mental health (and vice versa). Extended periods when the athlete is unable to participate in practice and competition due to injury or illness offer an illustrative example [341]. It is not uncommon for injured athletes to report symptoms of depression and other mental health issues [342].

Given that such trials are a feature of most athletic careers, it follows that we should do our best to help equip athletes with appropriate *athlete life skills*, including tools and coping strategies to cope with the myriad stressors that high level sport entails. *Cognitive-behavioural* stress management interventions have been investigated with athletes to help them better cope with the various stressors they face, such periods of illness and injury [341]. Studies have similarly explored these tools to help performers better cope with organisational stressors and group dynamics [343]. There has been some preliminary investigation of these themes for leaders and coaches in sport [344], including coaching performance under pressure [345] and stress management for sport coaches [346]. Whilst this is given less attention, the need to develop appropriate coping skills and stress management strategies extends to practitioners and professionals in all realms of human performance.

Given the propensity of the mind to shape what we feel in our bodies and the power of perception in shaping our thoughts and how we experience the sensations we feel, it follows that our cognitive processes are a key part of the solution. In essence, our cognitions represent the route by which we can unlock the puzzle of how we can better engage with and respond to the stressors we encounter in our environment and through our interactions with others. If we can become more rational (or at least less irrational) in how we appraise and interpret both external events and what is occurring in our own mind and body, we should be able to exert some influence over how these things affect us.

SCOPE OF PRACTICE...

On a personal and professional level I am leery of labels; however, for the purposes of this discussion, let us for now call me a performance coach. Beyond the physical and athletic preparation process, performing in competition has a significant mental component. The psychological and emotional aspects encompassed in the mental game can profoundly affect the athlete's expression of the physical and athletic qualities we have sought to develop. On that basis, it would seem highly remiss to neglect such portentous performance factors.

On a more fundamental level, I do not simply coach athletes; I coach humans who happen to be athletes. An integral part of working with humans is gaining an appreciation of how different individuals think and becoming attuned to their emotional state. For leaders and coaches in sport (and other realms of human performance) a command of subjects such as cognition and emotion should be considered a prerequisite, in the same way as knowledge in physiology or motor learning. Effecting a positive change in thinking habits and associated behaviours requires a deep knowledge and understanding in these areas. There is a need to understand both the human concerned and the complexities of mental performance if we are to guide the performer towards cognitive strategies that better serve them.

That apart, I am not only a coach of humans but also a human myself. As a human coach of humans, my effectiveness is contingent on the success of my interactions with others (particularly the athlete); hence the need to be highly cognisant of my own cognitions and emotions, particularly with regard to my conduct towards others. As with athletes, being successful as a coach requires that I am attuned to my own habits of thinking and emotional state, so that I am able to exercise the necessary vigilance to self-regulate in real-time and avoid costly missteps. These are essential qualities that require our continual attention as leaders and managers of people in our respective realms; and this equally applies to any profession that requires successful interaction with other humans.

That said, an important caveat is that whilst as coaches we might be best placed to offer early support to help performers to equip themselves, it is critical that we recognise and respect the limits of what we are equipped and qualified to deal with. When there is any indication of a need for clinical intervention or counselling, we must be ready to refer to a mental health specialist. To that end, it is important that we have an established referral pathway and protocol under the direction of a medical professional. Such instances would include suspected clinical depression and other conditions, such as eating disorders.

THE ILLUSIONS WE CREATE IN OUR MINDS...

It has been identified that performers' efforts under high stress conditions are often impeded by their own irrational beliefs in relation to the situation [347]. Our cognitions are very powerful in shaping our subjective reality and how we perceive things in the moment. These fabrications constructed from our thoughts and reasoning are given depth by the emotions they create. The underpinning cognitions do not need to reflect objective reality in order for what we construct in our mind to seem and feel very real.

On occasion the illusions and subjective reality we create in our minds does not serve us and can actively sabotage our efforts. Studies cite 'irrational beliefs' as a factor contributing to negative performance effects under stress [347] and as a cause for negative stress and adverse mental health outcomes [348]. Steps of illogic and warped perceptions of events and circumstances are part of the *cognitive distortions* that create unhelpful illusions and adversely affect the mindset of the performer.

What compounds the issue is that these illusions generate their own reinforcing thoughts and feelings. These influences can shape our internal representation of the situation and even how we view the world and ourselves. Irrespective of the objective reality, the fabrications we conjure in our minds can nevertheless have a very real bearing on how we perceive things and our emotional state. The feelings that we experience as a result are no less tangible, irrespective the fact that the underlying thoughts and reasoning may have no rational basis.

INCAPACITATING EFFECTS OF A NEGATIVE HEAD SPACE...

Given the propensity for our cognitions to shape our subjective reality, it is easy to fall prey to the beguiling influence of our own thoughts. We are all human and as such we all feel less than rosy about the world from time to time. The bigger danger is that once we find ourselves in a negative head space we are not always able to break out of it. When we become trapped in this cycle it can be incredibly debilitating, so that descriptions such as 'crippling anxiety' can seem apt.

An example of how this scenario might play out: at the outset, the prospect of the challenge we are facing may conjure doubts and troubling thoughts, eliciting associated feelings of dread and anxiety. The mere fact that we are having such thoughts and feelings may in turn provoke negative judgements; this can serve to further taint our subjective view of both ourselves and the task that faces us.

The effect on our perspective when we are in a negative head space has been likened to looking through binoculars [349]. In the one hand, our view of what we are facing can become magnified out of all proportion, whereas our view of ourselves is distorted as if we are looking through the opposite end of the binoculars.

A negative head space hereby adversely affects how we evaluate our own capabilities, particularly when we have blown the size of the challenge out of all proportion. When the challenge we face appears so daunting in our minds naturally this can affect our resolve. The magnitude of the task we face can loom so large that the odds of a successful outcome seem small. Against such apparently overwhelming odds our motivation to address the situation is thus impacted as our prospects can appear somewhat hopeless, leading to a sense of apathy.

On a practical level, our distorted thinking and somewhat irrational judgements on the situation also present a barrier to actually getting a handle on the problem. In this head space it becomes hard to know where to start. Without a realistic or objective evaluation it is naturally difficult to break down what we need to address in order to come up with actionable steps towards a solution. As the prospect inspires a level of aversion, there is consequently a tendency to defer the task or employ avoidance tactics.

DOWNWARD SPIRAL...

Once we find ourselves in a negative head space there are various forces that can make it difficult to climb back out. For instance, at these times we can become withdrawn, particularly in the face of negative outcomes. This only compounds the issue, as it reduces the opportunity to receive external input that might give us the perspective to lift our mood. The tendency towards introspection just dials up the volume and saturates our exposure to the distortions provided by our internal commentary, with less and less contrasting input to counterbalance it. As we withdraw into our own heads and isolate ourselves from others this also robs us of the in-person interaction we thrive on as social animals, which likewise contributes to the negative cascade.

Self-defeating thoughts have the potential to elicit self-defeating emotions and inspire self-defeating behaviours. In turn, this serves to generate further self-defeating thoughts, so that the cycle has a tendency to repeat. With each cycle the downward spiral gains strength, providing confirming evidence so that our negative judgements and pessimistic attitudes appear increasingly valid.

As the reader might appreciate, there is often a strange circular logic at play in our internal dialogue: I suspect that I am going to fail; this thought triggers negative feelings and in this negative emotional state my belief that I am going to fail starts to seem more real and believable. These growing doubts and attendant negative beliefs then sabotage my preparation and undermine my efforts when I come to perform, causing me to fail to execute to my potential when the time comes. All of which seems to confirm that I was correct in thinking I would fail. I take from the experience that I can expect to fail when I come to attempt this particular trial in future. I therefore label myself as 'bad at this', fuelling negative expectations and internal commentary when I come to encounter a similar situation at a later date.

BREAKING THE CYCLE: 'COGNITIVE TRAINING'...

To tackle these issues, the sports psychology literature and applied practitioners have made some preliminary efforts to borrow from therapeutic approaches such as 'cognitive therapy' or 'cognitive behavioural therapy' more commonly used to treat mental health disorders. Given the efficacy of these approaches in managing anxiety-related disorders in the clinical realm, it would seem to follow that they might have application in helping performers to manage the anxiety and associated issues that they experience.

Attempts have thus been made to apply the principles and underlying premise of cognitive therapy to performance sport. Central to this is approach is the simple but powerful realisation that our cognitions shape our emotional state and related behaviours [350]. From this starting point, researchers and practitioners have sought to devise and implement interventions to foster the 'mental skills' required to sustain performing at the highest level and cope with the associated stresses. Authors have described this approach as 'cognitive-behavioural training' to differentiate the application to mental performance, as opposed to mental health [351]. Related approaches employed in a performance context similarly emphasise the element of cognition and once again a central aspect of these interventions is reframing how performers appraise pressure situations. To that end, a specific focus is challenging the irrational beliefs that underpin much of the anxiety and aversion that performers might be feeling at the prospect of tackling the particular endeavour [348].

It should be noted that the application of cognitive-behavioural approaches in a performance context is still in its infancy. Moreover the support of sport psychologists or mental skills consultants is not widely available to most of us. Nevertheless, taking a self-directed approach with these methods has shown notable success [349]. Individual performers in different realms can thus take steps to employ these principles. An important first step in this endeavour is to bring awareness to our cognitions.

"The greatest weapon against stress is our ability to choose one thought over another"

– William James

Given that our thinking is at the centre of our distorted perceptions, it follows that we might break the cycle by taking action to alter our cognitions and our perceptions. The fact that the illusions we create in our mind do not stand up to scrutiny offers us a way out when we are trapped in a negative head space. The starting point is to get our swirling thoughts out of our head and onto paper. Once captured on paper, we can expose the version of reality we have created in our mind to daylight. As well as exposing these thoughts to some scrutiny, this also helps to bring some objectivity so that we can see how the logic stacks up. Engaging in action provides the means to disprove the untruths our psyche has been feeding us and this exercise provides tangible evidence to contradict the distorted reasoning that these thoughts are built upon.

Some common cognitive distortions are generally evident when performers get trapped in a negative head space and these same distortions tend to be a feature of our anxieties in general [349]. To illustrate the degree to which these cognitive distortions to do harm, *absolutist* statements indicative of *all or nothing thinking* (see below) feature prominently in what is expressed by those suffering with depression [352]. Becoming familiar with the common cognitive distortions is a crucial first step in order to bring awareness and permit us to exercise vigilance to avoid falling into the trap in the first instance. By extension, being armed with this understanding provides the means to escape the debilitating effects of our own thoughts when we do find ourselves in a negative head space and engage with situations in a more rational manner [348].

THE COMMON DISTORTIONS...

Absolutist, Binary, All or Nothing Thinking (e.g. less than perfection or total success represents complete failure)

Over-generalising (blanket generalisations, always statements, or assuming what is now will always be)

Labelling (affixing labels that define others or ourselves, generally based scant evidence - i.e. single act, event, interaction)

Jumping to Conclusions #1: Mind Reading Fallacy (assuming other's thoughts or motivations behind their actions)

Jumping to Conclusions #2: Forecasting the Future (definitive statements about future unknowable events or outcomes)

Selective Recollection (Filtering out the positive, capturing and storing only the negative)

Binocular Distortion (Magnifying negatives/weakness, minimising positives/strengths)

Reasoning Based on Felt Emotions (I feel this way therefore it must be the case)

Dismissing Success and Discrediting Praise

Attribution Errors (assuming fault or personal responsibility for external events or other's decisions or actions)

False Expectations, Assumed Obligations (how things should be, what I should be doing, provoking indignation towards others, guilt towards oneself)

TWO-PRONGED STRATEGY...

Addressing the above cognitive distortions and negative thought patterns calls for a two-pronged strategy. The first prong tackles the 'top-down' component, which means examining our thought patterns and modifying them as necessary. The second prong addresses 'bottom-up aspects' in the shape of our response to events and how we deal with the feelings and emotions that are elicited.

A major area of focus for sport psychology and mental performance skills for athletes is 'self-talk' [353]. The stories we tell ourselves are very powerful and how we engage with ourselves similarly exerts a major influence. Our self-talk includes both what we verbalise and our internal narrative in relation to ourselves and external events. The performer's dialogue with themselves throughout their preparations and during the event itself has a big impact on their mental state and in turn how they perform.

It can also be particularly problematic when what we verbalise outwardly about ourselves is negative or even abusive. What this signals to others can be exploited by opponents and also tends to cause disquiet amongst our team-mates and colleagues. It follows that recognising when our self-talk is unhelpfully negative and does not serve us is clearly important. Equally, taking steps to modify our self-talk requires not only becoming more aware but also tackling the root cause to address the cognitions from which this self-defeating behaviour originates.

Returning to the bottom up part of the two pronged strategy, in the context of how we deal with stressors emotional regulation effectively means learning how to deal with what we feel in a different way. This encompasses how we perceive the experiences we encounter, the bodily sensations we feel, what labels we give these aspects, and our appraisal of what it all means.

Marshalling our cognitions involves our executive functions and the 'meta-abilities' we introduced earlier. In particular, exercising awareness and gaining a command of our own minds calls for 'meta-cognition'. The meta-abilities that underpin emotional regulation are also central to the quest to shift our perception and modify our response to external events in ways that better serve us.

DEPLOYING META-COGNITION...

Meta-cognition describes our awareness of how we think. Exploring our cognitions provides the means to unmask the cognitive distortions. If we are systematic in our approach we can identify the distortions in our thinking that are creating the illusion in our minds and generating the negative feelings we are experiencing.

To that end, a simple but powerful practice is to keep a log of our thoughts so that we can become more aware of our habits of cognition and self-talk, including those that do not serve us [353]. Capturing our thoughts on paper allows us to shine a torch on whatever cognitive distortions are present to expose the flaws in reasoning and faults in our logic. We can interrogate each step of our reasoning to highlight unsupported leaps and suspect conclusions.

The next step in this exercise then provides the opportunity to summon more objective and rational thoughts to counter the distortions. In doing so we can bring our subjective reality closer to the objective truth of the matter. Whilst this is a retrospective exercise, it nevertheless helps to relieve lingering negative feelings and dispel the ongoing urge to ruminate. Regardless, the discipline of capturing our thoughts on paper remains important to download them, rather than allowing them to continue circling in our heads. Transcribing our thoughts onto paper also lends a degree of detachment.

Over time regularly engaging in this practice also helps to effect lasting changes in our habits of thinking. The practice of regularly engaging in the above exercise to capture and re-examine negative thoughts will help athletes and coaches to become highly familiar with commonly occurring cognitive distortions so that over time we may acquire the ability to recognise them in real-time.

From an emotional regulation viewpoint, developing a heightened level of self-awareness is clearly important to allow performers to be aware of their emotions in the moment. Fostering the ability to catch ourselves in real-time provides the means to deal with our thoughts and feelings in a more rational manner.

On a fundamental level, it is also crucial for performers to accept that the thoughts and feelings they are experiencing are both natural and entirely understandable in the circumstances. This acceptance alone helps neutralise much of the angst and rumination that stems from the unrealistic expectations and surrounding judgements that tend to accompany our thoughts and emotions.

By definition in sport the outcome is uncertain, so it is natural for there to be doubt and for performers to feel anxious to some degree. Given what is at stake and how invested we are in the endeavour it is likewise natural and appropriate to feel nervous. The physiological arousal that goes along with feeling nervous can also serve our mental and physical performance in a positive way, so from this viewpoint these feelings are not only natural but desirable. If performers (and coaches) are able to accept the premise that nerves can assist their performance this will help them to embrace whatever they are feeling.

A further element of metacognition concerns how we appraise situations, scenarios, and the sensations we are feeling. The labels we use and the meaning we attach to external events and scenarios go a long way to shaping our thought patterns and emotional responses. This is manifested in our tendency to perceive scenarios in terms of threat versus reward.

APPRAISAL AND RE-APPRAISAL...

As we outlined, one of the common cognitive distortions is the tendency to label things in a certain way, which influences (often in an unhelpful way) how we think about ourselves in relation to external events. Accordingly, a major focus of cognitive-behavioural interventions with performers is addressing how the individual appraises performing in competition [354]. More broadly, how both coaches and performers alike appraise the stressors they face (what labels they use and how they think about things) likewise has a major influence on their stress response, and in turn how they cope with the stresses that are part of operating in high performance setting [343, 344].

When our impression of a situation is dominated by the potential threat it constitutes (i.e. a potential loss), clearly this will shape how we anticipate the event, and by extension our cognitions and behaviour during the event. The prospect of doing something that we appraise in terms of threat will naturally provoke greater anxiety. Perceiving the situation as a threat prompts an aversive response, and will likely lead us to adopt a defensive approach as we seek to avoid the apparent risks.

Conversely, appraising the same scenario in terms of the potential rewards (i.e. opportunity for a potential win) shapes our perception and experience in a dramatically different way. Such an interpretation leads us to a think about the event in terms of the opportunities. In this scenario the prospect of tackling the task elicits very different thoughts and feelings – we might actually look forward to it, rather than experiencing feelings of dread. When the situation is framed in terms of challenge and rewards this likewise tends to alter our approach in terms of choices and actions when we perform, and by extension our overall experience of the endeavour.

If our appraisal has such a dramatic influence it follows that altering how we evaluate the situation will similarly have a major impact. Conceivably this could change the level of anxiety we feel at the prospect, and in turn our behaviour and experience when the event comes around. Our subjective judgements and how we evaluate different scenarios situations are not set in stone [355]. Returning to the tendency to assign labels, it follows we can hack this process by using different labels. By changing the story we tell ourselves and using different language we might therefore be empowered to change our state and alter how we respond to whatever it is we are facing.

Performers can switch from a threat to a challenge state by harnessing the power of reappraisal, as demonstrated by a growing number of investigations. In particular, changing our internal dialogue offers us a way to reframe our judgements on the situation and this alone can help improve our ability to perform under pressure [356]. Performers who struggle under pressure tend to label the prospective performance in terms of threat (and use negative labels in relation to themselves and their ability to cope). It has been demonstrated that it is possible to prompt these individuals to re-evaluate the situation at hand and instead switch to focus on the challenge and opportunity it presents. In doing so, performers are able to find new confidence and approach the task with a more positive mindset [354].

The power of appraisal also concerns the sensations we feel in our own body. The same physical sensations of physiological arousal can be experienced in different ways. Part of what determines the difference in how sensations are manifested is based on the labels we attach and the meaning we ascribe to them. We might perceive and interpret these bodily sensations as feeling anxious, or we might attribute these feelings to excitement. The experience we have as a result of the differing labels (anxious versus excited) are very different, despite the original sensations being identical. Clearly the thoughts that accompany the interpretation 'I am anxious' versus 'I am excited' are very different. These differing cognitions have downstream effects on our thoughts, feelings, and emotional state, in accordance with our expectations and the judgements that follow. With prompting, performers can successfully reappraise their feelings of physiological arousal during a task designed to elicit a stress response. Studies demonstrate that doing so has measurable positive effects on recorded cardiovascular responses and performers also show significantly improved attention allocation as a result [93].

Once again, whilst the support of sports psychologists or mental skills coaching to direct such interventions might not be readily available to many of us, we can still use this knowledge to empower ourselves. Whilst an external perspective is often helpful in the endeavour, it is nevertheless within our power to evaluate things differently and use more helpful labels for events and experiences. We can reframe how we appraise the sensations that will naturally be elicited as we anticipate and encounter high arousal situations. When we think about the physical symptoms of physiological arousal that accompany high stakes situations as functional and adaptive this alone can benefit how we respond under stress. In this way we can feel more in control and acquire some mastery over how we engage with events, so that our experience becomes more akin to excitement rather than aversion.

SELF TALK AND 'SELF COMPASSION'...

Given how our self-talk can influence our levels of anxiety and feelings of self confidence in a performance setting, it seems sensible to use this power for good. We certainly need to respect the power of what we verbalise to ourselves and resist beating ourselves up, particularly in public given what these expressions signal to others. As noted earlier, the simple practice of keeping a logbook to record our self-talk is a highly effective tool for becoming more aware of what we verbalise when preparing and performing [353]. Beyond recognising the potential harm and become more aware of our inner commentary, we can leverage the potential benefits of self-talk in mobilising and directing our attention towards the task. By harnessing self-talk in ways that serve us we also reduce our level of anxiety and enhance the sense of self confidence we bring in the process [357].

As noted in an earlier section, an important aspect of self-talk is how we relate and engage with ourselves. In the psychology literature this is described in terms of *self-compassion*. There have been some preliminary investigations attempting to apply self-compassion based interventions in athlete populations [358]. On a pragmatic level, whilst 'self-compassion' might be descriptive, using this language could also conceivably create a barrier to engagement with athletes and potentially with performers in other realms.

An approach I have found has more traction (particularly with male athletes) is presenting the concept as treating oneself as a valued team-mate – after all performers are ultimately reliant upon themselves. If we are reliant on ourselves it follows we merit being treated with respect, especially from ourselves. When a team-mate whom we respect is having difficulties it is generally more beneficial support them than tear them down. This same principles applies to how we treat ourselves during a slump in performance or when we are having a hard time in general.

I vividly recall such a scenario involving a squash player who I had worked with before moving overseas to New Zealand. The athlete was starting out on the professional circuit and somewhat bizarrely he was making a habit of publicly crucifying himself on social media after suffering a loss in tournaments. I reached out to the athlete to see if I could persuade him to desist this destructive behaviour, not least because he was exhibiting weakness in a public forum, which prospective opponents were sure to exploit. Whilst squash is an individual sport, each year selected players from the national programme competed in team events (European team championships and World team championships on alternate years). Given he had experienced these events I decided to use the team-mate metaphor when I made in my attempt to counsel him from afar. The case I put to him was that he would not be so negative and abusive towards another member of the team, so why did he deem it acceptable to treat himself in such a manner (particularly publicly)? I went on to walk him through the argument that aside from being an act of disrespect and highly inappropriate, it would also be demotivating and counterproductive to abuse a team-mate that he would later need to rely on. This led us to the obvious conclusion that if this logic applies to a team-mate, then this argument should equally apply to his conduct towards himself. An unlovely habit of those who are driven is that on occasion we treat ourselves far worse than we would another human, particularly one we care about.

OTHER COUNTERMEASURES...

Higher ratings of 'dispositional mindfulness' among elite junior athletes are found to be positively related to wellbeing in a way that protects against burnout in these young performers [359]. The ways in which mindfulness supports coping with stress in elite athletes has started to receive some study. One particular mechanism that has been highlighted is helping to combat the tendency to ruminate on negative events, thus limiting the lingering effects that can otherwise trap performers in a negative head space [85].

Aside from tackling the narrative provided by our minds head-on by capturing and interrogating our thinking, mindfulness practices essentially permit us to dial down the volume of the internal chatter to provide periods of respite. Effectively these practices divert our attention towards more purposeful activity and channel our awareness to alternative foci, which is a large part of what permits us to escape our own thoughts and ruminations.

What 'mindfulness practice' immediately calls to mind is yoga and meditation, and it is true that many athletes derive benefits from these practices. However, mindfulness simply means tuning into our own body, a mundane task, or our surroundings, rather than having our attention captured by the thoughts swirling in our mind. On that basis, essentially any routine activity can serve for these purposes; this might simply mean going out for a walk, or preparing a meal can be meditative for some. Why this is important is it allows us to engage in relevant 'mind-body' practice in a variety of settings, whilst avoiding the connotations that come with the labels of 'yoga' or 'meditation'. Indeed, even 'mindfulness' can be a barrier for some of us, as it is with athletes and coaches in certain instances. We can avoid much of this by avoiding the use of such labels and simply employ activities that serve the same purpose.

Of course physical activity also has the power to change our emotional state: exercise in humans elicits a host of beneficial neurochemical and neurophysiological effects that support cognitive and behavioural aspects [360]. For athletes, physical training offers a ready outlet that can help to favourably influence both mood and cognition. Equally, given the utility of exercise as a tool to provide mental refreshment, dedicated recovery workouts might be used for this specific purpose in a way that is perceived to be separate from the 'grind' of training (an unhelpful label that is in prevalent use currently). Beyond sport, performers in other realms can certainly utilise recreational exercise and physical activity as tools to support mental performance (and indeed mental health), alongside the physical and physiological benefits.

IN CLOSING...

There are persisting misconceptions and false expectations in relation to stress and anxiety among high performing athletes and coaches. On the other hand there is growing awareness of the increasing prevalence of health challenges such as chronic anxiety and depression among student athletes particularly, and it is increasingly evident that those in the elite and professional ranks are similarly affected. From both perspectives, this points to a need to take a more proactive approach to understanding and investing in the mental game that is a major part of competition and operating in a performance setting. These themes apply to human performance in the widest sense: there is a need to reckon with issues of stress and anxiety for performers across all realms given the magnitude of the performance and mental health implications.

Those who compete in individual pursuits are familiar with the notion of competing against themselves. We can be our biggest ally and paradoxically also our own worst enemy. Even the highest performers are still mortal. All of us can fall prey to habits of thought and narratives within our own minds that do not serve us. Our cognitions create the world within our minds and subjective reality is very powerful. In the moment it feels very real, and whilst our thoughts and feelings might not make something objectively true, when under stress our cognitions nevertheless affect us in very real ways.

In view of the power of our cognitions to influence our emotional state and shape our subjective reality, it follows there is a real need to bring some awareness to our habits of thought. Simply recognising that there are instances when our cognitions and self-talk do not serve our objectives is an important first step. Using this understanding as our starting point we can take steps to intervene and liberate ourselves from our own thoughts before they overwhelm us. We might think of this as 'cognitive training' and we should consider this practice an integral part of developing the mental fortitude required to perform under stress.

There are some very practical methods we can adopt to help regulate our thoughts, allowing us to identify dysfunctional thinking and cognitive distortions at play. The first part involves how we **appraise** stress both in general, but also in relation to specific circumstances. A simple yet powerful practice is to **capture** these cognitions on paper to bring our swirling thoughts out of the dark recesses of our mind and into the daylight. In this way we can scrutinise our thoughts and **examine** our reasoning in a rational way and with a degree of detachment. To complete this ongoing cyclical process, some form of systematic review or debrief to **reflect** after the event is critical to facilitate learning over time in order to progressively change our behaviour. In turn we can develop strategies and ways of thinking that better serve us. Along the way we can also acquire the capability to deploy our mental resources more effectively, facilitating the clutch performances that athletes aspire to.

REFLECTING AND CONNECTING THE DOTS...

How do you tend to think about stress and stressful situations? Would you say you have a positive, neutral, or negative attitude towards stress in general, and the specific stressors you encounter?

Is your response to stress 'domain specific'? For instance, do you engage with stressful situations in a different way in a professional setting versus your personal life?

Does the idea that the prospect of doing something is typically more daunting than the reality when you come to tackle it resonate with you?

Have there been specific any instances where your own thoughts and perceptions have compounded the difficulty of the challenge you were facing or actively sabotaged your efforts?

The saying goes that we are own worst enemy; to what extent do you feel you have been guilty of this in the past?

Have you encountered individuals in a competitive situation who are so critical with their self-talk that it borders on abuse? What were your thoughts at the time, and what are your reflections as you recall these instances?

Do you feel you might benefit from some sort of structured approach such as a log book to get a handle on how your thoughts help or hinder your efforts when performing under conditions of stress?

What activities do you employ to escape or tune out your own thoughts from time to time? Do you think you would benefit from a regular practice to serve this purpose?

What thoughts do you have on how you might implement each element of the cyclical process proposed (appraise, capture, examine, reflect), and ultimately integrate this practice into how you operate in a professional capacity and in your personal life?

Acknowledgements

Writing a book is always an iterative process, but it was all the more so the case with this one (on that note I was grateful to read *Creativity Inc* by Ed Catmull at a very timely point in the process!). I would like to acknowledge those who graciously took the time to read early drafts and provide feedback. The project began with a simple but compelling idea, and whilst it all made perfect sense in my own mind, the back and forth was crucial in helping me to put it on the page in a coherent way. On a similar theme, the manuscript also cycled through a number of different titles, so many thanks to those who took part in the vote to help me settle on the final selection! In particular, I would like to thank my wife Sian – as everybody who knows Sian would testify she is the brains of the outfit, and her support and insights were indispensable to this project, as in all things. I would like to say I always received the suggestions and critical feedback with good grace, but sadly this is a nonfiction book. For the record, I remain amazed, delighted, and very grateful to be your husband.

References

1. Kendellen K, Camiré M. Applying in life the skills learned in sport: A grounded theory. Psychology of Sport and Exercise. 2019;40:23-32.
2. Kellett P. Organisational leadership: Lessons from professional coaches. Sport Management Review. 1999;2(2):150-71.
3. Burnes B, O'Donnell H. What can business leaders learn from sport? Sport, Business and Management: An International Journal. 2011;1(1):12-27.
4. Jones G. Performance Excellence: A Personal Perspective on the Link Between Sport and Business. Journal of Applied Sport Psychology. 2002;14(4):268-81.
5. Coutu D, Kauffman C, Charan R, Peterson D, Maccoby M, Scoular P. What can coaches do for you. harvard business review. 2009;87(1):91-7.
6. Cruickshank A, Collins D. Culture Change in Elite Sport Performance Teams: Examining and Advancing Effectiveness in the New Era. Journal of Applied Sport Psychology. 2012;24(3):338-55.
7. Collins J. Good to Great: Why Some Companies Make the Leap and Others Don't. Harper Business; 2011.
8. Molan C, Kelly S, Arnold R, Matthews J. Performance Management: A Systematic Review of Processes in Elite Sport and Other Performance Domains. Journal of Applied Sport Psychology. 2018;31(1):87-104.
9. Fletcher D, Arnold R. A Qualitative Study of Performance Leadership and Management in Elite Sport. Journal of Applied Sport Psychology. 2011;23(2):223-42.
10. Callow N, Smith MJ, Hardy L, Arthur CA, Hardy J. Measurement of Transformational Leadership and its Relationship with Team Cohesion and Performance Level. Journal of Applied Sport Psychology. 2009;21(4):395-412.
11. Stenling A, Tafvelin S. Transformational Leadership and Well-Being in Sports: The Mediating Role of Need Satisfaction. Journal of Applied Sport Psychology. 2014;26(2):182-96.
12. Charbonneau D, Barling J, Kelloway EK. Transformational Leadership and Sports Performance: The Mediating Role of Intrinsic Motivation. Journal of Applied Social Psychology. 2001;31(7):1521-34.
13. van Dierendonck D. Servant Leadership: A Review and Synthesis. Journal of Management. 2011;37(4):1228-61.
14. Kim M, Kim Y, Won D. From commanding to serving athletes: Nurturing the coach–athlete relationship. International Journal of Sports Science & Coaching. 2018;13(6):891-901.
15. Rieke M, Hammermeister J, Chase M. Servant Leadership in Sport: A New Paradigm for Effective Coach Behavior. International Journal of Sports Science & Coaching. 2008;3(2):227-39.
16. Tuan LT. Coach humility and player creativity: The roles of knowledge sharing and group diversity. Sport Management Review. 2019.
17. Yu M, Vaagaasar AL, Müller R, Wang L, Zhu F. Empowerment: The key to horizontal leadership in projects. International Journal of Project Management. 2018;36(7):992-1006.

18. Price MS, Weiss MR. Relationships among Coach Leadership, Peer Leadership, and Adolescent Athletes' Psychosocial and Team Outcomes: A Test of Transformational Leadership Theory. Journal of Applied Sport Psychology. 2013;25(2):265-79.

19. Yukelson D, Rose R. The Psychology of Ongoing Excellence: An NCAA Coach's Perspective on Winning Consecutive Multiple National Championships. Journal of Sport Psychology in Action. 2014;5(1):44-58.

20. Price MS, Weiss MR. Peer Leadership in Sport: Relationships among Personal Characteristics, Leader Behaviors, and Team Outcomes. Journal of Applied Sport Psychology. 2011;23(1):49-64.

21. Fransen K, Delvaux E, Mesquita B, Van Puyenbroeck S. The Emergence of Shared Leadership in Newly Formed Teams With an Initial Structure of Vertical Leadership: A Longitudinal Analysis. The Journal of Applied Behavioral Science. 2018;54(2):140-70.

22. Fransen K, Decroos S, Broek GV, Boen F. Leading from the top or leading from within? A comparison between coaches' and athletes' leadership as predictors of team identification, team confidence, and team cohesion. International Journal of Sports Science & Coaching. 2016;11(6):757-71.

23. Arnold R, Fletcher D, Hobson JA. Performance Leadership and Management in Elite Sport: A Black and White Issue or Different Shades of Grey? Journal of Sport Management. 2018;32(5):452-63.

24. Cruickshank A, Collins D. Illuminating and Applying "The Dark Side": Insights From Elite Team Leaders. Journal of Applied Sport Psychology. 2015;27(3):249-67.

25. Scott K. Radical Candor: Fully Revised & Updated Edition: Be a Kick-Ass Boss Without Losing Your Humanity. St. Martin's Press; 2019.

26. Collins D, Cruickshank A. 'Multi-directional management': exploring the challenges of performance in the World Class Programme environment. Reflective Practice. 2012;13(3):455-69.

27. Silver N. The signal and the noise: the art and science of prediction. Penguin UK; 2012.

28. Parayitam S, Papenhausen C. Strategic decision-making. Management Research Review. 2018;41(1):2-28.

29. Wang D, Su Z, Guo H. Top management team conflict and exploratory innovation: The mediating impact of market orientation. Industrial Marketing Management. 2019.

30. Reynolds A, Lewis D. Teams solve problems faster when they're more cognitively diverse. Harvard Business Review. 2017;30.

31. Younis R. Cognitive Diversity and Creativity: The Moderating Effect of Collaborative Climate. International Journal of Business and Management. 2019;14(1).

32. Rahmi DY, Indarti N. Examining the relationships among cognitive diversity, knowledge sharing and team climate in team innovation. Team Performance Management: An International Journal. 2019;25(5/6):299-317.

33. Aggarwal I, Woolley AW, Chabris CF, Malone TW. The Impact of Cognitive Style Diversity on Implicit Learning in Teams. Front Psychol. 2019;10(112):112.

34. Meissner P, Wulf T. The effect of cognitive diversity on the illusion of control bias in strategic decisions: An experimental investigation. European Management Journal. 2017;35(4):430-9.

35. Kahneman D. Thinking, fast and slow. Macmillan; 2011.

36. Kahneman D, Lovallo D, Sibony O. Before You Make That Big Decision. Harvard Business Review. 2011;89(6):50-60.

37. Parayitam S, Papenhausen C. Agreement-seeking behavior, trust, and cognitive diversity in strategic decision making teams. Journal of Advances in Management Research. 2016;13(3):292-315.

38. Grant A. Originals: How Non-conformists Move the World. New York, NY: Viking Press; 2016.

39. Harari YN. Sapiens: A brief history of humankind. Random House; 2014.

40. Sapolsky R. This Is Your Brain on Nationalism: The Biology of Us and Them. Foreign Affairs. 2019;98(2):42-7.

41. Mason L. Ideologues without Issues: The Polarizing Consequences of Ideological Identities. Public Opinion Quarterly. 2018;82(S1):866-87.

42. Murray D. The Madness of Crowds: Gender, Race and Identity. Bloomsbury Publishing USA; 2019.

43. Epley N, Gilovich T. The Mechanics of Motivated Reasoning. Journal of Economic Perspectives. 2016;30(3):133-40.

44. Lukianoff G, Haidt J. The Coddling of the American Mind. (cover story). Atlantic Media Company; 2015. p. 42-52.

45. Gawande A. The Checklist Manifesto: How To Get Things Right. Profile Books; 2010.

46. Gamble P. Informed: The Art of the Science of Preparing Athletes. Informed in Sport publishing; 2018.

47. Williams S, Whatman C, Hume PA, Sheerin K. Kinesio taping in treatment and prevention of sports injuries: a meta-analysis of the evidence for its effectiveness. Sports medicine. 2012;42(2):153-64.

48. Cameron WB. Informal sociology: a casual introduction to sociological thinking. Random House; 1963.

49. Catmull E, Wallace A. Creativity, Inc: overcoming the unseen forces that stand in the way of true inspiration. Random House; 2014.

50. Lewis M. Moneyball: The art of winning an unfair game. WW Norton & Company; 2004.

51. Martindale A, Collins D. Enhancing the Evaluation of Effectiveness with Professional Judgment and Decision Making. The Sport Psychologist. 2007;21(4):458-74.

52. Goleman D. Emotional intelligence. Bantam; 2006.

53. Lee H, Wasche H, Jekauc D. Analyzing the Components of Emotional Competence of Football Coaches: A Qualitative Study from the Coaches' Perspective. Sports (Basel, Switzerland). 2018;6(4).

54. Hodgson L, Butt J, Maynard I. Exploring the psychological attributes underpinning elite sports coaching. International Journal of Sports Science & Coaching. 2017;12(4):439-51.

55. Kopp A, Jekauc D. The Influence of Emotional Intelligence on Performance in Competitive Sports: A Meta-Analytical Investigation. Sports (Basel, Switzerland). 2018;6(4):175.

56. Kerdijk C, van der Kamp J, Polman R. The Influence of the Social Environment Context in Stress and Coping in Sport. Front Psychol. 2016;7(875):875.

57. Davis L, Appleby R, Davis P, Wetherell M, Gustafsson H. The role of coach-athlete relationship quality in team sport athletes' psychophysiological exhaustion: implications for physical and cognitive performance. Journal of sports sciences. 2018;36(17):1985-92.

58. Hogue CM, Fry MD, Fry AC. The differential impact of motivational climate on adolescents' psychological and physiological stress responses. Psychology of Sport and Exercise. 2017;30:118-27.

59. Castro-Sánchez M, Zurita-Ortega F, García-Marmol E, Chacón-Cuberos R. Motivational Climate in Sport Is Associated with Life Stress Levels, Academic Performance and Physical Activity Engagement of Adolescents. International Journal of Environmental Research and Public Health. 2019;16(7):1198.

60. Isoard-Gautheur S, Trouilloud D, Gustafsson H, Guillet-Descas E. Associations between the perceived quality of the coach–athlete relationship and athlete burnout: An examination of the mediating role of achievement goals. Psychology of Sport and Exercise. 2016;22:210-7.

61. Hoffmann S, Borges U, Broker L, Laborde S, Liepelt R, Lobinger BH et al. The Psychophysiology of Action: A Multidisciplinary Endeavor for Integrating Action and Cognition. Front Psychol. 2018;9(1423):1423.

62. Holmes PS, Wright DJ. Motor cognition and neuroscience in sport psychology. Curr Opin Psychol. 2017;16:43-7.

63. Bachmann J, Munzert J, Kruger B. Neural Underpinnings of the Perception of Emotional States Derived From Biological Human Motion: A Review of Neuroimaging Research. Front Psychol. 2018;9(1763):1763.

64. Lerner JS, Li Y, Valdesolo P, Kassam KS. Emotion and decision making. Annual review of psychology. 2015;66(1):799-823.

65. Raab M. Motor heuristics and embodied choices: how to choose and act. Curr Opin Psychol. 2017;16:34-7.

66. Vastfjall D, Slovic P, Burns WJ, Erlandsson A, Koppel L, Asutay E et al. The Arithmetic of Emotion: Integration of Incidental and Integral Affect in Judgments and Decisions. Front Psychol. 2016;7(325):325.

67. Frankl VE. Man's search for meaning: The classic tribute to hope from the Holocaust. Random House; 2004.

68. Pena-Sarrionandia A, Mikolajczak M, Gross JJ. Integrating emotion regulation and emotional intelligence traditions: a meta-analysis. Front Psychol. 2015;6:160.

69. Ludwig RJ, Welch MG. Darwin's Other Dilemmas and the Theoretical Roots of Emotional Connection. Front Psychol. 2019;10(683):683.

70. van Kleef GA, Cheshin A, Koning LF, Wolf SA. Emotional games: How coaches' emotional expressions shape players' emotions, inferences, and team performance. Psychology of Sport and Exercise. 2019;41:1-11.

71. Torrence BS, Connelly S. Emotion Regulation Tendencies and Leadership Performance: An Examination of Cognitive and Behavioral Regulation Strategies. Front Psychol. 2019;10(1486):1486.

72. Barlow A, Banks AP. Using emotional intelligence in coaching high-performance athletes: a randomised controlled trial. Coaching: An International Journal of Theory, Research and Practice. 2014;7(2):132-9.

73. Schutte NS, Malouff JM, Bobik C, Coston TD, Greeson C, Jedlicka C et al. Emotional intelligence and interpersonal relations. J Soc Psychol. 2001;141(4):523-36.

74. Kozlowski D, Hutchinson M, Hurley J, Rowley J, Sutherland J. The role of emotion in clinical decision making: an integrative literature review. BMC Med Educ. 2017;17(1):255.

75. Kiely J. Essay: A New Understanding of Stress and the Implications for Our Cultural Training Paradigm. New Studies in Athletics. 2016;34:69-74.

76. Dimitroff SJ, Kardan O, Necka EA, Decety J, Berman MG, Norman GJ. Physiological dynamics of stress contagion. Scientific Reports. 2017;7(1):6168.

77. Lea RG, Davis SK, Mahoney B, Qualter P. Does Emotional Intelligence Buffer the Effects of Acute Stress? A Systematic Review. Front Psychol. 2019;10(810):810.

78. Lee YH, Chelladurai P. Emotional intelligence, emotional labor, coach burnout, job satisfaction, and turnover intention in sport leadership. European Sport Management Quarterly. 2017;18(4):393-412.

79. Tyng CM, Amin HU, Saad MNM, Malik AS. The Influences of Emotion on Learning and Memory. Front Psychol. 2017;8(1454):1454.

80. Headrick J, Renshaw I, Davids K, Pinder RA, Araújo D. The dynamics of expertise acquisition in sport: The role of affective learning design. Psychology of Sport and Exercise. 2015;16:83-90.

81. Carson HJ, Collins D. Implementing the Five-A Model of Technical Refinement: Key Roles of the Sport Psychologist. J Appl Sport Psychol. 2016;28(4):392-409.

82. Breske MP, Fry MD, Fry AC, Hogue CM. The effects of goal priming on cortisol responses in an ego-involving climate. Psychology of Sport and Exercise. 2017;32:74-82.

83. Sánchez-Álvarez N, Extremera N, Fernández-Berrocal P. The relation between emotional intelligence and subjective well-being: A meta-analytic investigation. The Journal of Positive Psychology. 2015;11(3):276-85.

84. Jackson RC, Ashford KJ, Norsworthy G. Attentional focus, dispositional reinvestment, and skilled motor performance under pressure. Journal of sport & exercise psychology. 2006;28(1):49-68.

85. Josefsson T, Ivarsson A, Lindwall M, Gustafsson H, Stenling A, Boroy J et al. Mindfulness Mechanisms in Sports: Mediating Effects of Rumination and Emotion Regulation on Sport-Specific Coping. Mindfulness (N Y). 2017;8(5):1354-63.

86. Guendelman S, Medeiros S, Rampes H. Mindfulness and Emotion Regulation: Insights from Neurobiological, Psychological, and Clinical Studies. Front Psychol. 2017;8(220):220.

87. Kral TRA, Schuyler BS, Mumford JA, Rosenkranz MA, Lutz A, Davidson RJ. Impact of short- and long-term mindfulness meditation training on amygdala reactivity to emotional stimuli. Neuroimage. 2018;181:301-13.

88. Osypiuk K, Thompson E, Wayne PM. Can Tai Chi and Qigong Postures Shape Our Mood? Toward an Embodied Cognition Framework for Mind-Body Research. Front Hum Neurosci. 2018;12(174):174.

89. Sullivan MB, Erb M, Schmalzl L, Moonaz S, Noggle Taylor J, Porges SW. Yoga Therapy and Polyvagal Theory: The Convergence of Traditional Wisdom and Contemporary Neuroscience for Self-Regulation and Resilience. Front Hum Neurosci. 2018;12(67):67.

90. Fischer D, Messner M, Pollatos O. Improvement of Interoceptive Processes after an 8-Week Body Scan Intervention. Front Hum Neurosci. 2017;11(452):452.

91. Kabir RS, Haramaki Y, Ki H, Ohno H. Self-Active Relaxation Therapy (SART) and Self-Regulation: A Comprehensive Review and Comparison of the Japanese Body Movement Approach. Front Hum Neurosci. 2018;12(21):21.

92. Krohler A, Berti S. Taking Action or Thinking About It? State Orientation and Rumination Are Correlated in Athletes. Front Psychol. 2019;10(576):576.

93. Jamieson JP, Nock MK, Mendes WB. Mind over matter: reappraising arousal improves cardiovascular and cognitive responses to stress. Journal of experimental psychology General. 2012;141(3):417-22.

94. Uphill MA, Rossato CJL, Swain J, O'Driscoll J. Challenge and Threat: A Critical Review of the Literature and an Alternative Conceptualization. Front Psychol. 2019;10(1255):1255.

95. Moore LJ, Wilson MR, Vine SJ, Coussens AH, Freeman P. Champ or chump? Challenge and threat states during pressurized competition. Journal of sport & exercise psychology. 2013;35(6):551-62.

96. Sammy N, Anstiss PA, Moore LJ, Freeman P, Wilson MR, Vine SJ. The effects of arousal reappraisal on stress responses, performance and attention. Anxiety, stress, and coping. 2017;30(6):619-29.

97. Moore LJ, Vine SJ, Wilson MR, Freeman P. Reappraising Threat: How to Optimize Performance Under Pressure. Journal of sport & exercise psychology. 2015;37(3):339-43.

98. Haggard P. Sense of agency in the human brain. Nat Rev Neurosci. 2017;18(4):196-207.

99. Borhani K, Beck B, Haggard P. Choosing, Doing, and Controlling: Implicit Sense of Agency Over Somatosensory Events. Psychological science. 2017;28(7):882-93.

100. Haggard P. The Neurocognitive Bases of Human Volition. Annual review of psychology. 2019;70(1):9-28.

101. Chambon V, Sidarus N, Haggard P. From action intentions to action effects: how does the sense of agency come about? Front Hum Neurosci. 2014;8:320.

102. Beck B, Di Costa S, Haggard P. Having control over the external world increases the implicit sense of agency. Cognition. 2017;162:54-60.
103. Taleb NN. Antifragile: Things that gain from disorder. Random House Incorporated; 2012.
104. Barlas Z, Hockley WE, Obhi SS. The effects of freedom of choice in action selection on perceived mental effort and the sense of agency. Acta psychologica. 2017;180:122-9.
105. McNamara JM, Stearne DJ. Flexible nonlinear periodization in a beginner college weight training class. Journal of strength and conditioning research / National Strength & Conditioning Association. 2010;24(8):2012-7.
106. Mann JB, Thyfault JP, Ivey PA, Sayers SP. The effect of autoregulatory progressive resistance exercise vs. linear periodization on strength improvement in college athletes. Journal of strength and conditioning research / National Strength & Conditioning Association. 2010;24(7):1718-23.
107. Coughlan EK, Williams AM, McRobert AP, Ford PR. How experts practice: a novel test of deliberate practice theory. Journal of experimental psychology Learning, memory, and cognition. 2014;40(2):449-58.
108. Webster LV, Hardy J, Hardy L. Big Hitters: Important Factors Characterizing Team Effectiveness in Professional Cricket. Front Psychol. 2017;8(1140):1140.
109. Ewing T, Heilgenberg K, Pitt L. How to demotivate your top performers: Lessons from professional cricket. Business Horizons. 2019;62(2):149-55.
110. Peterson MD, Rhea MR, Alvar BA. Maximizing strength development in athletes: a meta-analysis to determine the dose-response relationship. Journal of strength and conditioning research / National Strength & Conditioning Association. 2004;18(2):377-82.
111. McPhee JS, Lightfoot AP. Post-exercise recovery regimes: blowing hot and cold. The Journal of physiology. 2017;595(3):627-8.
112. Wilson LJ, Dimitriou L, Hills FA, Gondek MB, Cockburn E. Whole body cryotherapy, cold water immersion, or a placebo following resistance exercise: a case of mind over matter? European journal of applied physiology. 2019;119(1):135-47.
113. Roberts LA, Raastad T, Markworth JF, Figueiredo VC, Egner IM, Shield A et al. Post-exercise cold water immersion attenuates acute anabolic signalling and long-term adaptations in muscle to strength training. The Journal of physiology. 2015;593(18):4285-301.
114. Nadarajah S, Ariyagunarajah R, Jong ED. Cryotherapy: not as cool as it seems. The Journal of physiology. 2018;596(4):561-2.
115. Vaso M, Weber A, Tscholl PM, Junge A, Dvorak J. Use and abuse of medication during 2014 FIFA World Cup Brazil: a retrospective survey. BMJ Open. 2015;5(9):e007608.
116. Holgado D, Hopker J, Sanabria D, Zabala M. Analgesics and Sport Performance: Beyond the Pain-Modulating Effects. PM & R : the journal of injury, function, and rehabilitation. 2018;10(1):72-82.

117. Lilja M, Mandic M, Apro W, Melin M, Olsson K, Rosenborg S et al. High doses of anti-inflammatory drugs compromise muscle strength and hypertrophic adaptations to resistance training in young adults. Acta physiologica (Oxford, England). 2018;222(2):e12948.

118. Cardinale DA, Lilja M, Mandic M, Gustafsson T, Larsen FJ, Lundberg TR. Resistance Training with Co-ingestion of Anti-inflammatory Drugs Attenuates Mitochondrial Function. Front Physiol. 2017;8(1074):1074.

119. Lundberg TR, Howatson G. Analgesic and anti-inflammatory drugs in sports: Implications for exercise performance and training adaptations. Scandinavian journal of medicine & science in sports. 2018;28(11):2252-62.

120. Kristensen DM, Desdoits-Lethimonier C, Mackey AL, Dalgaard MD, De Masi F, Munkbol CH et al. Ibuprofen alters human testicular physiology to produce a state of compensated hypogonadism. Proceedings of the National Academy of Sciences of the United States of America. 2018;115(4):E715-E24.

121. Kooijman MK, Buining EM, Swinkels ICS, Koes BW, Veenhof C. Do therapist effects determine outcome in patients with shoulder pain in a primary care physiotherapy setting? Physiotherapy. 2020;107:111-7.

122. van Melick N, Hoogeboom T, Pronk Y, Rutten B, van Tienen T, van Cingel R et al. Only 19% of pivoting athletes after anterior cruciate ligament reconstruction meets return-to-play (RTP) criteria when their physical therapist releases them to RTP. Physical Therapy in Sport. 2017;28:e20-e1.

123. Nawasreh Z, Logerstedt D, Cummer K, Axe M, Risberg MA, Snyder-Mackler L. Functional performance 6 months after ACL reconstruction can predict return to participation in the same preinjury activity level 12 and 24 months after surgery. British journal of sports medicine. 2017.

124. Gray R. Differences in Attentional Focus Associated With Recovery From Sports Injury: Does Injury Induce an Internal Focus? Journal of sport & exercise psychology. 2015;37(6):607-16.

125. de Oliveira Silva D, Barton CJ, Briani RV, Taborda B, Ferreira AS, Pazzinatto MF et al. Kinesiophobia, but not strength is associated with altered movement in women with patellofemoral pain. Gait & posture. 2019;68:1-5.

126. Czuppon S, Racette BA, Klein SE, Harris-Hayes M. Variables associated with return to sport following anterior cruciate ligament reconstruction: a systematic review. British journal of sports medicine. 2014;48(5):356-64.

127. Burland JP, Lepley AS, Cormier M, DiStefano LJ, Arciero R, Lepley LK. Learned Helplessness After Anterior Cruciate Ligament Reconstruction: An Altered Neurocognitive State? Sports medicine. 2019;49(5):647-57.

128. Uehara S, Mawase F, Therrien AS, Cherry-Allen KM, Celnik P. Interactions between motor exploration and reinforcement learning. Journal of neurophysiology. 2019;122(2):797-808.

129. Davids K, Glazier P, Araujo D, Bartlett R. Movement systems as dynamical systems: the functional role of variability and its implications for sports medicine. Sports medicine. 2003;33(4):245-60.

130. Hardy LL, Barnett L, Espinel P, Okely AD. Thirteen-year trends in child and adolescent fundamental movement skills: 1997-2010. Medicine and science in sports and exercise. 2013;45(10):1965-70.

131. O' Brien W, Belton S, Issartel J. Fundamental movement skill proficiency amongst adolescent youth. Physical Education and Sport Pedagogy. 2015;21(6):557-71.

132. Handford C, Davids K, Bennett S, Button C. Skill acquisition in sport: some applications of an evolving practice ecology. Journal of sports sciences. 1997;15(6):621-40.

133. Carson HJ, Collins D. Refining and regaining skills in fixation/diversification stage performers: the Five-A Model. International Review of Sport and Exercise Psychology. 2011;4(2):146-67.

134. Chow JY, Davids K, Hristovski R, Araújo D, Passos P. Nonlinear pedagogy: Learning design for self-organizing neurobiological systems. New Ideas in Psychology. 2011;29(2):189-200.

135. Bernstein N. The co-ordination and regulation of movements. Pergamon-Press; 1967.

136. Newell KM, McDonald, P.V. Practice: A Search for Task Solutions. Enhancing Human Performance in Sport: New Concepts and Developments (American Academy of Physical Education Papers). Human Kinetics; 1992.

137. Seifert L, Button C, Davids K. Key properties of expert movement systems in sport : an ecological dynamics perspective. Sports medicine. 2013;43(3):167-78.

138. Seifert L, Komar J, Araujo D, Davids K. Neurobiological degeneracy: A key property for functional adaptations of perception and action to constraints. Neurosci Biobehav Rev. 2016;69:159-65.

139. Latash ML. The bliss (not the problem) of motor abundance (not redundancy). Experimental brain research. 2012;217(1):1-5.

140. Latash ML. Towards physics of neural processes and behavior. Neurosci Biobehav Rev. 2016;69:136-46.

141. Fox AS. Change-of-Direction Biomechanics: Is What's Best for Anterior Cruciate Ligament Injury Prevention Also Best for Performance? Sports medicine. 2018;48(8):1799-807.

142. Dempsey AR, Lloyd DG, Elliott BC, Steele JR, Munro BJ, Russo KA. The effect of technique change on knee loads during sidestep cutting. Medicine and science in sports and exercise. 2007;39(10):1765-73.

143. Dai B, Garrett WE, Gross MT, Padua DA, Queen RM, Yu B. The effects of 2 landing techniques on knee kinematics, kinetics, and performance during stop-jump and side-cutting tasks. The American journal of sports medicine. 2015;43(2):466-74.

144. Donnelly CJ, Elliott BC, Doyle TL, Finch CF, Dempsey AR, Lloyd DG. Changes in knee joint biomechanics following balance and technique training and a season of Australian football. British journal of sports medicine. 2012;46(13):917-22.

145. Folland JP, Allen SJ, Black MI, Handsaker JC, Forrester SE. Running Technique is an Important Component of Running Economy and Performance. Medicine and science in sports and exercise. 2017;49(7):1412-23.

146. Frank BS, Hackney AC, Battaglini CL, Blackburn T, Marshall SW, Clark M et al. Movement profile influences systemic stress and biomechanical resilience to high training load exposure. Journal of science and medicine in sport / Sports Medicine Australia. 2019;22(1):35-41.

147. Liao CM, Masters RS. Analogy learning: a means to implicit motor learning. Journal of sports sciences. 2001;19(5):307-19.

148. Lam WK, Maxwell JP, Masters RS. Analogy versus explicit learning of a modified basketball shooting task: performance and kinematic outcomes. Journal of sports sciences. 2009;27(2):179-91.

149. Abrahamson D, Sánchez–García R, Smyth C. Metaphors are projected constraints on action: An ecological dynamics view on learning across the disciplines. Singapore: International Society of the Learning Sciences; 2016.

150. Toner J, Moran A. Enhancing performance proficiency at the expert level: Considering the role of 'somaesthetic awareness'. Psychology of Sport and Exercise. 2015;16:110-7.

151. Adkins DL, Boychuk J, Remple MS, Kleim JA. Motor training induces experience-specific patterns of plasticity across motor cortex and spinal cord. Journal of applied physiology. 2006;101(6):1776-82.

152. Dayan E, Cohen LG. Neuroplasticity subserving motor skill learning. Neuron. 2011;72(3):443-54.

153. Dhawale AK, Smith MA, Olveczky BP. The Role of Variability in Motor Learning. Annu Rev Neurosci. 2017;40(1):479-98.

154. Weast JA, Shockley K, Riley MA. The influence of athletic experience and kinematic information on skill-relevant affordance perception. Quarterly journal of experimental psychology. 2011;64(4):689-706.

155. Withagen R, de Poel HJ, Araújo D, Pepping G-J. Affordances can invite behavior: Reconsidering the relationship between affordances and agency. New Ideas in Psychology. 2012;30(2):250-8.

156. Gibson JJ. The ecological approach to visual perception: classic edition. Psychology Press; 2014.

157. Masters R, Maxwell J. The theory of reinvestment. International Review of Sport and Exercise Psychology. 2008;1(2):160-83.

158. Bellomo E, Cooke A, Hardy J. Chunking, Conscious Processing, and EEG During Sequence Acquisition and Performance Pressure: A Comprehensive Test of Reinvestment Theory. Journal of sport & exercise psychology. 2018;40(3):135-45.

159. Swann C, Crust L, Vella SA. New directions in the psychology of optimal performance in sport: flow and clutch states. Curr Opin Psychol. 2017;16:48-53.

160. Galloway MT, Lalley AL, Shearn JT. The role of mechanical loading in tendon development, maintenance, injury, and repair. The Journal of bone and joint surgery American volume. 2013;95(17):1620-8.

161. Kiely J. Planning for physical performance: the individual perspective: Planning, periodization, prediction, and why the future ain't what it used to be! In: Button A, Richards H, editors. Performance Psychology. Edinburgh: Churchill Livingstone; 2011. p. 139-60.

162. Selye H. The stress of life. 1956.

163. Gems D, Partridge L. Stress-response hormesis and aging:"that which does not kill us makes us stronger". Cell metabolism. 2008;7(3):200-3.

164. Leak RK, Calabrese EJ, Kozumbo WJ, Gidday JM, Johnson TE, Mitchell JR et al. Enhancing and Extending Biological Performance and Resilience. Dose Response. 2018;16(3):1559325818784501.

165. Emery CA, Meeuwisse WH. The effectiveness of a neuromuscular prevention strategy to reduce injuries in youth soccer: a cluster-randomised controlled trial. British journal of sports medicine. 2010;44(8):555-62.

166. Lauersen JB, Bertelsen DM, Andersen LB. The effectiveness of exercise interventions to prevent sports injuries: a systematic review and meta-analysis of randomised controlled trials. British journal of sports medicine. 2014;48(11):871-7.

167. Steib S, Rahlf AL, Pfeifer K, Zech A. Dose-Response Relationship of Neuromuscular Training for Injury Prevention in Youth Athletes: A Meta-Analysis. Front Physiol. 2017;8(920):920.

168. Lauersen JB, Andersen TE, Andersen LB. Strength training as superior, dose-dependent and safe prevention of acute and overuse sports injuries: a systematic review, qualitative analysis and meta-analysis. British journal of sports medicine. 2018;52(24):1557-63.

169. Sugimoto D, Myer GD, Foss KD, Hewett TE. Dosage effects of neuromuscular training intervention to reduce anterior cruciate ligament injuries in female athletes: meta- and sub-group analyses. Sports medicine. 2014;44(4):551-62.

170. Stearns KM, Powers CM. Improvements in hip muscle performance result in increased use of the hip extensors and abductors during a landing task. The American journal of sports medicine. 2014;42(3):602-9.

171. Bowers C, Kreutzer C, Cannon-Bowers J, Lamb J. Team Resilience as a Second-Order Emergent State: A Theoretical Model and Research Directions. Front Psychol. 2017;8(1360):1360.

172. Fletcher D, Sarkar M. Mental fortitude training: An evidence-based approach to developing psychological resilience for sustained success. Journal of Sport Psychology in Action. 2016;7(3):135-57.

173. Collins DJ, Macnamara A, McCarthy N. Putting the Bumps in the Rocky Road: Optimizing the Pathway to Excellence. Front Psychol. 2016;7(1482):1482.

174. Sandvik AM, Bartone PT, Hystad SW, Phillips TM, Thayer JF, Johnsen BH. Psychological hardiness predicts neuroimmunological responses to stress. Psychology, health & medicine. 2013;18(6):705-13.

175. Jones G. What Is This Thing Called Mental Toughness? An Investigation of Elite Sport Performers. Journal of Applied Sport Psychology. 2010;14(3):205-18.

176. Meggs J, Ditzfeld C, Golby J. Self-concept organisation and mental toughness in sport. Journal of sports sciences. 2014;32(2):101-9.

177. Meggs J, Chen MA, Koehn S. Relationships Between Flow, Mental Toughness, and Subjective Performance Perception in Various Triathletes. Perceptual and motor skills. 2019;126(2):241-52.

178. Moran A, Campbell M, Toner J. Exploring the cognitive mechanisms of expertise in sport: Progress and prospects. Psychology of Sport and Exercise. 2019;42:8-15.

179. Swann C, Crust L, Jackman P, Vella SA, Allen MS, Keegan R. Performing under pressure: Exploring the psychological state underlying clutch performance in sport. Journal of sports sciences. 2016:1-9.

180. Davis L, Stenling A, Gustafsson H, Appleby R, Davis P. Reducing the risk of athlete burnout: Psychosocial, sociocultural, and individual considerations for coaches. International Journal of Sports Science & Coaching. 2019;14(4):444-52.

181. Al-Yaaribi A, Kavussanu M. Teammate Prosocial and Antisocial Behaviors Predict Task Cohesion and Burnout: The Mediating Role of Affect. Journal of sport & exercise psychology. 2017;39(3):199-208.

182. Hartley C, Coffee P. Perceived and Received Dimensional Support: Main and Stress-Buffering Effects on Dimensions of Burnout. Front Psychol. 2019;10(1724):1724.

183. Wagstaff C, Hings R, Larner R, Fletcher D. Psychological Resilience's Moderation of the Relationship Between the Frequency of Organizational Stressors and Burnout in Athletes and Coaches. The Sport Psychologist. 2018;32(3):178-88.

184. Chapman MT, Lines RLJ, Crane M, Ducker KJ, Ntoumanis N, Peeling P et al. Team resilience: A scoping review of conceptual and empirical work. Work & Stress. 2018;34(1):57-81.

185. Morgan PBC, Fletcher D, Sarkar M. Defining and characterizing team resilience in elite sport. Psychology of Sport and Exercise. 2013;14(4):549-59.

186. Morgan PBC, Fletcher D, Sarkar M. Understanding team resilience in the world's best athletes: A case study of a rugby union World Cup winning team. Psychology of Sport and Exercise. 2015;16:91-100.

187. McLaren CD, Spink KS. Team Member Communication and Perceived Cohesion in Youth Soccer. Communication & Sport. 2018;6(1):111-25.

188. Diamond A. Executive functions. Annual review of psychology. 2013;64:135-68.

189. Baker J, Young B. 20 years later: deliberate practice and the development of expertise in sport. International Review of Sport and Exercise Psychology. 2014;7(1):135-57.

190. MacIntyre TE, Igou ER, Campbell MJ, Moran AP, Matthews J. Metacognition and action: a new pathway to understanding social and cognitive aspects of expertise in sport. Front Psychol. 2014;5(1155):1155.

191. Kruger J, Dunning D. Unskilled and unaware of it: how difficulties in recognizing one's own incompetence lead to inflated self-assessments. Journal of personality and social psychology. 1999;77(6):1121-34.

192. Kim YH, Chiu CY, Bregant J. Unskilled and Don't Want to Be Aware of It: The Effect of Self-Relevance on the Unskilled and Unaware Phenomenon. PloS one. 2015;10(6):e0130309.

193. Dorjee D. Defining Contemplative Science: The Metacognitive Self-Regulatory Capacity of the Mind, Context of Meditation Practice and Modes of Existential Awareness. Front Psychol. 2016;7(1788):1788.

194. Webb TL, Miles E, Sheeran P. Dealing with feeling: a meta-analysis of the effectiveness of strategies derived from the process model of emotion regulation. Psychological bulletin. 2012;138(4):775-808.

195. Kuss DJ, Kanjo E, Crook-Rumsey M, Kibowski F, Wang GY, Sumich A. Problematic Mobile Phone Use and Addiction Across Generations: the Roles of Psychopathological Symptoms and Smartphone Use. J Technol Behav Sci. 2018;3(3):141-9.

196. Pivetta E, Harkin L, Billieux J, Kanjo E, Kuss DJ. Problematic smartphone use: An empirically validated model. Computers in Human Behavior. 2019;100:105-17.

197. Elhai JD, Dvorak RD, Levine JC, Hall BJ. Problematic smartphone use: A conceptual overview and systematic review of relations with anxiety and depression psychopathology. J Affect Disord. 2017;207:251-9.

198. Canale N, Vieno A, Doro M, Rosa Mineo E, Marino C, Billieux J. Emotion-related impulsivity moderates the cognitive interference effect of smartphone availability on working memory. Scientific Reports. 2019;9(1):18519.

199. Ward AF, Duke K, Gneezy A, Bos MW. Brain Drain: The Mere Presence of One's Own Smartphone Reduces Available Cognitive Capacity. Journal of the Association for Consumer Research. 2017;2(2):140-54.

200. Shin M, Webb A, Kemps E. Media multitasking, impulsivity and dual task ability. Computers in Human Behavior. 2019;92:160-8.

201. Wilmer HH, Chein JM. Mobile technology habits: patterns of association among device usage, intertemporal preference, impulse control, and reward sensitivity. Psychon Bull Rev. 2016;23(5):1607-14.

202. Lieberman A, Schroeder J. Two social lives: How differences between online and offline interaction influence social outcomes. Curr Opin Psychol. 2019;31:16-21.

203. Chotpitayasunondh V, Douglas KM. How "phubbing" becomes the norm: The antecedents and consequences of snubbing via smartphone. Computers in Human Behavior. 2016;63:9-18.

204. Tamir DI, Templeton EM, Ward AF, Zaki J. Media usage diminishes memory for experiences. Journal of Experimental Social Psychology. 2018;76:161-8.

205. Sanderson J, Browning B, Schmittel A. Education on the Digital Terrain: A Case Study Exploring College Athletes' Perceptions of Social-Media Training. International Journal of Sport Communication. 2015;8(1):103-24.

206. Hayes M, Filo K, Riot C, Geurin A. Athlete Perceptions of Social Media Benefits and Challenges During Major Sport Events. International Journal of Sport Communication. 2019;12(4):449-81.

207. Geurin AN. Elite Female Athletes' Perceptions of New Media Use Relating to Their Careers: A Qualitative Analysis. Journal of Sport Management. 2017;31(4):345-59.

208. Browning B, Sanderson J. The Positives and Negatives of Twitter: Exploring How Student-Athletes Use Twitter and Respond to Critical Tweets. International Journal of Sport Communication. 2012;5(4):503-21.

209. Newport C. Deep work: Rules for focused success in a distracted world. Hachette UK; 2016.

210. Ralph BCW, Seli P, Wilson KE, Smilek D. Volitional media multitasking: awareness of performance costs and modulation of media multitasking as a function of task demand. Psychol Res. 2018;84(2):404-23.

211. Wilmer HH, Sherman LE, Chein JM. Smartphones and Cognition: A Review of Research Exploring the Links between Mobile Technology Habits and Cognitive Functioning. Front Psychol. 2017;8(605):605.

212. Stothart C, Mitchum A, Yehnert C. The attentional cost of receiving a cell phone notification. J Exp Psychol Hum Percept Perform. 2015;41(4):893-7.

213. Elhai JD, Rozgonjuk D, Alghraibeh AM, Yang H. Disrupted Daily Activities From Interruptive Smartphone Notifications: Relations With Depression and Anxiety Severity and the Mediating Role of Boredom Proneness. Social Science Computer Review. 2019;0(0):089443931985800.

214. Kang S, Kurtzberg TR. Reach for your cell phone at your own risk: The cognitive costs of media choice for breaks. Journal of behavioral addictions. 2019;8(3):395-403.

215. Leroy S. Why is it so hard to do my work? The challenge of attention residue when switching between work tasks. Organizational Behavior and Human Decision Processes. 2009;109(2):168-81.

216. Mendoza JS, Pody BC, Lee S, Kim M, McDonough IM. The effect of cellphones on attention and learning: The influences of time, distraction, and nomophobia. Computers in Human Behavior. 2018;86:52-60.

217. Lee J, Cho B, Kim Y, Noh J, editors. Smartphone Addiction in University Students and Its Implication for Learning2015; Berlin, Heidelberg: Springer Berlin Heidelberg.

218. Mills KL. Possible Effects of Internet Use on Cognitive Development in Adolescence. Media and Communication. 2016;4(3):4.

219. Crone EA, Konijn EA. Media use and brain development during adolescence. Nat Commun. 2018;9(1):588.

220. Hu Y, Long X, Lyu H, Zhou Y, Chen J. Alterations in White Matter Integrity in Young Adults with Smartphone Dependence. Front Hum Neurosci. 2017;11(532):532.

221. Cain MS, Leonard JA, Gabrieli JD, Finn AS. Media multitasking in adolescence. Psychon Bull Rev. 2016;23(6):1932-41.

222. Singer Trakhman LM, Alexander PA, Berkowitz LE. Effects of Processing Time on Comprehension and Calibration in Print and Digital Mediums. The Journal of Experimental Education. 2019;87(1):101-15.

223. Singer LM, Alexander PA. Reading Across Mediums: Effects of Reading Digital and Print Texts on Comprehension and Calibration. The Journal of Experimental Education. 2017;85(1):155-72.

224. Ugur NG, Koc T. Time for Digital Detox: Misuse of Mobile Technology and Phubbing. Procedia - Social and Behavioral Sciences. 2015;195:1022-31.

225. Konrath SH, O'Brien EH, Hsing C. Changes in dispositional empathy in American college students over time: a meta-analysis. Pers Soc Psychol Rev. 2011;15(2):180-98.

226. Li J, Hao J, Shi B. From moral judgments to prosocial behavior: Multiple pathways in adolescents and different pathways in boys and girls. Personality and Individual Differences. 2018;134:149-54.

227. Allemand M, Steiger AE, Fend HA. Empathy development in adolescence predicts social competencies in adulthood. J Pers. 2015;83(2):229-41.

228. James C, Davis K, Charmaraman L, Konrath S, Slovak P, Weinstein E et al. Digital Life and Youth Well-being, Social Connectedness, Empathy, and Narcissism. Pediatrics. 2017;140(Suppl 2):S71-S5.

229. Edwards L, Kontostathis AE, Fisher C. Cyberbullying, Race/Ethnicity and Mental Health Outcomes: A Review of the Literature. Media and Communication. 2016;4(3):71.

230. Twenge JM, Campbell WK. Associations between screen time and lower psychological well-being among children and adolescents: Evidence from a population-based study. Prev Med Rep. 2018;12:271-83.

231. Orben A, Przybylski AK. Screens, Teens, and Psychological Well-Being: Evidence From Three Time-Use-Diary Studies. Psychological science. 2019;30(5):682-96.

232. Orben A, Przybylski AK. The association between adolescent well-being and digital technology use. Nat Hum Behav. 2019;3(2):173-82.

233. Kross E, Verduyn P, Demiralp E, Park J, Lee DS, Lin N et al. Facebook use predicts declines in subjective well-being in young adults. PloS one. 2013;8(8):e69841.

234. Marino C, Gini G, Vieno A, Spada MM. The associations between problematic Facebook use, psychological distress and well-being among adolescents and young adults: A systematic review and meta-analysis. J Affect Disord. 2018;226:274-81.

235. Booker CL, Kelly YJ, Sacker A. Gender differences in the associations between age trends of social media interaction and well-being among 10-15 year olds in the UK. BMC Public Health. 2018;18(1):321.

236. Verduyn P, Lee DS, Park J, Shablack H, Orvell A, Bayer J et al. Passive Facebook usage undermines affective well-being: Experimental and longitudinal evidence. Journal of experimental psychology General. 2015;144(2):480-8.

237. Phu B, Gow AJ. Facebook use and its association with subjective happiness and loneliness. Computers in Human Behavior. 2019;92:151-9.

238. Stieger S. Facebook Usage and Life Satisfaction. Front Psychol. 2019;10(2711):2711.

239. Rus HM, Tiemensma J. Social Media under the Skin: Facebook Use after Acute Stress Impairs Cortisol Recovery. Front Psychol. 2017;8(1609):1609.

240. Hu X, Kim A, Siwek N, Wilder D. The Facebook Paradox: Effects of Facebooking on Individuals' Social Relationships and Psychological Well-Being. Front Psychol. 2017;8(87):87.

241. Rotondi V, Stanca L, Tomasuolo M. Connecting alone: Smartphone use, quality of social interactions and well-being. Journal of Economic Psychology. 2017;63:17-26.

242. Shensa A, Sidani JE, Escobar-Viera CG, Switzer GE, Primack BA, Choukas-Bradley S. Emotional support from social media and face-to-face relationships:

Associations with depression risk among young adults. J Affect Disord. 2020;260:38-44.

243. Lima ML, Marques S, Muinos G, Camilo C. All You Need Is Facebook Friends? Associations between Online and Face-to-Face Friendships and Health. Front Psychol. 2017;8(68):68.

244. Newport C. Digital Minimalism: Choosing a Focused Life in a Noisy World. Penguin; 2019.

245. Markowitz DM, Hancock JT, Bailenson JN, Reeves B. Psychological and physiological effects of applying self-control to the mobile phone. PloS one. 2019;14(11):e0224464.

246. Fitz N, Kushlev K, Jagannathan R, Lewis T, Paliwal D, Ariely D. Batching smartphone notifications can improve well-being. Computers in Human Behavior. 2019;101:84-94.

247. Beland L-P, Murphy R. Ill Communication: Technology, distraction & student performance. Labour Economics. 2016;41:61-76.

248. O'Donnell S, Beaven CM, Driller MW. From pillow to podium: a review on understanding sleep for elite athletes. Nature and science of sleep. 2018;10:243-53.

249. Ritland BM, Simonelli G, Gentili RJ, Smith JC, He X, Mantua J et al. Effects of sleep extension on cognitive/motor performance and motivation in military tactical athletes. Sleep Med. 2019;58:48-55.

250. Barnes CM, Watson NF. Why healthy sleep is good for business. Sleep Med Rev. 2019;47:112-8.

251. Simpson NS, Gibbs EL, Matheson GO. Optimizing sleep to maximize performance: implications and recommendations for elite athletes. Scandinavian journal of medicine & science in sports. 2017;27(3):266-74.

252. Knufinke M, Nieuwenhuys A, Geurts SAE, Coenen AML, Kompier MAJ. Self-reported sleep quantity, quality and sleep hygiene in elite athletes. J Sleep Res. 2018;27(1):78-85.

253. Roberts SSH, Teo WP, Warmington SA. Effects of training and competition on the sleep of elite athletes: a systematic review and meta-analysis. British journal of sports medicine. 2019;53(8):513-22.

254. Mah CD, Kezirian EJ, Marcello BM, Dement WC. Poor sleep quality and insufficient sleep of a collegiate student-athlete population. Sleep Health. 2018;4(3):251-7.

255. Lastella M, Roach GD, Halson SL, Gore CJ, Garvican-Lewis LA, Sargent C. Sleep at the helm: A case study of how a head coach sleeps compared to his team. International Journal of Sports Science & Coaching. 2017;12(6):782-9.

256. Walker M. Why we sleep: The new science of sleep and dreams. Penguin UK; 2017.

257. Raysmith BP, Drew MK. Performance success or failure is influenced by weeks lost to injury and illness in elite Australian track and field athletes: A 5-year prospective study. Journal of science and medicine in sport / Sports Medicine Australia. 2016;19(10):778-83.

258. Milewski MD, Skaggs DL, Bishop GA, Pace JL, Ibrahim DA, Wren TA et al. Chronic lack of sleep is associated with increased sports injuries in adolescent athletes. Journal of pediatric orthopedics. 2014;34(2):129-33.

259. Besedovsky L, Lange T, Haack M. The Sleep-Immune Crosstalk in Health and Disease. Physiol Rev. 2019;99(3):1325-80.

260. Prather AA, Hall M, Fury JM, Ross DC, Muldoon MF, Cohen S et al. Sleep and antibody response to hepatitis B vaccination. Sleep. 2012;35(8):1063-9.

261. Lasselin J, Ingre M, Regenbogen C, Olsson MJ, Garke M, Brytting M et al. Sleep during naturally occurring respiratory infections: A pilot study. Brain, behavior, and immunity. 2019;79:236-43.

262. Prather AA, Janicki-Deverts D, Hall MH, Cohen S. Behaviorally Assessed Sleep and Susceptibility to the Common Cold. Sleep. 2015;38(9):1353-9.

263. Cohen S, Doyle WJ, Alper CM, Janicki-Deverts D, Turner RB. Sleep habits and susceptibility to the common cold. Arch Intern Med. 2009;169(1):62-7.

264. Walsh NP. Recommendations to maintain immune health in athletes. European journal of sport science. 2018;18(6):820-31.

265. Peake JM, Neubauer O, Walsh NP, Simpson RJ. Recovery of the immune system after exercise. Journal of applied physiology. 2017;122(5):1077-87.

266. Keaney LC, Kilding AE, Merien F, Dulson DK. The impact of sport related stressors on immunity and illness risk in team-sport athletes. Journal of science and medicine in sport / Sports Medicine Australia. 2018;21(12):1192-9.

267. Fullagar HH, Skorski S, Duffield R, Hammes D, Coutts AJ, Meyer T. Sleep and athletic performance: the effects of sleep loss on exercise performance, and physiological and cognitive responses to exercise. Sports medicine. 2015;45(2):161-86.

268. Kolling S, Duffield R, Erlacher D, Venter R, Halson SL. Sleep-Related Issues for Recovery and Performance in Athletes. Int J Sports Physiol Perform. 2019;14(2):144-8.

269. Reyner LA, Horne JA. Sleep restriction and serving accuracy in performance tennis players, and effects of caffeine. Physiol Behav. 2013;120:93-6.

270. Kirschen GW, Jones JJ, Hale L. The Impact of Sleep Duration on Performance Among Competitive Athletes: A Systematic Literature Review. Clinical journal of sport medicine : official journal of the Canadian Academy of Sport Medicine. 2018.

271. Mah CD, Mah KE, Kezirian EJ, Dement WC. The effects of sleep extension on the athletic performance of collegiate basketball players. Sleep. 2011;34(7):943-50.

272. Schwartz J, Simon RD, Jr. Sleep extension improves serving accuracy: A study with college varsity tennis players. Physiol Behav. 2015;151:541-4.

273. Suppiah HT, Low CY, Choong G, Chia M. Effects of a Short Daytime Nap on Shooting and Sprint Performance in High-Level Adolescent Athletes. International Journal of Sports Physiology & Performance. 2019;14(1):76-82.

274. Lowe CJ, Safati A, Hall PA. The neurocognitive consequences of sleep restriction: A meta-analytic review. Neurosci Biobehav Rev. 2017;80:586-604.

275. Williamson AM, Feyer AM. Moderate sleep deprivation produces impairments in cognitive and motor performance equivalent to legally prescribed levels of alcohol intoxication. Occup Environ Med. 2000;57(10):649-55.
276. Goel N, Rao H, Durmer JS, Dinges DF. Neurocognitive consequences of sleep deprivation. Semin Neurol. 2009;29(4):320-39.
277. Knufinke M, Nieuwenhuys A, Maase K, Moen MH, Geurts SA, Coenen AM et al. Effects of Natural Between-Days Variation in Sleep on Elite Athletes' Psychomotor Vigilance and Sport-Specific Measures of Performance. Journal of Sports Science & Medicine. 2018;17(4):515.
278. Kusztor A, Raud L, Juel BE, Nilsen AS, Storm JF, Huster RJ. Sleep deprivation differentially affects subcomponents of cognitive control. Sleep. 2019;42(4):zsz016.
279. Bolin DJ. Sleep Deprivation and Its Contribution to Mood and Performance Deterioration in College Athletes. Current sports medicine reports. 2019;18(8):305-10.
280. Meridew C, Athey A, Killgore W, Gehrels J, Alfonso-Miller P, Grandner M. 0190 Academic Performance Associated with Sleep Duration among Student Athletes: Impact of Insomnia, Fatigue, and Depression. Sleep. 2018;41(suppl_1):A74-A5.
281. Jones JJ, Kirschen GW, Kancharla S, Hale L. Association between late-night tweeting and next-day game performance among professional basketball players. Sleep health. 2019;5(1):68-71.
282. Dutil C, Walsh JJ, Featherstone RB, Gunnell KE, Tremblay MS, Gruber R et al. Influence of sleep on developing brain functions and structures in children and adolescents: A systematic review. Sleep Med Rev. 2018;42:184-201.
283. Gruber R, Laviolette R, Deluca P, Monson E, Cornish K, Carrier J. Short sleep duration is associated with poor performance on IQ measures in healthy school-age children. Sleep Med. 2010;11(3):289-94.
284. Short MA, Blunden S, Rigney G, Matricciani L, Coussens S, C MR et al. Cognition and objectively measured sleep duration in children: a systematic review and meta-analysis. Sleep Health. 2018;4(3):292-300.
285. Urrila AS, Artiges E, Massicotte J, Miranda R, Vulser H, Bezivin-Frere P et al. Sleep habits, academic performance, and the adolescent brain structure. Scientific Reports. 2017;7:41678.
286. Maski KP. Sleep-Dependent Memory Consolidation in Children. Semin Pediatr Neurol. 2015;22(2):130-4.
287. Walker MP, Stickgold R. Sleep-dependent learning and memory consolidation. Neuron. 2004;44(1):121-33.
288. Mazza S, Gerbier E, Gustin MP, Kasikci Z, Koenig O, Toppino TC et al. Relearn Faster and Retain Longer. Psychological science. 2016;27(10):1321-30.
289. Stickgold R. Sleep-dependent memory consolidation. Nature. 2005;437(7063):1272-8.
290. Walker MP, Stickgold R. It's practice, with sleep, that makes perfect: implications of sleep-dependent learning and plasticity for skill performance. Clinics in sports medicine. 2005;24(2):301-17, ix.

291. Walker MP, Stickgold R. Sleep, memory, and plasticity. Annual review of psychology. 2006;57(1):139-66.

292. Stickgold R. Parsing the role of sleep in memory processing. Curr Opin Neurobiol. 2013;23(5):847-53.

293. Walker MP, Brakefield T, Morgan A, Hobson JA, Stickgold R. Practice with sleep makes perfect: sleep-dependent motor skill learning. Neuron. 2002;35(1):205-11.

294. Appleman ER, Albouy G, Doyon J, Cronin-Golomb A, King BR. Sleep quality influences subsequent motor skill acquisition. Behav Neurosci. 2016;130(3):290-7.

295. Perogamvros L, Schwartz S. Sleep and Emotional Functions. In: Meerlo P, Benca RM, Abel T, editors. Sleep, Neuronal Plasticity and Brain Function. Berlin, Heidelberg: Springer Berlin Heidelberg; 2015. p. 411-31.

296. Spiegel K, Tasali E, Penev P, Van Cauter E. Brief communication: Sleep curtailment in healthy young men is associated with decreased leptin levels, elevated ghrelin levels, and increased hunger and appetite. Ann Intern Med. 2004;141(11):846-50.

297. Taheri S, Lin L, Austin D, Young T, Mignot E. Short sleep duration is associated with reduced leptin, elevated ghrelin, and increased body mass index. PLoS Med. 2004;1(3):e62.

298. Hogenkamp PS, Nilsson E, Nilsson VC, Chapman CD, Vogel H, Lundberg LS et al. Acute sleep deprivation increases portion size and affects food choice in young men. Psychoneuroendocrinology. 2013;38(9):1668-74.

299. Bos MM, van Heemst D, Donga E, de Mutsert R, Rosendaal FR, Blauw GJ et al. The Association between Habitual Sleep Duration and Sleep Quality with Glycemic Traits: Assessment by Cross-Sectional and Mendelian Randomization Analyses. Journal of Clinical Medicine. 2019;8(5):682.

300. Nedeltcheva AV, Kilkus JM, Imperial J, Schoeller DA, Penev PD. Insufficient sleep undermines dietary efforts to reduce adiposity. Ann Intern Med. 2010;153(7):435-41.

301. Goldstein AN, Walker MP. The role of sleep in emotional brain function. Annu Rev Clin Psychol. 2014;10(1):679-708.

302. Andrade A, Bevilacqua G, Casagrande P, Brandt R, Coimbra D. Sleep quality associated with mood in elite athletes. The Physician and sportsmedicine. 2019;47(3):312-7.

303. Lastella M, Lovell GP, Sargent C. Athletes' precompetitive sleep behaviour and its relationship with subsequent precompetitive mood and performance. European journal of sport science. 2014;14 Suppl 1(sup1):S123-30.

304. Ritchie HK, Knauer OA, Guerin MK, Stothard ER, Wright KP. 0183 Both Positive and Negative Affect Are Impacted by Sleep Deprivation. Sleep. 2018;41(suppl_1):A72-A.

305. O'Leary K, Small BJ, Panaite V, Bylsma LM, Rottenberg J. Sleep quality in healthy and mood-disordered persons predicts daily life emotional reactivity. Cogn Emot. 2017;31(3):435-43.

306. Altena E, Micoulaud-Franchi JA, Geoffroy PA, Sanz-Arigita E, Bioulac S, Philip P. The bidirectional relation between emotional reactivity and sleep: From disruption to recovery. Behav Neurosci. 2016;130(3):336-50.

307. Beattie L, Kyle SD, Espie CA, Biello SM. Social interactions, emotion and sleep: A systematic review and research agenda. Sleep Med Rev. 2015;24:83-100.

308. Famodu OA, Montgomery-Downs H, Thomas JM, Gilleland DL, Bryner RW, Olfert MD. 0083 Impact of A single Week of Sleep Extension on Performance, Mood, and Nutrition among Female College Track Athletes. Sleep. 2017;40(suppl_1):A32-A.

309. Weber M, Webb CA, Deldonno SR, Kipman M, Schwab ZJ, Weiner MR et al. Habitual 'sleep credit' is associated with greater grey matter volume of the medial prefrontal cortex, higher emotional intelligence and better mental health. J Sleep Res. 2013;22(5):527-34.

310. Nowack K. Sleep, emotional intelligence, and interpersonal effectiveness: Natural bedfellows. Consulting Psychology Journal: Practice and Research. 2017;69(2):66-79.

311. Yap Y, Rice-Lacy RC, Bei B, Wiley JF. 0178 Bidirectional Relations between Stress and Sleep: An Intensive Daily Study. Sleep. 2018;41(suppl_1):A70-A.

312. Walker MP, van der Helm E. Overnight therapy? The role of sleep in emotional brain processing. Psychological bulletin. 2009;135(5):731-48.

313. Vandekerckhove M, Wang Y. Emotion, emotion regulation and sleep: an intimate relationship. Aims Neuroscience. 2018;5(1):1-17.

314. McCall CA, Turkheimer E, Tsang S, Avery A, Duncan GE, Watson NF. 0177 Sleep and Resilient Coping: A Twin Study. Sleep. 2018;41(suppl_1):A69-A70.

315. Chakravorty S, Siu HY, Lalley-Chareczko L, Brown GK, Findley JC, Perlis ML et al. Sleep Duration and Insomnia Symptoms as Risk Factors for Suicidal Ideation in a Nationally Representative Sample. Prim Care Companion CNS Disord. 2015;17(6):10.4088/PCC.13m01551.

316. Haghighi A, Athey A, Killgore W, Gehrels J, Alfonso-Miller P, Grandner M. 0979 Insufficient Sleep Duration and Insomnia Symptoms Independently Predict Suicide Ideation in Student Athletes and Non-Athletes. Sleep. 2018;41(suppl_1):A363-A.

317. Irwin MR. Why sleep is important for health: a psychoneuroimmunology perspective. Annual review of psychology. 2015;66(1):143-72.

318. Wolk R, Somers VK. Sleep and the metabolic syndrome. Exp Physiol. 2007;92(1):67-78.

319. Shi L, Chen SJ, Ma MY, Bao YP, Han Y, Wang YM et al. Sleep disturbances increase the risk of dementia: A systematic review and meta-analysis. Sleep Med Rev. 2018;40:4-16.

320. Sargent C, Lastella M, Halson SL, Roach GD. The impact of training schedules on the sleep and fatigue of elite athletes. Chronobiol Int. 2014;31(10):1160-8.

321. Sargent C, Halson S, Roach GD. Sleep or swim? Early-morning training severely restricts the amount of sleep obtained by elite swimmers. European journal of sport science. 2014;14 Suppl 1(sup1):S310-5.

322. Bonnar D, Bartel K, Kakoschke N, Lang C. Sleep Interventions Designed to Improve Athletic Performance and Recovery: A Systematic Review of Current Approaches. Sports medicine. 2018;48(3):683-703.

323. Stutz J, Eiholzer R, Spengler CM. Effects of Evening Exercise on Sleep in Healthy Participants: A Systematic Review and Meta-Analysis. Sports medicine. 2019;49(2):269-87.

324. Dunican IC, Higgins CC, Jones MJ, Clarke MW, Murray K, Dawson B et al. Caffeine use in a Super Rugby game and its relationship to post-game sleep. European journal of sport science. 2018;18(4):513-23.

325. Jones MJ, Dawson B, Gucciardi DF, Eastwood PR, Miller J, Halson SL et al. Evening electronic device use and sleep patterns in athletes. Journal of sports sciences. 2019;37(8):864-70.

326. Robey E, Dawson B, Halson S, Gregson W, King S, Goodman C et al. Effect of evening postexercise cold water immersion on subsequent sleep. Medicine and science in sports and exercise. 2013;45(7):1394-402.

327. Whitworth-Turner C, Di Michele R, Muir I, Gregson W, Drust B. A shower before bedtime may improve the sleep onset latency of youth soccer players. European journal of sport science. 2017;17(9):1119-28.

328. Britton DM, Kavanagh EJ, Polman RCJ. A Path Analysis of Adolescent Athletes' Perceived Stress Reactivity, Competition Appraisals, Emotions, Coping, and Performance Satisfaction. Front Psychol. 2019;10(1151):1151.

329. Clarke P, Sheffield D, Akehurst S. Personality Predictors of Yips and Choking Susceptibility. Front Psychol. 2019;10(2784):2784.

330. Liu JJW, Reed M, Vickers K. Reframing the individual stress response: Balancing our knowledge of stress to improve responsivity to stressors. Stress Health. 2019;35(5):607-16.

331. Meijen C, Turner M, Jones MV, Sheffield D, McCarthy P. A Theory of Challenge and Threat States in Athletes: A Revised Conceptualization. Front Psychol. 2020;11(126):126.

332. Dhabhar FS. The short-term stress response - Mother nature's mechanism for enhancing protection and performance under conditions of threat, challenge, and opportunity. Front Neuroendocrinol. 2018;49:175-92.

333. Lupien SJ, Juster RP, Raymond C, Marin MF. The effects of chronic stress on the human brain: From neurotoxicity, to vulnerability, to opportunity. Front Neuroendocrinol. 2018;49:91-105.

334. Kotler S, Wheal J. Stealing fire: How Silicon Valley, the Navy SEALs, and maverick scientists are revolutionizing the way we live and work. HarperCollins; 2017.

335. Swann C, Crust L, Jackman P, Vella SA, Allen MS, Keegan R. Psychological States Underlying Excellent Performance in Sport: Toward an Integrated Model of Flow and Clutch States. Journal of Applied Sport Psychology. 2017;29(4):375-401.

336. Schucker L, Hagemann N, Strauss B. Attentional processes and choking under pressure. Perceptual and motor skills. 2013;116(2):671-89.

337. Stults-Kolehmainen MA, Bartholomew JB. Psychological stress impairs short-term muscular recovery from resistance exercise. Medicine and science in sports and exercise. 2012;44(11):2220-7.

338. Stults-Kolehmainen MA, Bartholomew JB, Sinha R. Chronic psychological stress impairs recovery of muscular function and somatic sensations over a 96-hour period. Journal of strength and conditioning research / National Strength & Conditioning Association. 2014;28(7):2007-17.

339. Ivarsson A, Johnson U, Andersen MB, Tranaeus U, Stenling A, Lindwall M. Psychosocial Factors and Sport Injuries: Meta-analyses for Prediction and Prevention. Sports medicine. 2017;47(2):353-65.

340. Guo T, Ni Y, Li Q, Hong H. The Power of Faith: The Influence of Athletes' Coping Self-Efficacy on the Cognitive Processing of Psychological Stress. Front Psychol. 2019;10(1565):1565.

341. Perna FM, Antoni MH, Baum A, Gordon P, Schneiderman N. Cognitive behavioral stress management effects on injury and illness among competitive athletes: a randomized clinical trial. Ann Behav Med. 2003;25(1):66-73.

342. Putukian M. The psychological response to injury in student athletes: a narrative review with a focus on mental health. British journal of sports medicine. 2016;50(3):145-8.

343. Didymus FF, Fletcher D. Effects of a cognitive-behavioral intervention on field hockey players' appraisals of organizational stressors. Psychology of Sport and Exercise. 2017;30:173-85.

344. Didymus FF. Olympic and international level sports coaches' experiences of stressors, appraisals, and coping. Qualitative Research in Sport, Exercise and Health. 2016;9(2):214-32.

345. Olusoga P, Maynard I, Hays K, Butt J. Coaching under pressure: a study of Olympic coaches. Journal of sports sciences. 2012;30(3):229-39.

346. Taylor J. Coaches are people too: An applied model of stress management for sports coaches. Journal of Applied Sport Psychology. 1992;4(1):27-50.

347. Chadha NJ, Turner MJ, Slater MJ. Investigating Irrational Beliefs, Cognitive Appraisals, Challenge and Threat, and Affective States in Golfers Approaching Competitive Situations. Frontiers in Psychology. 2019;10(2295).

348. Turner MJ. Rational Emotive Behavior Therapy (REBT), Irrational and Rational Beliefs, and the Mental Health of Athletes. Front Psychol. 2016;7:1423.

349. Burns DD. Feeling good. Signet Book; 1981.

350. Hofmann SG, Asmundson GJ, Beck AT. The science of cognitive therapy. Behav Ther. 2013;44(2):199-212.

351. Gustafsson H, Lundqvist C, Tod D. Cognitive behavioral intervention in sport psychology: A case illustration of the exposure method with an elite athlete. Journal of Sport Psychology in Action. 2016;8(3):152-62.

352. Al-Mosaiwi M, Johnstone T. In an Absolute State: Elevated Use of Absolutist Words Is a Marker Specific to Anxiety, Depression, and Suicidal Ideation. Clinical Psychological Science. 2018;6(4):529-42.

353. Hardy J, Roberts R, Hardy L. Awareness and Motivation to Change Negative Self-Talk. The Sport Psychologist. 2009;23(4):435-50.

354. Neil R, Hanton S, Mellalieu SD. Seeing Things in a Different Light: Assessing the Effects of a Cognitive-Behavioral Intervention upon the Further Appraisals and Performance of Golfers. Journal of Applied Sport Psychology. 2013;25(1):106-30.

355. Moore LJ, Freeman P, Hase A, Solomon-Moore E, Arnold R. How Consistent Are Challenge and Threat Evaluations? A Generalizability Analysis. Front Psychol. 2019;10(1778):1778.

356. Hase A, Hood J, Moore LJ, Freeman P. The influence of self-talk on challenge and threat states and performance. Psychology of Sport and Exercise. 2019;45:101550.

357. Hatzigeorgiadis A, Zourbanos N, Mpoumpaki S, Theodorakis Y. Mechanisms underlying the self-talk–performance relationship: The effects of motivational self-talk on self-confidence and anxiety. Psychology of Sport and Exercise. 2009;10(1):186-92.

358. Mosewich AD, Crocker PR, Kowalski KC, Delongis A. Applying self-compassion in sport: an intervention with women athletes. Journal of sport & exercise psychology. 2013;35(5):514-24.

359. Gustafsson H, Skoog T, Davis P, Kenttä G, Haberl P. Mindfulness and its relationship with perceived stress, affect, and burnout in elite junior athletes. Journal of Clinical Sport Psychology. 2015;9(3):263-81.

360. Basso JC, Suzuki WA. The Effects of Acute Exercise on Mood, Cognition, Neurophysiology, and Neurochemical Pathways: A Review. Brain Plast. 2017;2(2):127-52.

Printed in Great Britain
by Amazon